Truth, Knowledge and Causation

International Library of Philosophy and Scientific Method

EDITOR: TED HONDERICH
ADVISORY EDITOR: BERNARD WILLIAMS

A Catalogue of books already published in the
International Library of Philosophy and Scientific Method
will be found at the end of this volume.

Truth,
Knowledge and Causation

by

C. J. DUCASSE

LONDON

ROUTLEDGE & KEGAN PAUL

NEW YORK : HUMANITIES PRESS

First published 1968
by Routledge & Kegan Paul Limited
Broadway House, 68–74 Carter Lane
London, E.C.4

Printed in Great Britain
by Richard Clay (The Chaucer Press) Ltd
Bungay, Suffolk

SBN 7100 6333 4

CONTENTS

PREFACE

Many of the questions to which philosophers have addressed themselves through the centuries have great practical importance; for the answers made to those questions have implications as to what, in given circumstances, the wisest thing to do, to think, or to feel would on the whole be for a person having then and there a given set of powers and of incapacities.

Unfortunately, however, the answers philosophers have offered to the momentous questions on which they had reflected, have seldom if ever had the status of knowledge properly so called; which on the contrary is that of many of the answers reached by the natural and the formal sciences to the questions they ask. Rather, different philosophers have offered different answers to each of the classical philosophical questions, but have failed to prove these answers true. Hence the epistemic status of their answers has not been that of knowledge, but only that of opinions.

In this respect they resemble the differing dogmas of the various religions, which, like philosophical opinions, nevertheless have psychological leverage and therefore practical importance; and this resemblance accounts for the fact that, in classifications of topics of inquiry, philosophy and religion, or philosophy and theology, are often listed together as constituting one group. For instance, in the American Academy of Arts and Sciences' classification of the topics on which one or others of its Fellows are specialists, Class IV is '*Humanities*'; and Section 1 of Class IV is '*Philosophy and Theology*'. Also, among scientists, the belief that philosophy and theology belong together is widespread.

Nevertheless, that knowledge properly so called—even when only of probabilities—is what philosophical reflection really aims at, is shown by the fact that the grounds, whether sound or not, which philosophers advance for their contentions and against those of their opponents are of epistemic and logical kinds, not fideistic, aesthetic, or of other epistemically irrelevant kinds.

Why then is it that philosophical reflection has so generally yielded only diverse opinions?

The answer to this tormenting question is, I believe, that philosophers have so generally failed to employ the particular form of genuinely scientific method appropriate to the solving of philosophical problems; which particular form as I conceive it is described in my Howison Lecture, 'The Method of Knowledge in Philosophy.'

And what the other essays in the present collection attempt to do is to illustrate the application of that knowledge-yielding method to semantic analysis of a number of philosophical terms, of whose meaning a precise and non-arbitrary conception is indispensable if far-reaching yet rigorous inferences in which they are key terms are to be possible.

BROWN UNIVERSITY   C. J. DUCASSE
OCTOBER 12, 1967

ON THE NATURE AND THE OBSERVABILITY OF THE CAUSAL RELATION*

The aim of this paper is to set forth two related theses. The first is that the correct definition of the causal relation is to be framed in terms of one single case of sequence, and that constancy of conjunction is therefore no part of it, but merely, under certain conditions, a corollary of the presence of the causal relation. The second thesis is that the causal relation, when correctly defined, is as directly observable as many other facts, and that the alleged mysteriousness of the causal tie is therefore a myth due only to a mistaken notion of what a tie is.

1. *Meaning of 'a correct definition'*

The problem of giving a 'correct' definition of the causal relation is that of making analytically explicit the meaning which the term 'cause' has in actual concrete phrases that our language intuition acknowledges as proper and typical cases of its use. For obviously it is one thing to 'know what cause means' in the cheap sense of being able to understand intuitively such an assertion as that the Santa Barbara earthquake caused the collapse of numberless chimneys; and it is another and a much more difficult and rarer thing to 'know what cause means' in the sense of being able to give a correct definition of it. To say that a definition of it is correct means that that definition can be substituted for the word 'cause' in any such assertion as the above, in which the word occurs, *without in*

---

* *The Journal of Philosophy,* vol. XXIII, No. 3, 1926.

the least changing the meaning which the assertion is felt to have. Any ventured definition of such a philosophical term as cause is thus capable of being correct or incorrect in strictly the same sense as that
in which a scientific hypothesis is so, viz., either it fits the facts or
it does not. The only difference is that in the case of scientific hypotheses the facts are perceptual objects and their relations, while
in the case of philosophical hypotheses the facts are the intuited
meanings of actual phrases in which the word to be defined occurs.
The great inductive method of hypothesis-deduction-verification
is thus no less that of philosophy than that of science.

2. *Two preliminary remarks*

Before attempting to formulate a definition of the term 'cause',
attention must briefly be called to two essential preliminary
points.[1]

    1. The first is that nothing can, in strict propriety, ever be
spoken of as a cause or an effect, except an *event*. And by an event
is to be understood either a change or an absence of change
(whether qualitative or relational) of an object.[2] On the other hand,
objects themselves (in the sense of substances, e.g., gold; or
things, e.g., a tree) never can properly be spoken of as causes or
effects,[3] but only as agents or patients, as components or com-
pounds, as parts or wholes. These relations, although closely
allied to the causal relation, are nevertheless distinct from it, and
cannot be discussed here.

    2. The second point to be borne in mind is that when the term
'causal connection' is used, any one of four distinct objective relations may actually be meant, namely, objectively sufficient to,
necessary to, necessitated by, contingent upon. And to these four
relations correspond respectively the four functional terms, cause,
condition, effect, resultant. So that, more explicitly, if a given par-

---

[1] In a monograph on causation by the writer, these two points are argued
at some length. See *Causation and the Types of Necessity,* Univ. of Washington
Press, 1924, pp. 52 ff.

[2] More technically, an event can be defined as either a change or an absence
of change in the relation of an object to either an intensive or an extensive
standard of reference, during a specified time interval.

[3] cf. Schopenhauer, *The Fourfold Root of the Principle of Sufficient Reason,*
trans. Hillebrand, pp. 38 ff.; and Wundt, *Logik,* Third Ed., vol. I, p. 586.

ticular event is regarded as having been *sufficient to* the occurrence of another, it is said to have been its *cause*; if regarded as having been *necessary to* the occurrence of another, it is said to have been a *condition of* it; if regarded as having been *necessitated by* the occurrence of another, it is said to have been its *effect*; and if regarded as having been *contingent upon* the occurrence of another, it is said to have been a *resultant* of that other. Much confusion has resulted in discussions of causality from the failure to keep these four relations at all times clearly distinguished, Mill, indeed, pushing perversity to the point of convincing himself and some of his readers that there was no sound basis for a distinction between cause and condition. But it is, on the contrary, essential to remember that to be sufficient is one thing, to be necessary another thing, and to be *both* sufficient and necessary (which is what Mill's definition would make cause mean) yet a third thing.

Of the four relations, cause, condition, effect, resultant, which a given particular event may have to another with which it is connected, we shall have space here to discuss only the first, namely, cause. And we shall, moreover, confine ourselves to cases—much the more frequent—where the events contemplated are changes, rather than absences of change.

3. *Definition of cause*

Taking it as an admitted fact of the language that if the occurrence of a particular change sufficed to the occurrence of a given other it is then said to have caused that other, the all-important question now arises how such sufficing is to be defined. I suggest that the correct definition of it, framed in terms of a hypothetical situation, is as follows:

Considering two changes, C and K (which may be either of the same or of different objects), the change C is said to have been sufficient to, i.e., to have caused, the change K, if :

1. The change C occurred during a time and through a space terminating at the instant I at the surface S.[1]

2. The change K occurred during a time and through a space beginning at the instant I at the surface S.

3. No change other than C occurred during the time and

---

[1] The limit of a change of a solid is obviously a surface, not a point.

through the space of C, and no change other than K during the time and through the space of K.

More roughly, but in briefer and more easily intuited terms, we may say that *the cause of the particular change K was such particular change C as alone occurred in the immediate environment of K immediately before.*

4. Some bearings of the definition

A number of important points may be noted in connection with the above definition of cause.

1. The first is that it presents the causal relation as involving not two terms only, but essentially three terms, namely, (a) the environment of an object, (b) some change in that environment, (c) the resulting change in the object. As soon as it is clearly realized that the expression 'the cause of an event' thus has any meaning at all only in terms of some definite environment, either concretely given or abstractly specified, Mill's contention that the distinction between cause and conditions is arbitrary and capricious, is seen to be absurd. To take up the environment into the 'cause', as Mill's definition of cause[1] tries to do, is impossible because the cause consists of a change in that environment. No event can be spoken of as the cause of anything, except relatively to certain conditions; and vice versa, as regards conditions.

2. The second remark for which the definition of cause above gives occasion concerns the immediate spatial and temporal contiguity of cause and effect. The alleged impossibility of such immediate contiguity is the chief ground upon which Russell has advocated the extrusion of the term 'cause' from the philosophical vocabulary.[2] The difficulties raised by him, however, are easily disposed of if two things are kept in mind. The first is that the terms 'a time' and 'a place' are ambiguous. It is essential to distinguish clearly 'a time' in the sense of an instant, i.e., a *cut* of the time series, from 'a time' in the sense of a *segment* of the time series, limited by

---

[1] 'The cause . . . is the sum total of the conditions, positive and negative taken together . . . which being realized, the consequent invariably follows' (*Syst. of Logic*, bk. III, ch. v, No. 3). This definition is obviously in flagrant contradiction with Mill's characterization of the cause as the single difference in the circumstances, in the canon of the 'Method of Difference'.

[2] *Proc. Arist. Soc.*, vol. XIII, 'On the Notion of Cause'.

two cuts. And similarly with regard to the space order, the cuts of it (viz., points, lines, or surfaces according as one, two, or three dimensional space is considered) are to be carefully distinguished from the *parts* of space, which have such cuts as limits. The second thing to bear in mind is that an event (whether a change or an 'unchange'[1]) cannot be said to occur *at* a time (cut), but only *during* a time (segment); nor *at* a point (or other cut of space), but only *through* a space (between cuts). Thus, a change is essentially a process which has extent both in time and in space, and is therefore divisible; any division yielding segments of the process that are themselves extended in time and space and therefore further divisible, *ad infinitum*.[2] The immediate contiguity of cause and effect in space and time, specified in our definition, then means only that one identical space-time *cut* marks both the end of the cause process and the beginning of the effect process; the one extending up to, and the other from, that cut; the cut itself, however (by the very nature of a cut as distinguished from a segment), having no space-time dimension at all.[3] With cause and effect and their space-time relation[4] so conceived, there is no possibility that, as Russell contended, some other event should creep in between the cause and the effect and thwart the production of the effect. Nor are we compelled, as he also contended, to trim down indefinitely the beginning part of the cause (and, *mutatis mutandis*, the end part of the effect) on the ground that the early part of the cause is not necessary to the effect so long as the end part of the cause

---

[1] The apt term 'unchange' is borrowed from Dr. Charles Mercier's book, *Causation and Belief*.

[2] A stage might, however, conceivably be reached, at which the parts obtained by the division of a change, would, *in terms of the particular test of changing used at the previous stages of division,* be themselves not changes, but unchanges (though, of course, nonetheless extended in time and space and therefore divisible). That is, the assertion that something changes, or, equally, does not change, remains ambiguous so long as some definite test of such change has not been specified as standard. Thus the assertion might be true in terms of one test and false in terms of another. Cf. 'A Liberalistic View of Truth', by the writer, in the *Philos. Review* for November, 1925.

[3] In practice, no space-time dimension of a relevant order of magnitude. Clock ticks and graduation lines as used are never perfectly dimensionless.

[4] This view of the space-time relation of cause and effect, I was gratified to find, is also that set forth by Mr. Johnson in vol. III of his *Logic* (p. 74), which appeared at virtually the same time as the monograph on causation referred to above.

occurs. For, once more, the cause means something which was sufficient, and not as the objection assumes something which was both sufficient and necessary, to the effect. Thus the space-time limit of the cause process at the outer end is as elastic as we please, and varies with the space-time scope of the particular description of the cause that we give in each concrete case. And the same is true of the outer end of the effect process.[1]

3. The third observation to be made on the definition of cause proposed is that it defines the cause of a particular event in terms of but a single occurrence of it, and thus in no way involves the supposition that it, or one like it, ever has occurred before or ever will again. The supposition of recurrence is thus wholly irrelevant to the meaning of cause; that supposition is relevant only to the meaning of law. And recurrence becomes related at all to causation only when a law is considered which happens to be a generalization of facts themselves individually causal to begin with. A general proposition concerning such facts is, indeed, a causal law, but it is not causal because general. It is general, i.e., a law, only because it is about a class of resembling facts; and it is causal only because each of them already happens to be a causal fact individually and in its own right (instead of, as Hume would have it, by right of its co-membership with others in a class of pairs of successive events). The causal relation is essentially a relation between concrete individual events; and it is only so far as these events exhibit likeness to others, and can therefore be grouped with them into kinds, that it is possible to pass from individual causal facts to causal laws. On the other hand, in the case of laws obtained, not by experimentation and generalization of the result of it by abstraction, but in a purely statistical manner (the only manner directly relevant to Hume's notion of cause), it is only quite accidentally that the terms of such 'constant conjunctions' as these laws

---

[1] It is interesting to note that the analysis of the space-time relation of cause and effect given above reveals an essential connection between the two notions of Change and of Causation. For, taking any given change process, by specifying a space-time cut of it, one splits it into a cause and an effect; and, on the other hand, taking any given cause and its effect, by abstracting from the particular space-time cut in terms of which as common limit the cause process is distinguished from the effect process, one obtains a process describable as one change. This calls to mind Kant's very inadequately argued contention in the Second Analogy, that (objective) change involves the category of causation.

describe stand one to the other as cause and effect. Much more frequently they are not such and are not regarded as such; and uniformity of succession thus constitutes not at all the meaning of the cause-effect relation, but at the most only evidence of the existence of some causal connection, perhaps very remote and indirect, *and yet to be discovered,* between the terms of the succession. A causal connection explains the regularity of the succession, but is not constituted by such regularity, which is but a corollary of the causal connection whenever the cause or the chain of causes happens to occur again. Hume himself, indeed, on the very page of the *Enquiry* where he gives his definition of cause (in terms of regularity of succession), says that that definition is 'drawn from circumstances foreign to the cause'; 'from something extraneous and foreign to it.' And it was to avoid having to say, as Hume's definition would require, that day was the cause of night and night the cause of day, that Mill added, in his own definition, the requirement of 'unconditionality' to that of invariability of sequence—without perceiving, however, that as soon as 'unconditionality' was introduced, invariability became superfluous. For if the effect 'unconditionally' follows from the cause, i.e., is *necessitated by* the cause, then, obviously, as often as the cause recurs the effect *must* recur also. But this so-called unconditionality of an effect upon a cause, i.e., the necessitation of the effect by the cause, was the very thing which Mill had declared was not revealed by mere observed regularity of sequence. It must then be ascertained by the experimental 'method of difference', i.e., by the analytical observation of an individual case. But Mill never sees that this amounts to *defining* cause in terms of single difference in one experiment. Hume refers to single difference as a 'Rule' by which to judge of causes and effects,[1] and Mill, borrowing the blunder, throughout persists in regarding single difference as a 'method' for the roundabout ascertainment of something other than itself, viz., of invariable sequence; instead of, and properly, regarding it as the very definition of cause. This is perhaps in part explicable by the fact that Mill never clearly perceived the difference between experimentation and generalization[2] by abstraction; he never was adequately conscious that it is one thing to introduce a single difference, i.e.,

---

[1] *Treatise,* bk. I, part III, No. 15.
[2] This has been noted by Jevons, *Pure Logic and Other Minor Works,* p. 251.

make a single change, in a given concrete set of circumstances, and note what happens; and a very different thing to compare two such experiments, one of which yielded a certain effect and the other failed to, and note what single difference there was between the single antecedent changes introduced in the two cases into the (same) set of circumstances.

4. As a last remark upon the definition of cause in terms of a single case given above, it may be noted that it is the only one which is faithful to the manner in which the word 'cause' is actually used by every person whose English has not been contaminated by Hume. As Russell himself notes, we cannot without 'intolerable circumlocution'[1] avoid speaking of one particular event as causing another particular event. And, I ask, why seek to avoid it, when just that is so plainly what we do mean? When any philosophically pure-minded person sees a brick strike a window and the window break, he judges that the impact of the brick was the cause of the breaking, *because* he believes that impact to have been the only change which took place then in the immediate environment of the window. He may, indeed, have been mistaken, and acknowledge that he was mistaken, in believing that impact to have been the only change in the environment. But if so he will nevertheless maintain that *if* it had been the only change, it would have been the cause. That is, he will stand by the definition of cause, and admit merely that what he perceived was not a true case of what he meant and still means by cause.

5. *The observability of the causal relation*

This now brings us to the second of the two theses mentioned at the beginning of this paper, namely, that concerning the observability of the causal relation. Hume's view that no connection between a cause and its effect is objectively observable would be correct only under the assumption that a 'connection' is an entity of the same sort as the terms themselves between which it holds, that is, for Hume and his followers, a sense impression. For it is true that neither a colour, nor an odour, not a sound, nor a taste, nor any other sense impression, 'connecting' the cause and the effect, is observable between them. Indeed, we must even add that if a sense impression were present between those said to constitute the

---

[1] *Scientific Method in Philosophy*, p. 220.

cause and the effect, it would, from its very nature as a sense impression, be quite incapable of doing any connecting and would itself but constitute one more of the entities to be connected. This is true in particular of the feeling of expectation which Hume would have us believe is what the words 'necessary connection' ultimately denote.

But there is fortunately no need for us to attempt to persuade ourselves that whenever people during the past centuries have talked of objective connection they thus have not really meant it at all. For the fact is that causal connection is not a sensation at all, but a relation. The nature of that relation has already been minutely described above. It is, as we have seen, a relation which has individual concrete events for its terms; and, as analysed by us, its presence among such events is to be observed every day. We observe it whenever we perceive that a certain change is the *only* one to have taken place immediately before, in the immediate environment of another.

But at this point it becomes necessary for us to consider two apparently weighty objections, which can be urged against the observability of what we have defined as constituting the causal relation. One of them is that we are never theoretically certain that we have observed as much as the definition demands; and the other is that, on the other hand, we are often certain that the cause is less than the definition would permit us so to call. Each of these difficulties in turn must be carefully examined.

1. The first of them, more explicitly stated, is this: We never can be certain that the change which we have observed in any given case was, as the definition requires, the *only* change that occurred then and there, and therefore it is always possible that a part of the cause has escaped us. In considering this objection, it is, of course, well to bear in mind that our definition specifies contiguity in space as well as in time of the cause to the effect, and in addition permits us to set the *outer* space-time limit of the environment to be observed as near to the effect as we find convenient; so that the definition relieves us of the sometimes alleged obligation to observe the antecedent change of the entire universe. But even confining our observation to as externally limited a region of the contiguous space-time as we please, the possibility still always remains that we have not in a given case observed the whole of the change in that environment.

This predicament, it must frankly be admitted, is inescapable. But we must state also, and with all possible emphasis, that it is not peculiar to the definition of causation proposed.[1] Nor, indeed, is it, in its essence, peculiar even to definitions of cause. Rather it is a predicament involved *in every attempt to observe a universal negative*. Thus, even such an assertion as that 'this man is Mr. So-and-so' is theoretically always precarious in exactly the same manner, for there is no theoretically absolute guarantee that the man before us is not someone else, who merely happens to be exactly like Mr. So-and-so in the particular respects to which our observation has turned.[2] The predicament mentioned, thus, does not constitute the least evidence against the correctness of our definition of cause, for the very same difficulty would arise no matter what other definition were proposed.

All that we are then called upon to do in connection with that predicament is, first, to call attention to its existence and nature, and sagely class it as a fact illustrating the platitude that life is a precarious business in many ways; and, second, to state explicitly the proviso subject to which cases of causation as defined are observable. This proviso is obviously that *the change which we observed in the antecedently contiguous space-time was really the only change which occurred in it*. That is not something which we know to be true, but only something which we hope is true, and which for *practical* purposes we must suppose true; i.e., it is a *postulate*—the first of those underlying the present theory of causation. There is, however, no doubt that when, as in the laboratory, we have a high degree of control over the environment, and good opportunity to observe what occurs in it at a given moment, we do make the assumption just stated.

2. The second of the difficulties which we have to examine is of a logical rather than of a practical nature. It arises from the fact

---

[1] The corresponding difficulty with the Humian definition of cause as regular sequence is that experience never can guarantee that exceptions to the regularity of the sequence have not escaped our observation; or, more generally, that the sample of the character of the sequence, which we have observed, is a 'fair sample'.

[2] This difficulty becomes particularly acute when the opportunity for observation is limited, as, e.g., in establishing one's identity over the telephone; or, again, in the endeavour of psychical researchers to check up the alleged identity of the 'controls' of their mediums.

that in the face of the definition of cause given, we cannot without a contradiction refuse to take into the cause *any part* of the total change observed in the contiguous space-time environment of the effect; while, on the contrary, we very frequently in fact seem so to use the word 'cause' as to do just that. Thus, at the instant a brick strikes a window pane, the pane is struck, perhaps by the air waves due to the song of a canary near by. Yet we usually would say that the cause of the breakage was the impact of the brick, and that the impact of the air waves, although it was part of the prior total change in the contiguous space-time, was no part of the cause. This being the way in which the word 'cause' actually is used, how, then, can a definition which forbids us to call the cause anything less than *the whole* of the prior change in the contiguous space-time be regarded as a correct analysis of the meaning which the term 'cause' actually possesses?

The contradiction, however, is only apparent, and depends upon a confusion between two different questions, due in turn to a certain ambiguity in the expression 'the cause of an event'. The first of the two questions is, *what did cause, i.e., what did then and there suffice to, the occurrence of that concrete individual event?* The second question, on the other hand, is really a double question, for it assumes the answer to the first as already possessed, and goes on to ask, *which part of what did suffice would be left if we subtracted from what did suffice such portions of it as were unnecessary to such an effect?* This is a perfectly significant question, for to say 'sufficient to' is one thing; and to say 'no more than sufficient to' is another thing: a hundred-pound rock may well have been that which sufficed to the crushing of a worm, but it cannot be said to have been no more than what would have sufficed, since the tenth part of it would also have been enough. The second and double question, moreover, is usually that which we mean to ask when we inquire concerning the cause of an event; but, as will appear directly, it is not, like the first, really an inquiry after the cause of one individual concrete event strictly as such. It is, on the contrary, an inquiry concerning *what is common to it and to the causes of certain other events of the same kind.* This much of a generalization, indeed, is indissolubly involved in the mere assigning of *a name* to the cause and to the effect perceived; although *it is not involved in the merely perceiving them.* This is an extremely important point, which constitutes the very key to the whole matter. That this is so will become fully evident if the significance of the second of the two questions above is more explicitly analysed.

If we inquire what exactly is required to define the meaning of that (double) question, we find that at least *two* hypothetical cases are needed. For to say that in a given case a certain change *sufficed* to the occurrence of a given event, means, as we have seen, that no other change than it did occur in the prior contiguous space-time; and to say that a certain portion of that change was *unnecessary* means that in a case where that portion of the change did *not* occur —*which case therefore cannot be the very identical case, but only a case that is otherwise similar*—an (other) event of the same sort as the effect considered nevertheless did result. But now the fact that at least two hypothetical cases are thus necessary to define the meaning of our second question above, implies that that question is wholly meaningless with regard to one single concrete event. It is a question not, like the first, concerning the cause of one single concrete event, but concerning what was, or would be, *common to the causes* of at least two such.

The apparent contradiction which we faced is therefore now disposed of, for if, by 'the cause of an event', we really mean the cause of one individual concrete event, and not merely of some case of a sort of event, then we must include in our answer *the whole* of the antecedent change in the contiguous space-time. And if, on the other hand, our answer leaves out any part of that change (as it often does), then the only question to which it can be a correct answer is one as to *what was common to the individual causes* of two or more individual events of a given sort. Thus, if we say that the impact of a brick was the cause of the breaking of the window, and that the song of the canary had no part in it, then the words 'the breaking of the window' do not refer to an individual event considered in its full concreteness, but only to a *case-of-a-kind*, uniquely placed and dated indeed, but not qualitatively specified otherwise than by the characters that define its kind, viz., 'breaking of window'. And it is solely owing to this that we can truly say that the song of the canary had nothing to do with it, for that means, then, nothing to do with what occurred *in so far as what occurred is viewed merely as a case of breakage of a window*. As already explained, to say that the song of the canary was unnecessary is not to say that it was not part of what did then and there suffice; it *is* to say only that in *another* case, otherwise similar, where the song did not occur, an effect of the *same sort,* viz., breaking, nevertheless did occur.

The whole of our answer to the objection we have been discussing may, after all this detail, be summarized by saying that the expression 'the cause of the breaking of this window' has two senses, one strict, and the other elliptical. In the strict sense, it means 'the fully concrete individual event which caused all the concrete detail of this breaking of this window.' In the elliptical (and indeed more practically interesting) sense, it means 'that which the cause of this breaking of this window has in common with the individual causes of certain other individual events of the same sort.'

6. *The generalization of observed causal facts*

It is, of course, to be acknowledged that, as the parenthesis in the last sentence suggests, we are interested in causes and effects primarily for practical purposes, and that for such purposes causal knowledge is of direct value only so far as it has been generalized. This means that the interest of strictly concrete individual facts of causation to us is chiefly the indirect one of constituting raw material for generalization. And this explains why we so naturally and so persistently confuse the question, what did cause one given concrete event, with the very different question, in what respects does that cause resemble the causes of certain other events of the same sort previously observed in similar environments. For it is from the answer to this second question that we learn, what in such environments is the most we must do to cause the occurrence of another event of the given sort. And evidently just that is the very practically valuable information that we desire ultimately to obtain. But although it is true that, as practical beings, we are not directly interested in concrete individual facts of causation, it is not true that there are no such facts; nor, as we have seen, is it true that generality or recurrence is any part of the meaning of cause.

To round out the outline of the theory of the causal relation which this paper sets forth, there remains only to state the two postulates which condition, respectively, the validity of the descriptions by names which we formulate to fit sets of individual causal facts, and the validity of the applications we make of such generalizing descriptions to new cases.

The postulate which conditions the correctness of any answer we venture to give to the problem of description, viz., the problem in what respects the cause of a given concrete event resembles the causes of certain others of the same sort previously observed in similar environments,[1] is that *the respects of resemblance which we include in our answer* (through the name by which we describe the cause) *are really the only ones that there were*. This postulate, which may be called that of the *descriptibility* of our causal observations, is then the second postulate of our theory. The first, which it will be recalled was that no change that was not observed occurred in the prior contiguous space-time environment, may be called that of the *observability* of causal facts. And the third postulate, which we may term that of the *applicability* of our descriptions of our observations of causal facts to new cases, is that *the new case (or cases) differs from those on the basis of which the description was formulated not otherwise nor more widely than they differed among themselves.*

---

[1] Mill correctly states that 'It is inherent in a description to be the statement of a resemblance, or resemblances,' *Logic*, p. 452.

2.

ON THE ANALYSIS OF
CAUSALITY*

In a recent issue of *The Journal of Philosophy*,[1] Professor Arthur Pap calls attention to the fact that critics of the regularity theory of causation have more than once pointed out that two events may be 'constantly conjoined' without being causally connected, but have mostly been silent as to an alternative analysis of the concept of causation. He then mentions as an exception the analysis of it offered in Chapters 8 and 9 of my book, *Nature, Mind, and Death*. But he goes on to say that that analysis seems to him completely untenable, for reasons he then proceeds to set forth.[2]

If those reasons indeed invalidate it and no valid other analysis of the concept is in sight, then, in view of the ubiquity and importance to us of the Causality relation, there can hardly be a more pressing task in the whole field of philosophy than that of formulating an adequate analysis of that relation. And to do so ought not really to be very difficult, for the notion of Causality is used many times every day by each of us, whether explicitly or implicitly. All such verbs as 'to break', 'to bend', 'to heat', 'to kill', 'to twist', 'to melt', 'to prevent', 'to steer', 'to remind', 'to irritate', etc., are verbs of causation. Moreover in the majority of cases, we seem to have little or no difficulty in identifying concrete instances of the causal relationships those verbs designate as between events of the kinds respectively concerned. Hence we must have an adequate working notion of Causality, and it should be possible to analyse it.

---

* *The Journal of Philosophy*, vol. LIV, No. 13, 1957.

[1] 'A Note on Causation and the Meaning of "Event",' vol. LIV, No. 6, March 14, 1957, pp. 155–9.

[2] That analysis is also set forth in the present collection's first paper: *On the Nature and the Observability of the Causal Relation*.

The difficulty which has chiefly stood in the way of reaching an analysis of it that would stand up has been, I believe, that instead of attending to the obvious, the searchers have gratuitously assumed that Causality must be something recondite and therefore hard to detect. But what in fact was needed for the task was not superior ingenuity, but ingenuousness—the ingenuousness which, in the familiar story of the courtiers vying in admiration of the king's subtly fine garments, enabled the innocent child to perceive that the king was simply naked!

I believe that Pap's criticisms of the analysis of Causality I offered can be shown to be based only on certain misapprehensions. Before turning to this, however, and irrespective of the correctness or incorrectness of Pap's surmises as to how I arrived at that analysis, it will be well to state briefly what it is.

1. *The Causality relation*

What I contend is that Causality is *the relation which obtains between the three terms of a perfect experiment*—the relation, namely, between a given *state of affairs S* and two *changes* (whether simple or complex) in it that are the *only* two changes in it: one of them a change C at a time T_1, and the other a change E at an *immediately sequent* time T_2. To say that this triadic relation obtains between S, C, and E is to say that C in S is etiologically both sufficient and necessary to E in S (i.e., both *cause* of and *condition* of E in S); and, conversely, that E in S is etiologically both necessitated by and contingent upon C in S (i.e., both *effect* of and *resultant* of C in S). This definition of Causality, being framed in terms of but one occurrence of the sequence in S of C and E, does not require the supposition that it ever occurred before or ever will again. But it entails that whenever, if ever, S, and C in S recur, then E in S also recurs.

2. *Pap's first criticism*

Pap writes: 'Ducasse overlooks that the observation of a solitary change preceding the event to be explained may not be the sufficient ground of the causal judgement.' The ground which Pap says may be required and actually employed in addition is: (i) elimination of alternative explanatory hypotheses—e.g., in the instance of the parcel that glowed when I touched it, the hypothesis that the parcel's continuing contact with the table was the cause; and (ii) the assumption that causality is universal—'cause' being conceived as regular immediately antecedent event.

Now, as regards (i), what Pap apparently overlooks is that, simply under the definition of Causality stated in Sec. 1, i.e., *without any tacit additional premises* such as he suggests, the supposition that C (my touching the parcel) was the *only* change immediately preceding E (the parcel's glowing) automatically eliminates as alternative the hypothesis that some *other* change could be the cause of E. And further, the hypothesis that the *continuing* contact of the parcel with the table might be the cause of the glowing is automatically eliminated too, as alternative explanatory hypothesis, by the definition's requirement that the cause be a *change* in the given, otherwise continuing, state of affairs S.

As regards (ii), since, admittedly, some cases of regularity of sequence exist that are *not* cases of causation, regularity of sequence cannot, merely as such, be what Causality consists in. Hence to suppose that 'Causality', conceived as merely regularity of sequence, is universal, is to suppose that something, *which does not constitute Causality,* is universal. And such a supposition is not needed for, nor is it relevant to, the conclusion that if C (my touching the parcel) was indeed, as my analysis of Causality requires, the only change occurring in the situation S immediately before the change E (the glowing), then C was what caused E.

Whether the only change one *observed* was the only change that *really occurred* at the time in the given state of affairs is of course a different question. What can be said about it is only that, the more carefully we look for additional changes without finding any, the more *probable* it becomes that there were no others. To analyse the concept of Causality is one task; and to identify empirically concrete exemplifications of it is another task. The outcome of the latter always remains theoretically precarious in some degree. But this is nothing peculiar to Causality. Rather, it is a feature of every attempt to identify in experience concrete cases of something one has defined abstractly—for example, Straightness, or Equality, etc.

3. *Pap's criticism under his (a) heading*

Pap states there that, on my analysis of Causality, 'it is self-contradictory to suppose that an event which is immediately preceded by more than one change in its neighbourhood is caused at all.' But what really follows from my analysis is only that the change in S, which immediately preceded the event, was then a *complex* change; for in order that at a time T a change C in S be the *single* change there, it does not have to be a *simple* change.

Pap writes next: 'If one antecedent event is causally irrelevant to e, then all of them are, since a change which is one of several concurrent changes in S cannot be said to be the only change in S.' But any appearance that that conclusion follows is due only to the ambiguous phrase, 'causally irrelevant to', which invites confusion between etiologically *sufficient to* (i.e., 'cause of') and etiologically *necessary to* (i.e., 'condition of'). That a complex change abc in S, which was the single change immediately preceding a complex single other change def in S, was sufficient to cause it, entails that it was *sufficient* to cause all the parts of def, but does not entail that the *whole* of abc was a *necessary* condition of, say, occurrence of the part d of def. For no contradiction is involved in supposing, for example, that, had the part a of abc been absent, the remainder, bc, would have been sufficient to cause, say, df.

The only way to find out whether or not it would have been sufficient—i.e., the only way to isolate sufficient cause from necessary condition—is to take a *new case* of the S state of affairs, but one in which the single change which occurs in it first is not abc but only bc; and then to observe whether or not d is again a part of the change which immediately follows in S. If it is, then the part a of the change abc was *not necessary* to the part d of the ensuing change in S—and this notwithstanding that the *whole* of abc in S was *both* sufficient and necessary to the *whole* of def in S.

4. *Pap's criticism under his (b) heading*

Pap's contention, under the (b) heading of his criticism, is that my analysis of Causality would make the words 'cause' and 'effect' applicable only to concrete events, whereas 'in any ordinary and significant use' those words 'are applied to instances of definite kinds of events, not to what Ducasse calls "concrete events". '

What invalidates this criticism is the false assumption, on which it is based, that the *instances* of given kinds of events do not consist of concrete events. The truth is, on the contrary, that every state of affairs that exists, and every change in it that occurs, is fully concrete, no matter of what kinds that state of affairs and that change in it may respectively be instances. And of course, only changes *that occur*, in states of affairs *that exist,* can cause or be caused by anything. This is the sense in which it is true that my analysis of Causality makes the words 'cause' and 'effect' applicable only to concrete events; and this restriction constitutes not a defect but a virtue of that analysis, for it is a requirement which any correct analysis of Causality would have to satisfy.

That restriction, however, does not in the least stand in the way of either of the following two things:

One is—as pointed out in Sec. 3 above—that it is possible *to interest oneself* specifically in some concrete *part* of a given concrete occurrence, and to inquire as to what concrete *part* of the cause of that occurrence was sufficient to, and what concrete *part* of it was not necessary to, occurrence of that specific concrete part of the given total occurrence.

The other thing that is in no way precluded by the restriction mentioned is that one should choose to limit *the interest one takes* in a given concrete change, that is occurring in a given concrete state of affairs, to the fact that the change happens to be of a certain kind K, and the state of affairs in which it takes place, of a certain kind Z. If so, one is then simply *uninterested* in the characteristics, additional to those definitive of kinds K and Z, which the given concrete change and concrete state of affairs do possess notwithstanding one's disinterest in them—which additional characteristics differentiate from all other instances of K and of Z *the* individual instance, respectively of K and of Z, which the given concrete change and the given concrete state of affairs respectively constitutes.

Hence, when one asks for the cause of the given concrete change *of kind K* which took place in the given concrete state of affairs *of kind Z*, one is correspondingly *interested only* in discovering what *the kind Q* is, of which that concrete cause, like the concrete causes of the other concrete changes *of kind K* in other concrete states of affairs *of kind Z*, was an instance.

In the light of these remarks, it becomes evident that my analysis of Causality is perfectly consistent with the meaning of such a question as 'What caused this breakage of this window?' and of such an answer as 'The impact of this brick caused it'.

Also, statements of causal laws, which are what enable us to control or to anticipate events, can be interpreted without difficulty in terms of my analysis of Causality. For example, the rough causal generalization: 'Throwing bricks at windows ordinarily causes them to break' would be explicated as: 'Any concrete change that is an instance of the kind "throwing a brick at a window" does, under concrete circumstances that are an instance of the "ordinary" kind, cause a concrete change that is an instance of the kind "breakage of the window". '

3.

CAUSATION: PERCEIVABLE?
OR ONLY INFERRED?*

David Hume, in his *Enquiry Concerning Human Understanding*, rightly declares that 'if there be any relation between objects which it imports us to know perfectly, it is that of cause and effect.' And he goes on to say that 'the only immediate utility of all the sciences is to teach us how to control and regulate future events by their causes.'[1]

What, then, is this Causality relation, with which the sciences supposedly occupy themselves? If we turn to recent treatises on the methods and concerns of science, what we find discussed under the heading of Causality is what Nagel aptly terms 'the so-called "law of causality".' But, as he goes on to point out, 'there is no general agreement as to what it affirms'; that is, whether it is an empirical generalization, or an *a priori* truth, or a concealed definition, or perhaps a recommended maxim of procedure in inquiry.[2]

1. The 'principle of causality' in theoretical physics

The last of these conceptions seems to be the one now most favoured by philosophers of science. Nagel, for instance, writes that 'the principle (of causality) as a maxim expresses the general objective of theoretical science to achieve *deterministic* explanations in the now familiar sense of determinism according to which, given the state of a system for some initial time, the explanatory

---

* From *Philosophy & Phenomenological Research*, vol. XXVI, No. 2, 1965.
[1] Open Court edition, pp. 78–9.
[2] *The Structure of Science*, Harcourt Brace & World, New York 1961, pp. 316 ff.

theory logically establishes a unique state for the system for any other time' (p. 323).

Margenau similarly conceives the principle of causality to be what he terms 'a metaphysical requirement. It demands that (theoretical) constructs shall be so chosen as to *generate causal laws*.'[1] And more explicitly, 'We wish to regard causality as a relation (not between immediate experiences, but) between constructs, in particular as a relation between *states*, or conditions, of physical systems. The principle of causality asserts that a given state is invariably followed, in time, by another specifiable state ... causality is a property of physical laws and not of observations' (p. 95).

Accounts of the 'principle of causality', likewise in terms of strict functional relations between the state of a system at a given time and its state at any later or earlier time, are given by Northrop,[2] and by Lenzen.[3] The system, of course, is conceived as *isolated*. This is explicitly mentioned for instance by Philipp Frank when he writes that 'the applicability (of the principle of causality) ... depends on the possibility of isolating (*herausgreifen*) from the universe portions inside which (a state) Ao always recurs.'[4] And Margenau writes that 'the availability of finite "closed systems" is a precondition for causality to be meaningful.'[5]

In the chapter where he discusses various manners in which the term Cause has actually been used, Margenau insists on a distinction between 'total cause', which is what is in view in physical theories, and 'partial causes', which would be one or another part of the total cause that somehow specially engages the interest of a particular person. But Margenau insists that 'there is no causality among matters of fact ... even when the transition from partial to total causes is made' (pp. 395–6).

The upshot, then, of the various statements about causality by the contemporary philosophers of science quoted seems to be that when in theoretical physics something A is spoken of as cause of something B, what both A and B designate are total states of a theoretical system conceived as isolated, A being conceived as occurring at a time T_1 earlier than the time T_2 of B; the theoreti-

---

[1] *The Nature of Physical Reality*, McGraw-Hill, New York 1950, p. 96.
[2] *Philosophy of Science*, vol. 3, No. 2, April 1936, p. 226.
[3] *Causality in Natural Science*, Charles C. Thomas, Springfield, 1954, p. 21.
[4] *Das Kausalgesetz und seine Grenzen*, Wien, 1932, p. 230.
[5] Op. cit., p. 398.

cal system being itself so conceived as equally to warrant inference of occurrence of B at T_2 from occurrence of A at T_1, and inference of A at T_1 from occurrence of B at T_2.

In theoretical physics, causality is thus a conceptual relation, strictly dyadic, between conceived total states A and B of a conceptual system; and since concepts are not perceivable, neither is causation of B by A perceivable. This is what entails that, as Margenau stresses, among 'matters of fact', i.e., among perceivable occurrences, there is no causation. But of course, this only means no causation *in the sense assigned to the term in theoretical physics.*

Causation in this sense therefore has no relevance to matters of fact unless one is somehow able to identify certain perceived occurrences as being concrete instances of total states A and B of some particular isolated theoretical system.

Such identification, so far as it is possible at all, is effected by means of certain operational 'bridges' between the conceived and the perceived; that is, between theoretical constructs and concrete occurrences. These bridges are what Northrop has called 'epistemic correlations'; Margenau, 'rules of correspondence'; Bridgman, the 'text' as distinguished from the equations of a theory; Norman Campbell, the 'dictionary' as distinguished from the 'hypothesis' of a theory; C. W. Morris and J. H. Woodger, the 'semantics' of a theory as distinguished from its 'syntax'; and the present writer, a 'method of comparison' of something perceived and something defined.[1]

Thus, when causation is defined as in theoretical physics, concrete cases of it are *not perceived* to be such but are *inferred* to be such: They are ascertainable only by deductive inference from, together, the particular physical theory concerned, and the fact that

[1] F. S. C. Northrop, *The Meeting of East and West,* MacMillan, New York 1946, p. 443. H. Margenau, *The Nature of Physical Reality,* McGraw-Hill, New York 1950, pp. 60 ff. P. W. Bridgman, *The Logic of Modern Physics,* MacMillan, New York 1927, pp. 5, 6, and *The Nature of Physical Theory,* Princeton Univ. Press, 1936, p. 59. N. R. Campbell, *Physics, The Elements,* Cambridge Univ. Press 1920, p. 122. C. W. Morris, *Foundations of the Theory of Signs,* Internat. Encycl. of Unified Science, vol. I, No. 2, Univ. of Chicago Press 1938, p. 6. J. H. Woodger, *The Technique of Theory Construction, Internat. Encyc. of Unified Science,* vol. II, No. 5, Univ. of Chicago Press 1939, pp. 6, 7. C. J. Ducasse, 'A Liberalistic View of Truth', *Philosophical Review,* vol. XXXIV, No. 6, November 1925, pp. 583–5.

a certain concrete occurrence cA, perceived at a time t_1, and a certain other concrete occurrence cB perceived at a time t_2, were identified—each by means of a 'bridging' operation such as just referred to—as being concrete instances respectively of the antecedent 'total state' A, and of the sequent 'total state' B of the theoretical system envisaged.

What must now be emphasized, however, is that the capacity or incapacity of a particular operation to identify a perceivable instance of something defined depends on the relevance or irrelevance of the operation to the particular use one intends to make of the perceivable fact the operation picks out.

This becomes evident if one notes that the need for an operation to bridge the gap between definition and perception is not confined to occasions when 'cause A' and 'effect B' are the terms one had defined. Consider for example the task of ascertaining whether a given concrete object does or does not *weigh one kilogram*. By international stipulation, the definition of 'weighing one kilogram' is *being equal in weight* to a certain piece of platinum-iridium kept in the International Bureau of Weights and Measures.' But objects equal in weight to the standard kilogram can be identified only by comparing their weight with that of the standard kilogram by means of, typically, a balance; and some balances are far more sensitive than others. Which balance, then, shall one use?

The answer is that if on a given occasion one's purpose in weighing the object is to find out how much postage will be needed to mail it, then the balance at the Post Office is the authoritative one to use even if, when it says the object weighs one kilogram, the far more sensitive balance in a research laboratory or in the office of a dealer in precious metals were to say that the object weighs a little more than one kilogram. On the other hand, the latter balance would be the authoritative one if the object were a gold bar one was intending to buy or to sell.

Similarly, a particular operation by which to identify two perceivable occurrences as being instances, respectively, of 'a cause' and of 'its effect' as these two terms are defined in theoretical physics, will be authoritative, or not, according to the relevance or irrelevance of the information yielded by the operation to the particular use one intended to make of that information. For it might be too precise, or on the contrary not precise enough, to enable one to conclude from it whether, for instance, the death of a particular person was a case of suicide, or of murder, or of man-slaughter.

An additional important remark remains to be made concerning causation as defined in theoretical physics. It is that what is so defined is, *ex hypothesi, physical* causation; and hence that the theoretical physicist's definition of causation has no direct relevance, if any relevance at all, to cases of causation where the cause, or the effect, or both, are *mental* not physical events.

2. *The common verbs of causation, and the perceivability of causal connection*

Let us now turn from theoretical physics to the conception of causation implicit in the use everyone actually makes of the common verbs of causation. Causality as defined in theoretical physics is patently not the relation a person has in view when, in describing some ordinary occurrence he perceives, he employs transitively one or another of the many common verbs which are then verbs of causation; verbs, for example, such as to bend, to corrode, to push, to cut, to scratch, to break, to kill, to transform, to remind, to motivate, to irritate, to ignite, to create, to incite, to convey, etc.

Indeed, it is only because the relation contemplated in the physicist's concept of causality is *not* the relation of which particular cases are in view when such common verbs of causation are being employed, that it was possible for Margenau to assert without paradox that 'there is no causality among matters of fact' (p. 395); for otherwise this assertion would entail that there are no such occurrences as that of one particular thing being bent by, or pushed by, or ignited by, or scratched by, etc., another thing.

Beyond question, however, there are such occurrences; and the millions of persons who, in reporting them, employ these verbs of causation do so—and in most cases correctly—without drawing at all on the physicist's definition of causality; of which anyway the vast majority of the users of those common verbs have never even heard.

I therefore submit that the ability we all have, to employ and understand those ordinary verbs of causation, has its source in a fact which is obvious when attention is called to it, but which is usually ignored as automatically as each of us ordinarily ignores his sight of his own nose when writing or looking at his watch.

The plain fact to which I refer is that every person has *perceived*—and I say *perceived*, not *inferred*—that, for example, a particular tree branch was *being caused to bend* by a particular bird's alighting on it; that a particular bottle was *being caused to break* by the fall on it of a particular rock; that a particular billiard ball was *being caused to move* by a particular other billiard ball's rolling against it; that a particular match was *being caused to ignite* by friction of it on a particular rough surface; that a particular footprint was *being created*—that is, being caused to exist—by a particular man's foot walking on a beach, etc. Indeed, even a naïve dog who innocently approached a mother cat's kittens then *perceived* not only the cat and her movements, but also that he was *being scratched* by them!

My contention that in such cases what is *perceived* is not only two occurrences but also *causation* of one of them by the other, is based on two solid facts which, although crucial, are commonly neglected in discussions of causality.

(1) The first of them is that what is capable of being perceived includes not only various physical objects and the occurrences which the behaviour of those objects at particular moments constitutes, but also *various space and time relations between those occurrences*; and sometimes *the special one of these relations which constitutes causation of one concrete event by another*; namely, the special relation definitive of what is called an *experiment*. When in such a case the concrete events perceived are of the particular kinds concerned in one or another of the examples offered in what precedes, then the *causing* of one of the two events by the other is termed more specifically the bending, breaking, pushing, igniting, creating, or scratching of one of the two perceived objects by the other. In any such concrete case observed, the causation which occurred was *not inferred* but was as literally *perceived* as were the concrete events it connected.

Hume, it is true, asserted that no connection is ever perceived between a particular cause-event and its particular effect-event. But he then found himself forced to confess *that he did not even know what he was denying* under the name of 'connection'; for he declared that 'we have no idea of this connection, nor even any distinct notion of what it is we desire to know, when we endeavour at a conception of it.'[1]

---

[1] *Enquiry Concerning Human Understanding,* Open Court ed., p. 79.

What Hume failed to realize, of course, was that although sequence is not *eo ipso* consequence, yet, when sequence occurs under the special conditions distinctive of what is properly called *an experiment*—whether one performed by man or by Nature—then, *eo ipso*, the sequence is *causal sequence*; so that, in the many cases where an experiment is what one did perceive, causation of the sequent event by the antecedent event was itself perceived as truly as were the two events concerned.

Causation, then, i.e., proximate causation, is the *triadic* relation which obtains between the three factors that together constitute an experiment. They are: (1) a concrete *state of affairs S* in which only two changes, whether simple or complex, occur; (2) one of these a change C occurring at a time T; and (3) the other a change E that begins to occur after change C has begun to occur.[1] This triadic relation is *not a sign* that causation, in some mysterious sense, is occurring, but is *causation itself,* and is perceived by the performer or observer of a well-conducted experiment. Indeed, one may well ask what an experiment makes perceptually evident, if not that occurrence of the particular variation C at time T in the variables of the set up S of the experiment did cause the particular sequent variation E in those variables.

Moreover, *one single experiment* is sufficient in principle to make evident that the particular change C in S did cause the particular change E in S. For repetition of the experiment is called for, if at all, only to make sure that the experiment was conducted strictly, and its outcome observed accurately.

Causation is therefore not to be confused with causal law, as too often is done. An empirically discovered causal law is causal not because it asserts a uniformity of sequence (for some uniform sequences are admittedly not causal), but because it is an induction from perceived occurrences each of which, *in its own individual right,* was a case of causation and was perceived to be so. An occurrence therefore could be unique in the history of the universe, and yet be, and be known to be, a case of causation.

---

[1] Some writers have plausibly contended that an effect and its proximate cause are strictly simultaneous. But if so the question remains as to how we can decide which of the two events concerned is the cause and which the effect. The answer is that, as R. M. Gale has pointed out (p. 211, *The Review of Metaphysics,* December 1965), the cause is *the only one of the two related events that has a prior cause independent of the other event.*

(2) I pass now to the second of the two facts alluded to earlier, which support the contention that causation of one event by another is sometimes as literally perceived as are the two events themselves. The fact to which I refer is that, in order that a person be able to perceive that one of a pair of perceived events is causing the other, it is not at all necessary that he should know *discursively* —that is, that he should be able to describe—the special features which identify a certain space-time relation, perceived between two events, as being the causality relation. It is enough that, on occasions when that relation is present and is perceivable, his practical response to the occasion be such as is appropriate to a case of causation, not such as would be appropriate to a case of accidental sequence.

Capacity of a percipient thus to discriminate in practice between these two kinds of cases does not require that he should be able to describe the features distinctive of the causality relation, any more than does the capacity of a dog to respond differently to the approach of his master and to that of a stranger require that the dog should be able to describe his master.[1]

---

[1] cf. 'Tacit Knowing: Its Bearing on some Problems of Philosophy,' by Michael Polanyi—*Reviews of Modern Physics*, vol. 34, No. 4, Oct. 1962.

4.

CONCERNING THE
UNIFORMITY OF CAUSALITY*

In a paper entitled 'Professor Ducasse on Determinism' (*Philosophy and Phenomenological Research*, vol. XXII, No. 1, 1961), Professor Richard M. Gale refers to the contention in Chapter 9 of my book, *Nature, Mind, and Death*, that causation is both universal and uniform. He writes: 'Professor Ducasse develops the thesis that *every* event of *necessity* must have a cause from which it follows in a uniform manner. If it can be shown that causality is both uniform and universal, determinism will *ipso facto* be proven.' Then, referring to my definition of Causality on p. 106 of that book, as 'the relation which obtains between an event C at a time T_1, and another event E at a later time T_2 if C and E are two changes in a given state of affairs S and are the only two changes in it', Gale writes that 'the crucial question is whether this definition either includes or entails that causality is uniform'; and he then gives the reasons why he would answer that question in the negative.

The reply I offer to Gale's criticisms of the definition of Causality I have put forward depends for such force as it has on certain considerations and distinctions too often neglected in discussions of Causality, which had therefore better first be explicitly stated.

(a) Gale and I are I believe in agreement that nothing other than an *event* can be said without incongruity to cause, or to be caused by, anything—an 'event' meaning either a change or (to borrow Dr. Charles Mercier's term) an 'unchange', i.e., a state's enduring for some time unchanged. That is, to speak of a *thing*, e.g., of a knife, as causing something is permissible at all only if meant elliptically; for, literally, occurrence of a cut is caused not by what a knife *is* but by occurrence of a *motion* as between the

* *Philosophy and Phenomenological Research*, vol. XXII, No. 1, 1961.

knife and the substance cut; and occurrence of a motion is an event, and so is occurrence of a cut. On such an occasion, the knife is properly categorized not as cause but as *agent*, i.e., as that, of which a *motion* causes a cut in some substance, whose status is then so far that of *patient*, not of effect.

(b) I believe that Gale and I are also in agreement that, if only there be passage of time, then the definition of causality I have presented entails that every event is caused and in turn causes something.

(c) The first point to which attention must now be called is that if two events are causally connected, then there are *four*, not just two, more specific relations in which one of the two events may be standing to the other. These four relations are termed 'cause of', 'effect of', 'condition of', and 'resultant of'.[1]

More explicitly, that a given event functioned as 'cause of' a given other, and the other conversely as 'effect of' the first, means that, under the circumstances which then existed, occurrence of the first was *causally sufficient* (or we may prefer to say, synonymously, *etiologically sufficient*) to occurrence of the other; and conversely, occurrence of the other was *causally necessitated by* occurrence of the first.

And, that a given event functioned as 'condition of' a given other, and the other conversely as 'resultant of' the first, means that, under the circumstances which existed, occurrence of the first was *causally necessary to* occurrence of the other; and conversely, occurrence of the other was *causally contingent on* occurrence of the first.

(d) The use just made of the expressions 'sufficient to', 'necessitated by', 'necessary to', and 'contingent on', calls attention to a fact about which it is of cardinal importance to be perfectly clear in discussions of causality. It is that although these expressions sometimes designate *logical* relations (between truth-values of propositions), nevertheless they sometimes designate instead *causal* relations (between concrete occurrences); and further that the latter relations cannot be 'reduced to', i.e., are not special cases of, the former. This, if it should not be obvious, can be made so by the following illustrations.

---

[1] For the justification of using 'resultant of' to designate the fourth of these relations, see the writer's *Nature, Mind, and Death*, pp. 107–8 n.

An example of logical entailment would be: Truth of 'All M's are P's and S is an M' logically entails, i.e., is *logically sufficient to*, Truth of 'S is a P'; and conversely, truth of 'S is a P' is logically entailed by, i.e., is *logically necessitated by*, truth of 'All M's are P's and S is an M.' Again, Truth of 'S is an M' is logically presupposed by, i.e., is *logically necessary to*, truth of 'None but M's are P's and S is a P'; and conversely, truth of 'None but M's are P's and S is a P' logically presupposes, i.e, is *logically contingent on*, truth of 'S is an M.'

On the other hand, that, under the concrete circumstances which existed at a given time and place, a given concrete scratching of a given concrete object on a given concrete surface was *causally sufficient* to the given object's then catching on fire was discovered *by making the experiment and observing its outcome*; not by detecting a relation of logical entailment between the concrete scratching and the sequent concrete occurrence of fire. For no such relation existed or could have existed between them: relations of logical entailment and logical presupposition, whether formal or conceptual, are congruous to truth-values of propositions, but incongruous to concrete occurrences.

Or again, the relation which obtained between the actual motion of the executioner's axe and the actual coming off of the head of Charles I was not that of implicans to implicate, but that of cause to effect. To say that the movement of the axe *made* the head come off means that *causation not logical entailment*, of the second by the first is *what occurred then*. Actual causation always has a date (and so has actual inference) but logical entailment is not an event and therefore has no date.

In view then of the ambiguity of the expressions 'sufficient to', 'necessitated by', 'necessary to', 'contingent on', it is essential when employing them in discussions of causality to make them unambiguous by prefixing them either with 'causally' or with 'logically', according to what specifically one then means; and the same precaution is appropriate in the case of the expression 'impossible' and the expression 'possible'; the latter, it is important to notice, being ambiguous not only in the respect just mentioned, but also in that it sometimes means *not necessary*, but sometimes means *not impossible*.

(e) The expressions '*causally* sufficient to', '*causally* necessitated by', '*causally* necessary to', and '*causally* contingent on' are the ones whose definition by me is in view in Gale's comments. It will therefore be well now to state that definition precisely. It is formulated in terms of the relations which obtain between the three elements of a *perfect* experiment, as follows:

Suppose (i) a concrete i.e., completely determinate, state of affairs, and let S designate the nature and quantity of it. Suppose further (ii) that at a particular moment M of its existence, a completely determinate change occurs in it, C designating the nature and quantity of that change. Suppose further (iii) that, immediately after the occurrence of this change, there occurs in the given state of affairs another completely determinate change, E designating the nature and quantity of it. And finally suppose (iv) that these two changes are the only ones that occur in the given state of affairs during a period that includes both of them. Then occurrence of the first of these two changes in S was both *'causally sufficient to'* (i.e., was *'cause of'*), and *'causally necessary to'* (i.e., was *'condition of'*) occurrence of the second change in S; and conversely occurrence of the second change in S was both *'causally necessitated by'* (i.e., was *'effect of'*) and *'causally contingent on'* (i.e., was *'resultant of'*) occurrence in S of the first change.[1]

The causality relation thus analyses as irreducibly *triadic*, not *dyadic* as often tacitly assumed—an assumption which gives rise to various wholly gratuitous puzzles. The triadic character, moreover, extends to the notion of 'causally impossible' and to that of 'causally possible' whether in the sense of 'not causally necessary' or in the sense of 'not causally impossible'.

(f) A word must here be added concerning the adjective, 'determinate', which is employed in the definition; for otherwise confusion might arise between it and the adjective, 'determined'.

In the definition, 'determinate' is used in the sense which contrasts it with 'determinable', and which may be made clear by the following example. 'Colour' is the name of a determinable quality; 'Yellow', of a subdeterminable of it; and 'Dark Yellow', 'Greenish Yellow', etc., would in turn be names of subdeterminables of Yellow. But even these would be further determinable in respect of precise hue, of precise degree of lightness or darkness, and of precise degree of saturation. The yellow, on the other hand, of the

---

[1] For present purposes, there is no need to consider the rather obvious process by which 'sufficient to' can be separated from 'necessary to', and 'necessitated by' separated from 'contingent on'.

paper now in front of me is *completely determinate* in all three of these dimensions of any colour. The yellow of the paper is even then a *species* of yellow, but is an *infima species*, i.e., a species that has no sub-species. Yet it remains a species—a kind—inasmuch as it is capable of existing or not existing at any particular place-time.

Such, then, is the sense in which the term 'determinate', as distinguished from 'determinable' is used in the definition given in Sec. (e).[1] That the state of affairs S and the occurrences C and E, in terms of which is framed the definition of causality offered in Sec. (e), are hypothesized as 'concrete' in the sense of completely determinate both qualitatively and quantitatively, but are left completely indeterminate as regards date and place, is a feature of the definition which has direct bearing on Gale's criticism, which we are now in position to consider.

(g) Gale's contention, if I apprehend it correctly, is as follows, when formulated in the terms employed in the definition of the causality relation. He considers the supposition (i) that a state of affairs exists again, whose completely determinate nature and quantity is wholly identical with that which S was employed to designate; and (ii) that, at a particular moment M in the existence of that state of affairs there occurs a change in it which is the only change in it at the moment, and the determinate nature and quantity of which is wholly identical with that which C was employed to designate. He then contends that suppositions (i) and (ii) above, taken together with the definition given earlier of *causal* necessitation of change E in S by only change C in S, do not *logically* necessitate that, immediately after M, an only change whose determinate nature and quantity will be wholly identical with that which E was employed to designate, is *causally* necessitated to occur in the contemplated state of affairs.

I submit, however, that this contention is self-contradictory and therefore invalid, for it supposes that the requirements for *causal necessitation* of E in S, as these were defined, *are* strictly met, and

---

[1] The distinction between 'determinable' and 'determinate' is set forth by W. E. Johnson in ch. XI, 'The Determinable', of vol. I of his *Logic*. Misleadingly, however, he uses the names of various colours as illustrations of names of determinates; whereas obviously blue, for instance is a determinable having as subdeterminables cerulean blue, prussian blue, etc. Actually no names exist in the common language for the very many distinguishable completely determinate colours.

yet that this *does not logically necessitate* that occurrence of E in S is then *causally necessitated!*

More explicitly, the fact which *logically* necessitates that causation of E in S by C in S, as defined, is uniform, is that the definition of such causation makes no reference at all either explicitly or implicitly to any particular date or point in space. Hence the supposition that C in S did, in the sense defined, cause E in S yesterday, and yet that identical occurrence of S and of C in S today might not, in the sense defined, cause identical occurrence of E in S is incongruous exactly as would be the supposition, for instance, that a prime number is defined as one divisible without remainder only by itself and unity and that 7 is such a number, and yet that 7 might be prime today but perhaps not tomorrow. In both cases alike, particular date or place in space, merely as such, is totally irrelevant.

Gale, however, argues that particular date and place *are* relevant to the question whether causality, as defined by me, is uniform; and this because difference of date and place logically entails that we then have 'two different instances' of S and of C in S. But his conclusion that it is *logically* possible that in the later instance the effect will be different from what it was in the earlier ignores the fact that, *ex hypothesi,* the two instances are not different but strictly identical *in every one of the features in terms of which alone causal necessitation of E in S was defined*; and that particular date and place did not enter at all, explicitly or implicitly, in the definition, and are therefore logically altogether irrelevant to the question of causation of E in S by C in S. And, if something is causally necessitated to occur, it *does* necessarily occur!

Empirically, of course—as distinguished from theoretically as in the definition of causality in terms of a *perfect* experiment—one instance of a described kind of occurrence is practically certain to differ to some extent from another instance of it, no matter how minute is the description of the kind of occurrence concerned, for description is always in terms of *determinables*, whereas the qualitative and quantitative characteristics of each concrete actual instance are *completely determinate* and in all probability are not strictly the same determinates of the determinables alike instantiated in both cases. Also, in an actual experiment, the requirement that the change first occurring in the actual state of affairs, and the change observed to follow it, be the only two changes in that state of affairs, may not be strictly complied with, for they may actually be the only two changes that were noticed, though not the only two that did occur. Hence, empirically, the description of what, in an experiment performed, did cause what, is strictly speaking never more than approximate; and this entails that, empirically, sameness of effect, in repetitions of the experiment, is itself strictly never more than probable—and probable in a degree corresponding to that in which the several experiments approximate to being perfect experiments.

This situation, however, is not different in the case of causality from what it is in that of the theoretical concepts of physics—e.g., that of gravitation—which are defined in terms of conditions which, empirically, are never satisfied strictly but only approximated more or less—yet, in many cases, approximated enough to serve adequately the purposes of prediction or control in view on the particular occasion.

5.

EXPLANATION, MECHANISM, AND TELEOLOGY*

In an article in *The Journal of Philosophy*, (vol. XXI, No. 25), Dr. E. R. Guthrie considered Purpose and Mechanism as categories of explanation in psychology, his general conclusion being that teleological explanation is not so intrinsically despicable, after all, as it is often thought to be. The present writer is in thorough agreement with that conclusion, but it seems to him that Guthrie's distinction between mechanism and teleology is much too loose to be satisfactory, and that he classes as explanations many things which have no title to that name. It is obviously highly desirable to define explanation, purposiveness, and explanation in terms of purpose with precision, for otherwise clear and firm conclusions cannot possibly be reached. The present paper attempts such definitions briefly.

First, with regard to the logical nature of Explanation. Guthrie characterizes explanation as the 'assigning a fact or an event to a category of some sort.' Thus, 'the apple falls ... because every pair of physical objects will, under similar circumstances, approach each other. The dog seeks food because all living creatures do this.' And he quite rightly, although I believe with undue resignation, points out that these cases are, logically, exactly parallel to the classical horrible example, according to which the fact that a man who has taken opium sleeps, is 'explained' by saying that men who have taken opium always do. But the correct conclusion to be drawn from this parallelism is, I submit, that since admittedly nothing whatever is explained in the latter case, neither is anything explained at all in the former, and therefore that explanation

* *The Journal of Philosophy*, vol. XXII, No. 6, 1925.

cannot be defined as the 'assigning the event to be explained to a class of similar events.'

Explanation essentially consists in the offering of a hypothesis of fact, standing to the fact to be explained as case of antecedent to case of consequent of some already known law of connection (laws of bare conjunction statistically obtained, will not do). Thus, the hypothesis that the tree was shaken *does* explain the fact that an apple fell, under the general rule, already experimentally ascertained, that when an apple tree is shaken, ripe apples fall. We may, of course, go on and ask for an explanation of the *other* fact that they always fall then. And one can doubtless be given, but it will consist, once more, in the mention of something from which, under some already known law, the fact that apples do fall then, follows. Charles Peirce,[1] with great insight, pointed out something which seems never to have been adequately noticed before, and to have been largely forgotten since, namely that inferences are not of two sorts only, but *of three sorts*: From Rule and Case to Result (Deduction), from Case and Result to Rule (Induction), *and from Rule and Result to Case*. Peirce very unfortunately called this third sort of inference 'Hypothesis', while hypothesis in fact means the making of *any* sort of a conjecture. The word which exactly designates this third sort of inference in common usage, from which there is no occasion to depart, is *Diagnosis*, or inference from Circumstantial Evidence. Now, when the Rule under which a diagnosis is made is a law *of connection* (causal or logical), the diagnosis *explains* the observed fact from which it started. But (and Peirce did not perceive this) when the Rule is a law of bare *conjunction,* a merely statistical uniformity, the diagnosis *does not explain*. Thus, from the observation that an animal has cloven hoofs one frames, diagnostically, the hypothesis that it ruminates, under the statistical law that all ruminants have cloven hoofs. But that diagnosis, whether correct or not, *does not* in the least *explain* the cloven hoofs; it *merely predicts them* under the law.

My second point concerns certain cases referred to by Guthrie as cases of purposiveness, which, it seems to me, have no *a priori* title to that name, e.g., in particular those which he borrows from Haldane—'physiological states of equilibrium whose disturbance

---

[1] *Popular Science Monthly*, Aug., 1878, 'Deduction, Induction and Hypothesis'. *Johns Hopkins Studies in Logic*, 'A Theory of Probable Inference'.

causes their own re-establishment.' One cannot help wondering why the predictions on the basis of known normal causal sequences mentioned by Guthrie in the last paragraph on p. 676 are referred to by him as predictions 'in terms of purpose'. The only excuse for it would seem to be the perfectly gratuitous labelling of the effect an 'end result'. When the water level in a tank equipped with a ball float is lowered by the withdrawal of water, that disturbance causes the ball to fall and to open the intake pipe, and thus the disturbance itself causes the re-establishment of the original water level.[1] The process is automatic, but nonetheless purely mechanical, for automatism is one thing and purposiveness another. And the fact that, in the similar case of the maintenance of the proportion of blood salts to blood volume, we do not know the mechanism, does not warrant the conclusion that purpose is involved, but only the conclusion that we do not know what the explanation is (which the details of the mechanism would constitute). Prediction is one thing, and explanation of the predictability another thing. Moreover, it is not strictly correct to say, as Haldane apparently does, that the maintenance of the proportion is predictable. What can be said is, that either somehow the proportion will be maintained, or else the animal will sicken or die— which, as Guthrie notes, many have done. Of course, that an animal is *now* healthy, enables us to infer (predict) that, in spite of the ingestion of water, the proportion was somehow maintained— also, obviously, that somehow he escaped his enemies, etc.—but *not* that these various necessary conditions of life and health were provided by some intelligence *purposing* that it should live and be healthy. Again, that the soldiers in a hospital ward were all wounded in 'non-vital organs' was not, as a pious man thought, evidence of the purpose and mercy of God—unless perhaps none of the soldiers shot were to be found in the graveyard! The phenomenon of maintenance of an equilibrium, whether physical or physiological, is, like every other phenomenon, dependent upon the joint presence of various conditions, but is not on that account any more purposive than the rest. If we label it an 'end' or 'end result', rather than an 'effect', it is only because *we* then *import* into it our own interest in it and our desire that it occur, but not be-

---

[1] Stevenson Smith, 'Regulation in Behaviour', *Journal of Philosophy*, vol. XI, pp. 320–6.

cause we *find* a purpose objectively and intrinsically present in it as a necessary part of its description. In all cases of this sort, what we have as the law under which we infer, is a law of the type 'Only if X, Y,' instead of one of the type 'If X, Y', i.e., a law informing us of that in the *absence* of which Y *does not* occur, instead of one informing us of that on the *presence* of which Y *does* occur. And obviously, when the law is of the 'Only if X, Y' type, prediction is from the truth of the consequent to that of the antecedent, or from the falsity of the antecedent to that of the consequent.

But, in such cases, how about *explanation*? It is here, truly, that the methodological Devil puts forth his strongest and most subtle temptation, against which nothing but the most careful analysis will avail. The situation is this: Explanation, as we have seen, consists in the supposition of something that would have been *sufficient to* the existence of the observed fact under a given known law. This being so, *no explanation is possible under a law of the 'Only if X, Y' type* (e.g., Only if moisture is present will a plant live); for since the observed fact is here X (e.g., moisture is present), the factuality of X could under this type of law be explained, if at all, only by the hypothesis of the factuality of Y (e.g., that the plant will live). But the relation of Y *to* X under a law of this type is *not* 'sufficient to', but the very different one of '*contingent upon*'. Therefore the hypothesis that Y will be a fact cannot explain the factuality of X. How, indeed, could a fact that has not yet occurred explain, i.e., be a possible cause of, a fact that has already occurred? And it is here that the teleological temptation comes in: Obviously, whispers the Devil, only if an intelligence aware of the contingency of the second upon the first, and desiring the occurrence of the second, is thereby moved to bring about the first!

That is, in truth, a hypothesis explanatory of the occurrence of X, and it is a teleological one. And I do not mean to say that such an explanation is not, in some cases, a perfectly good and proper one and the only correct one. My only concern is to point out that *it is even then not what was asked for*, i.e., it is not an explanation of the occurrence of X under the law that 'Only if X occurs, does Y occur.' It is an explanation of X under *another* law, viz., the law that 'If an agent believes that Y is contingent upon X and desires Y, then that agent is likely to do X'; and this is still a law of the 'If' type, which is the only type under which explanations are possible. It is also, of course, the only sort of explanation of X in which the

39

dependence of Y on X enters, although it enters in it *not as something true*, but only *as something believed*. But then we may well ask, if all that is wanted is an explanation of X, why insist on dragging Y into it at any cost? Why not, in the absence of evidence of the existence of an agent and his purpose, frame an explanation of X under some other law known, e.g., under the law that 'If W, X' by the hypothesis that W occurred? The teleological explanation is certainly not forced on us *a priori* by the situation. It must compete with possible mechanical explanations, e.g., an evolutionary one, and the choice between them is to be made on precisely the usual grounds of choice between rival explanations, viz., relative antecedent probability, relative simplicity, etc.

The analysis of the distinction between purpose and mechanism has already been adumbrated in the above. To be able properly to speak of an act (or event) as purposive, it is neither necessary nor sufficient that the act be such that unless it occurs some specified result will not occur. What is essential, on the other hand, is that the following elements be present, or be supposed, by the speaker, to be present:

1. *Belief* by the performer of the act in a law (of either type), e.g., that If X occurs, Y occurs.

2. *Desire* by the performer that Y shall occur.

3. *Causation by that desire and that belief jointly,* of the performance of X.

It follows from this definition of purposiveness that only the acts of entities capable of belief and desire, are capable of being purposive, and therefore that the occurrences of 'inanimate nature' cannot be spoken of as purposive without contradiction, unless belief and desire be injected into nature, e.g., as often has been done, by viewing its occurrences as acts of God. And the disrepute into which teleological explanations have fallen is doubtless due to their having been so frequently thus put forth in cases where the existence of the agent appealed to and of his beliefs and desires, was not already known, but invented outright and purely *ad hoc*—this obviously constituting explanation of the *ignotum, per ignotius*. But when antecedent evidence for their existence is present (e.g., when the hypothetical agent is a human being), a teleological explanation is methodologically quite respectable, although, like any other, it may in a given case not happen to be the correct one.

It is interesting and quite important to note that it makes no essential difference to the definition of a purposive act given above, whether the words 'belief' and 'desire' which occur in it, be interpreted in terms of consciousness, or purely in terms of neurones and nerve currents. The essential point is, that unless it be *true* that belief and desire (no matter in what terms described), are present, there is no purposiveness. If belief and desire are given a description in terms of purely neural mechanisms, then what we have to say is that unless *just these particular types of neural mechanisms* are involved, the act performed cannot be spoken of as purposive, while if they are involved it must be so spoken of. And there is usually little dispute between the behaviourists and their opponents as to whether, in any given case, belief and desire *are* present; the dispute is as to how they shall be described. By way of illustration, we may take two examples used by Stevenson Smith (loc. cit., p. 324) as cases of what he calls 'positive regulation'. When a squirrel stores away food, I take it that neither behaviourists nor their opponents would assert that the squirrel *believes* that if he stores nuts he will not starve next winter, nor that he, at the time, *desires* not to starve next winter. Then, if that is not asserted, the squirrel's act may be 'positive regulation', but it is *not a purposive act*. On the other hand, when a prospector digs for gold, behaviourists and their opponents alike would grant that he *believes* that if he digs he will probably find gold and that he *desires* to find some. If both these things are granted, then the prospector's act may be 'positive regulation', but *it is a purposive act* all the same.

So much for the definition of purposive acts. Now an *explanation* of a fact, e.g., the fall of an apple, can be said to be teleological, or in terms of purpose, when the hypothetical cause offered as explanation (e.g., that a boy shook the tree) is regarded not as a 'blind' occurrence, but as a 'purposive' act, i.e., as being the *effect* in an agent of his *desire* for the fact (the fall of the apple) and of his *belief* that the act (shaking the tree) would cause the fact. Obviously that is sometimes the exact history of the occurrence of the fall of an apple, and in every such case none but a teleological explanation will be correct, and therefore no other can ever replace it. This remains so, as already stated, even if 'belief' and 'desire' are themselves capable of being described as special kinds of mechanisms. Mechanism and teleology are therefore not logically incompatible.

6.

ON THE ATTRIBUTES OF
MATERIAL THINGS*

This paper will attempt to show that qualities and properties are very different sort of entities, and that a neglect of the difference between them is in large measure responsible for the persistence of the controversy between idealism and realism. The term 'material things' will be used to refer to such entities as the tables, trees, books, houses, animals, minerals, mountains, rivers, etc., by which we are surrounded in the view of common sense, and the assumption of common sense also will be made, that we can well enough for ordinary purposes identify a place in space by pointing to it. Although the problem of the meaning of the terms 'space', 'time', and 'material thing' is raised by the views to be presented, no attempt to deal with it can be made within the limits of the present paper.[1]

In philosophical discussions, such simple statements as 'This tree is green', 'The table in my study is brown', etc., are frequently used as examples of information, obtained by perception, concerning attributes of material things. The present discussion will take as a starting point the statement 'This tree is green', and will be throughout largely worded in the terms of this particular statement. While this procedure may at first appear to entail some loss

---

* *The Journal of Philosophy*, vol. XXXI, No. 3, 1934.

[1] The writer, however, has elsewhere outlined the sort of analysis of the notion of 'material thing' that he would propose to give. The outcome of it is in brief that a material thing is nothing more or less than a set of properties (in the sense of that term to be stated below) possessed by a region of space between certain times, or, if we prefer, a region of space possessing between certain times a set of properties. See 'On Our Knowledge of Existents', *Proceedings of the Seventh International Congress of Philosophy,* pp. 37 ff.

of generality, it will have the great advantage of minimizing ambiguity and the consequent risk of misunderstanding. In the next two main divisions of this paper, two radically different senses, one or the other of which appears sufficient in all cases to interpret the assertion 'This tree is green', will be examined. And in the fourth main division, the bearing of the distinctions established upon the contentions of realism and idealism will be considered.

1. *The quality interpretation*

In the first of these senses the meaning of 'This tree is green' would be made explicit by saying 'The colour we see as we now look at this tree is the colour called green.' When the given statement is so interpreted, its true, as distinguished from its ostensible, subject is a certain immediately intuited colour-quality, and the tree enters into the story only as an adventitious means of indicating which one of the many colours at the moment seen is being talked about. That this is so becomes evident if we note that, instead of mentioning the tree, we could have taken a cardboard tube, pointed it in a certain direction, and said: 'The colour seen when one looks through this tube is the colour called green.' In spite of the fact that this statement is verbally different from the other, the very same directly intuited colour-quality is obviously indicated by the subject terms of the two; and it is this colour-quality that either of them asserts to be the colour called green.

2. *How the truth of assertions of this kind is tested*

Doubt as to the truth of the assertion 'This tree is green' as interpreted in the manner just described would be resolved by comparing the directly given colour-quality with a sample of the colour that all parties concerned are agreed to regard as constituting the definition-by-type of the word 'green', i.e., as constituting the standard of greenness. Or, putting the matter a little more generally, the truth of assertions of this kind is tested by observing whether the given concrete subject (in this case the particular colour intuited when one looks at the tree) does or does not conform to the agreed definition (in this case, definition-by-type) of the predicate asserted of it.

43

3. *A parallel but more plausible instance*

The above interpretation of the statement 'This tree is green' may seem forced, and the procedure just mentioned for testing the truth of the statement as so interpreted may seem artificial—a procedure, even, never actually used. Such an objection, however, would really have its root only in the fact that the statement used as an example, when taken out of any practical context, is so trivial that no one would be likely to utter it at all, or to dispute it if uttered. But it is easy to give other precisely parallel examples in which both the interpretation and the testing procedure described are obviously the appropriate ones and are the ones actually used in practice.

Such an example, likewise involving a colour, would be provided by the colours that have to be observed in the tempering of steel. The novice in that art is told that, to obtain the temper suitable for certain purposes, the steel must be chilled when it exhibits the colour 'light-straw'. But just because his idea of what colour is meant by 'light-straw' is likely to be vague, he is provided with a standard in the form of a chart of the principal colours that heated steel can take, each with its agreed name. The question 'Is this piece of steel light-straw colour?' obviously is for the man who would temper it a very real one, and the only meaning that it has for him is whether the colour he sees at the moment he looks at the steel is the colour called 'light-straw'. This question he does answer by comparing the colour he sees when he looks at the steel with the colour he sees when he looks at the place labelled 'light-straw' on the chart.

4. *Other examples*

Examples of assertions which are really of the same kind, but in which the predicate is such that its meaning would be defined otherwise than by type, would be: 'What this man is suffering from is typhoid fever', 'This animal is a ferret', 'This substance is gold', 'The relation of these two points is adjacence', 'This man is the former King of Spain', etc. The variety of these examples shows that the assertions that are tested in the manner considered may be, but need not be, about a quality. They may equally well be about a relation (adjacence), a stuff (gold), a complex state (typhoid fever), an organism (ferret), an individual (the King), or anything else given by direct or indirect indication.

5. *General character and function of the judgements leading to such statements*

The judgements as a result of which such statements as have been exemplified are made may all be described as judgements of *identification* or *classification*. That is to say, they represent attempts to determine whether or not some entity directly or indirectly indicated is of some suggested familiar kind, or is some familiar individual. The function of such judgements is to bring to bear upon the particular entity that one indicates knowledge already possessed about the kind to which one refers it, or about the individual with which one perceives it to be identical. That is, epistemically considered, they are *applicative* judgements—their role is to provide us with the minor premise for some syllogism of which the major is furnished by our already existing store of knowledge.

6. *The property interpretation*

When the statement 'This tree is green' is interpreted in the other of the two senses alluded to in the first division of this paper, its ostensible subject, namely, the tree pointed to at the moment, is then its true subject; and what is asserted of it is that it possesses the *property* of being green. To elucidate further this interpretation of the given statement, it is necessary to analyse in some detail the nature of a property.

7. *Property is an essentially causal concept*

Examples in which the essentially causal nature of properties is obvious would be fragility, malleability, fusibility, ductility, rigidity, impermeability, etc. No argument is needed to show that any attempt to make explicit what such properties consist in would have to take the form of an account of *what is caused when.* . . . To say that glass is *fragile*, for example, is to say that impact by a hard substance readily causes it to break; to say that gold is *malleable* is to say that hammering causes it to change shape without breaking, etc. Properties such as these two are describable in terms of kinds of effects produced *in the thing that has them* by certain causes under certain circumstances. Some other properties are describable in terms of kinds of effects caused *in another thing* when the thing that has the property is brought into a certain relation to that other thing. For example, sulphuric acid has the property of being *corrosive* of certain other substances under certain conditions; and, under analogous qualifications, carborundum, of being *abrasive*; arsenic, of being *poisonous*, etc. But whether they be of one or the other of these two sorts, all the properties that have been mentioned are evidently analysable in terms of *what is caused when.* . . .

8. *'Primary' and 'secondary' properties*

What the present paper is perhaps most fundamentally concerned to establish, however, is that such attributes of material things as 'being green', 'being fragrant', 'being noisy', etc., are properties of them in exactly the same essentially causal sense as are, for instance, 'being abrasive', or 'being corrosive', etc.; for it seems to the writer that neglect of this fact has been the source of endless difficulties in the theory of knowledge. To render the truth of that contention fully evident, three remarks have to be made:

The first concerns a distinction among properties, i.e., among 'effects that are caused in . . . when . . . ', on the basis of whether the effect in terms of which a given property is described is a *state of consciousness*—in particular, a sensation—or is a *physical state*. When for instance we speak of carborundum as being *abrasive*, we mean that friction of it against such other physical substances as steel, glass, etc., causes their surfaces to wear away. The effect which is caused when such friction takes place in no way requires for its occurrence the existence of a conscious being; nor does it for its description in any way require inclusion therein of the supposition that such beings exist. Its description can be given in purely physical terms.

But if, on the contrary, a rose is spoken of as being *fragrant*, this means that it is such that under certain conditions its near presence causes in human beings the *state of consciousness* designated as a pleasant olfactory sensation.[1] Again, if a person is spoken of

---

[1] The distinction between a sensation and what it is a sensation of—on the basis of which this assertion might be disputed—is analysed in detail in Section 13. Whether or not the validity of the particular example given above is

as being an *irritating* or an *unpleasant* individual, this means that he is such that in certain relations to other persons, he behaves in ways that cause in them the *feelings* called irritation or discomfort. In such cases, since the effect in terms of which the property is defined consists of a state of consciousness, it obviously cannot occur without the actual existence of some conscious being; nor can a description of it be given that does not include the supposition of the existence of such a being.

The same thing would be true of such other properties as 'being noisy', 'being green', 'being bitter', etc. Properties of this sort, viz., those where the effect in terms of which they are defined is a state of consciousness, may be called 'secondary' properties; and those where the defining effect is a physical state, 'primary' properties. The use of these terms is intended to suggest, not that Locke and others had this in mind when they spoke of primary and secondary qualities, but that the above distinction is the one which their untenable accounts of these terms were really groping for.

9. *Ambiguity of the terms 'sound', 'colour', 'heat', etc.*

The distinction proposed in the preceding section between properties in which the defining effect is physical and those in which it is psychological might be objected to by persons who would insist on taking such terms as sound, colour, heat, etc., in the sense they have in physics. To do this would of course be to grant automatically the point towards the establishment of which that distinction was made, namely, that such a property as 'being green' is essentially causal in exactly the same sense as, for instance, 'being malleable'. For to say that the tree is green would then mean that when struck by a beam of sunlight, it reflects light vibrations of one of the component frequencies, and absorbs the others. But, in the writer's view, this would be granting a right contention for a wrong reason: it would, that is, be granting that 'being green' is indeed a causal predicate, but granting it because the word 'green' is being taken in the physicist's sense, instead of the ordinary, psychological one, with which we are alone directly concerned in the present connection.

---

admitted, the argument in any case requires only the admission that there are *some* states of consciousness, and that some of them are regularly caused by certain relations of the organism to certain things.

The fact is that the terms 'sound', 'colour', 'heat', etc., and the more determinate ones that fall under them, e.g., 'green', have two, or rather three distinct meanings—one physical, one physiological, and one psychological. The first and the second of these meanings belong to these terms only in the technical languages of physics and of physiology. The third, on the contrary, namely, the psychological, is the one they had long before these sciences existed, and still have for everybody, including even physicists and physiologists not at the moment engaged in the pursuit of their sciences. Everyone understands the sort of effect meant when quinine is spoken of as being bitter. That effect is a certain psychological state, a certain taste sensation, perfectly known to everybody in the mere occurrence thereof, and knowable in no other way. That what constitutes the meaning which the word 'bitter' has for everyone is that kind of a psychological occurrence, and not some physical character or physiological event, is shown by the fact that, so far as the writer has heard, no one as yet knows just what the physical character is that distinguishes 'bitter' substances from others, nor just what the physiological events are that distinguish the effect of those substances on the gustatory nerves from the effects of others. But in spite of that universal, or at all events nearly universal, ignorance, the meaning of the word 'bitter' is universally known.

The fact is that the original and usual meaning of the word, and of such words as sound, colour, heat, etc., is the psychological one; and that much later these terms came to be borrowed by specialists to designate physical facts of the same sort as those which cause in conscious beings the normal sensations of sound, colour, etc., or to designate physiological events on which depends the occurrence of those sensations. And to admit this hardly deniable fact is at the same time to admit the legitimacy of the distinction on the basis proposed above, between primary and secondary properties.

10. *Latency and patency of the properties of material things*

We come now to the second of the three remarks needed to make evident the fact that the property 'being green' is, like any other, essentially causal, that is to say, is analysable in terms of a certain effect (viz., the sensation of green) which the material things said to possess the property have the power of causing in the consciousness of sentient beings.

What must now be remarked is that ordinarily the things that possess colour are presented to our attention visually, i.e., through the effect they produce at the time in our colour-consciousness. For example, when we say 'This tree is green', the chances are that by 'this tree' we mean 'the tree we are looking at', rather than 'the tree we are touching in the dark'; although we might, of course, well be meaning the latter. But if we were, the assertion that *that* tree is green would lose its triviality, because it would in this case no longer be an assertion of something at the time obvious. And in this case also, the account of the meaning of 'being green' that describes it as possession by the tree of a power or property, that, namely, of causing in us (under other conditions) the sensation of green, would lose the artificiality it seems to have when the conditions existing at the moment happen to be those under which that power is no longer latent but patent, i.e., is being exercised upon us by the tree.

That feeling of artificiality thus arises only from the unusualness (notwithstanding the correctness) of asserting of an effect which is *actually* being produced, that it is susceptible of being produced (namely, is produced whenever the circumstances are of such and such another nature). It would feel similarly artificial to speak of mercury as fusible or of granite as solidifiable, and for the same reason, namely, that under the conditions ordinarily present when these substances are observed, they are not merely potentially but actually liquid and solid respectively. A property is a power that a thing has to produce certain effects; but which particular one among the various powers which it possesses it happens to exercise at the moment depends on the particular set of conditions that happens to be present at that moment. We speak of the powers of a thing mostly at times when they are not being exercised by it; for there is seldom any occasion for us to utter concerning a thing the truism that it *can do* that which at the moment it is actually observed to be doing.[1]

---

[1] Readers under the influence of Hume's views on causation may balk at the use of the term 'powers'. Space will not permit here an attempt to vindicate it. The writer can only refer such readers to the criticism he has published elsewhere of Hume's doctrine of causation, and to the theory of

It may be observed at this point that, after the causal analysis of properties that has been given, there is no longer any paradox in saying that a tree, which at the moment happens to be in the dark, nevertheless is green. For it only means that that tree, which under the existing circumstances causes in the observer only tactual sensations, or possibly visual sensations only in the range of greys, is nevertheless such that, under certain other well-understood circumstances, it would cause in him the sensation of green.

11. *The real vs. the apparent colour of things*

The third of the remarks needed to vindicate our causal analysis of the property 'being green' concerns the fact that although maple trees, for instance, when seen a long distance away sometimes produce in us the sensation of blue, we nevertheless say that they are *really* green and only *appear* blue. This is a firm belief on our part and it cannot be lightly dismissed; there is undoubtedly a sense in which it is true, and our task is to define that sense and to show that it is consistent with the causal analysis proposed.

The fact need hardly be insisted upon that the production by the maples of the sensation of green in us is just as dependent on the nearness of the maples, the clearness of the intervening air, the sort of light that falls upon them, etc., as their production of the sensation of blue is dependent on their remoteness, the haziness of the intervening air, and other conditions. It is therefore obvious that the distinction between their real and their apparent colour cannot be that the latter is the colour they cause us to see under certain conditions and the former that which they cause us to see apart from any conditions. The colour we see *always* depends, not only on the thing looked at, but also on the conditions under which it is being observed. Painters, who have to attend to the colours that things actually make them see, are well aware that it

that relation which he has proposed, in which the notion of 'power' is analysed in terms more fully empirical than were Hume's own, when he supposedly exploded that notion. See *Causation and the Types of Necessity,* Univ. of Washington Press, 1924 (p. 87 for the analysis of 'power' which term is there, however, taken in a somewhat narrower sense than here); also the first paper in the present volume, 'On the Nature and the Observability of the Causal Relation,' and *Contemporary American Philosophy,* Geo. Allen & Unwin, 1930, vol. I, p. 321.

is only under certain conditions that the colour they see when looking at flesh is 'flesh colour', when looking at gold, yellow, etc.

Reflection on these facts leads us to perceive that the true distinction between the 'real' and the 'apparent' colour of a thing is one between the colour it causes us to see under what we consider *standard* conditions, and the colours it causes us to see under what we consider *accidental* or *abnormal* conditions. The question is then on what basis we come to consider certain conditions as standard, and others as abnormal.

That basis seems to be essentially practical; that is, the conditions we come to regard as standard or normal seem to be largely those under which we are observing the thing when we are using or are about to use it, or are to it in such other practical relation as it generally has to our lives, conditions, for instance, under which other important characters of the thing (e.g., the species to which a tree belongs) are discernible. Another factor, likewise practical, which also seems to enter into the determination of the conditions regarded as standard, is that of relative ease of duplication, which is important if our judgements are to be readily accessible to verification by others. This factor, for instance, would seem to be a governing one when we judge that the top of a table is 'really' square and only 'appears' trapezoidal. The angle of observation defined by a line perpendicular to the centre of the table surface is simpler to specify and to refer to than any other would be, and the 'real' shape of the table is therefore conceived in terms of it even though a table-top which causes us to perceive a square when observed from that angle does just as truly cause us to perceive a trapezium when observed from another angle.[1] It may be remarked incidentally that the distinction between the 'real' and the 'apparent' characters of a thing tends to disappear in many cases, when we pass from the ordinary practical to the scientific level of description, and this because science always attempts to include in the statement of its findings an explicit account of the conditions under which they were obtained, and to which they are strictly

---

[1] Determination of the 'real' shape of the table by means of yardstick and protractor presupposes that we have already ascertained, in the sort of way just indicated, that the changes of size and shape of those instruments themselves, which we see when we move them about in using them, are only 'apparent' changes.

relative. And just because the distinction in question has its significance primarily at the practical common sense level of knowledge which, it should be noted, is the level truly relevant to most of the ordinary situations in our lives, but which is inferior in explicitness and precision to the scientific, because of this, the set of conditions used as standard in judging, for instance, the 'real' colour of a thing is difficult to specify with complete definiteness.

Bearing in mind the nature of the distinction we have now discerned between the real and the apparent colour of things, it becomes evident that, instead of attending to the apparent colour as a painter would, what we generally do is to treat it only as a clue to the real colour. For instance, we judge the beard of an old man to be grey, in spite of the fact that the colour it actually causes us to see under the conditions existing at the moment is perhaps a light green. When we so judge we are using the light green actually seen only as a sign that we would see not green but grey if we looked at the beard under the conditions (of illumination, distance, absence of reflection from surrounding objects, absence of contrast effects, shadows, high lights, etc.) that constitute the standard in terms of which we define the 'real' (or what artists sometimes call the 'local') colour of the beard.

12. *Import and function of judgements of properties*

The considerations set forth in the preceding sections enable us now to state explicitly the meaning of the assertion 'This tree is green' when interpreted as expressing a judgement of property. It means, namely, that the tree, whether or not it be at the moment looked at, is such that under the conditions of observation that are the standard ones for such an object, it would cause a sentient observer of it to see the colour green; and hence, that, if at the moment those standard conditions happen to be present and the tree looked at, it then is causing the observer to see the colour 'green'.

It is obvious that when the problem to be solved is whether the tree considered has the *property* of being green in the sense just described, the question whether the colour *quality* seen at the moment one looks at it is the one called green is not at issue, for the answer to it is assumed to be self-evident. The problem in such a case, that is to say, is one to be solved not by a comparison of given colours, but by arranging the standard conditions and noting whether or not this causes in our consciousness the occurrence of the sensation of green.

The task that leads us to inquire into the *properties* of things is not as before that of applying knowledge we already possess concerning a kind to something indicated, which we identify as a case of that kind. The task that leads to such inquiry is on the contrary that of amplifying our store of applicable knowledge; and the function of our judgements in such cases may therefore be termed *amplificative* (of knowledge), as contrasted with the *applicative* function of the judgements first considered.

13. *Some implications of the position of some realists*

Neglect of the various considerations to which attention has been drawn above seems to be chiefly responsible for a certain unfortunate philosophical supposition, namely, that the green colour, for instance, which is seen when one looks at a tree may exist on the tree when no one looks at it, or perhaps even when the tree is in the dark.[1] This supposition bases itself upon a distinction between that which is seen, e.g., the colour-quality 'green', and the seeing of it.

That there is something radically wrong with such a doctrine becomes evident when its implications are traced out in detail in realms of sensation other than the treacherously favourite one of sight. For the same doctrine, when applied in a strictly parallel manner, for instance in the realm of hearing, requires us to say that the very noise-quality which we hear when we listen to a bell struck by a hammer may without contradiction be supposed to be itself literally present in the bell when no one hears it, or perhaps even when it is not being struck, just as it was declared that the very colour-quality which we see when we look at a tree struck by

---

[1] Some realists would not assert the later, but if not they would be depriving themselves of the possibility of giving to the common-sense belief that a green tree is green even in the dark any meaning in which it would be true. Also, some realists would say that when the tree is not looked at, the green colour (of it?) nevertheless exists, but not on the tree or not at the place where the tree is. The implications of such a position, however, are of no more acceptable a character than those, about to be exhibited, of the philosophical supposition mentioned above.

a beam of light could without contradiction be supposed to be itself literally present in the tree when no one sees it, or perhaps even when it is not being illuminated.

Again, carrying the doctrine in a precisely parallel manner to another neglected realm of sensations, viz., the kinaesthetic, we find ourselves required to say that the quality called nausea, of which we obtain experience when we bring the substance ipecac in the appropriate relation to the relevant inner sense organs—that that very nausea-quality may without contradiction be supposed to be literally present in the ipecac when it is still in the druggist's bottle. Indeed remorseless consistency would require us to go even farther, and to declare legitimate the supposition that that very nausea-quality is intrinsically present also in the waves of the sea, even when the semi-circular canals of some person subject to seasickness are not in the spatial relation to those waves necessary to procure him the experience of the nausea-quality.[1]

It is difficult to believe that anyone should continue to consider the doctrine in question plausible after he has clearly perceived such implications of it as have just been exhibited. Rather, these implications move one to inquire what subtle confusion it can be that gave the doctrine its initial plausibility.

14. *Ambiguity of 'to see', 'to hear', 'to smell', etc.*

A little reflection discovers that confusion to be one which arises from neglect of the fact that such verbs as 'to hear' and 'to see' are ambiguous, and that they are used in radically different senses when one says 'I hear a bell', or 'I see a tree', and when one says 'I hear sound' or 'I see colour'. The assertion 'I see a tree' means, in the light of the analysis given earlier in this paper, that I am at the moment having some sensations of colour and shape which I ac-

---

[1] It should be noted that it is not 'nauseousness' but the nausea-quality itself, that the doctrine would, if consistently carried through, assert to be possibly present in the ipecac and the waves; for nauseousness is not a quality, but a property of some material things, viz., that of, under certain conditions, causing sentient beings to have an experience of the nausea-quality. Nauseousness therefore could without absurdity be said to be a character of the ipecac and the waves; whereas the nausea-quality could not.

ept both as effects, and as signs, of the existence at a certain place
n space of what is meant by 'a tree'. But 'a tree' means much more
han something having the property of causing in one the sensa-
ions of colour and shape that I have at the moment; it means, for
nstance, something having also the property of hardness, viz., of
ausing in one, under other circumstances, certain tactual sensa-
ions. It is therefore obvious that, since hardness is observed not
hrough sight but through touch, one can speak only elliptically of
eeing a tree or any other material thing. 'Seeing' as so used is an
llipsis for judging, on the basis of visual signs, that a material
hing having also such and such other than visual properties exists
t a certain place.

But when one says 'I see colour', the meaning of the verb 'to see
s very different. It no longer means interpreting certain visual
ensations as signs of the existence of a material thing, for no
naterial thing is now in question, and no interpretation occurs.
What is now seen is colour, and it is seen, not, as material things
lways are, in an elliptical sense, but in the most literal sense, viz.,
that of being intuited. What is intuited is simply determinate colour, and not, as the tendency to reify even colours would tempt us
to say, the colour of a colour. The fact is that there are certain entities called feelings, sensations, simple qualities, immediate experiences or apprehensions, the whole being of which is known in
introspection and is exclusively psychological, whatever may happen to be their necessary physical and physiological antecedents or
concomitants. And if one leaves such physical and physiological
conditions out of the story, and confines oneself to facts accessible
at the time to the person who is seeing colour, viz., to psychological facts, then, to say for instance, 'I have a feeling of nausea, or of
pain', or 'I have a sensation of green', means nothing whatever
other than 'My feeling at this moment is of the sort called nausea,
or pain', or 'My sensation at this moment is of the sort called
green.'

What is experienced, sensed, felt, or seen, in the literal as distinguished from the elliptical sense of these words is only logically,
but not existentially, separable from the experiencing, sensing,
feeling, or seeing of it. When, as now, that literal sense alone is in
question, then, notwithstanding the treacherous little word 'of',
there is between experiencing and what the experiencing is of, between sensation and what is sensed, feeling and what is felt, seeing

and what is seen, no other difference than that between, for instance, waltzing and what is waltzed.[1] That sense does permit us to use the word 'of' in similar fashion, and speak of the waltzing *of* a waltz, or to say that what is danced on a certain occasion is a waltz. But it obviously does not warrant the supposition that a waltz may exist when no waltzing is taking place; indeed, the discerning of that sense renders manifest the absurdity of such a supposition, and likewise of the supposition that colour, nausea, etc., may exist when no seeing, feeling, etc. (in the literal sense) is taking place.

But when the terms 'experiencing', 'feeling', 'sensing', 'seeing', etc., are used in the elliptical sense described above, the situation is very different. The relation between the (elliptical) seeing of the tree, and the tree (elliptically) seen is not (except grammatically) in the least like the relation between the dancing of a waltz, and the waltz danced, nor therefore like the precisely similar relation between the (literal) seeing of colour and the colour (literally) seen or between the smelling of odour and the odour smelled. For the relation between the seeing of the tree and the tree seen has been shown by our earlier analysis to be a causal relation, the tree being the cause, or more accurately the agent that causes, the seeing; and the seeing is the effect, and therefore potentially the sign, of the existence at a certain place in space of a tree.

The relation, on the other hand, between the (literal) seeing of colour and the colour (literally) seen is not at all causal. For if we ask what is the cause of our seeing colour, the answer is in terms of the presence outside the body, not of colour, but of some material thing, and of the absorption and reflection by the surface of that material thing of certain vibratory frequencies of the form of energy called light; and further, in terms of certain physiological conditions within the body. Such physical and physiological facts are known to be the cause of our seeing colour; and to say that the cause of our seeing colour is a colour would therefore be simply to say something false, and would be possible only if one were ignorant of the facts, or if, blinded by an indiscriminating devotion to realism, one were to insist on making of colour a sub-

---

[1] Lest the ambiguity of the word 'waltz' should lead us into confusion, let us agree to take that word only in the sense in which it means a certain sort of series of movements, and not in the sense in which it means the sort of music that usually is heard while these movements are performed.

stance. But realism is in no need of having such logical monstrosities laid upon its altar.

Just what, then, is the relation between the seeing of colour, and the colour seen? or the relation between the waltzing of a waltz, and the waltz waltzed? Let us approach this question in terms of the latter example, since in it less strain is placed by pre-existing philosophical devotions upon our logical conscience.

Two distinct facts can be noted concerning the individual set of our movements on an occasion when we are said to be waltzing. One of these facts is that that set is very similar to certain sets of our movements at other times. By attending to the likenesses and neglecting the differences between these various individual sets of movements, we are able to form a certain concept of kind, namely, that represented by the word 'waltz'. And when we predicate 'being a waltz' of any actual or supposititious set of movements, we are then only saying of what nature, or kind, it is.

The other fact to be noted is that our individual set or movements on the occasion considered also belongs to a certain group. the members of which, however, are most heterogeneous as regards their intrinsic characters, namely, the group consisting of all and none but such entities as possess a unique place in time. This basis of grouping, or respect of likeness, we refer to by calling the members of the group 'events', or 'occurrences'; such terms predicating nothing whatever as to the individual nature of the members but only the bare fact that they have some unique place in time.

When, however, we wish to refer to our set of movements *both* as occupying some unique place in time, *and* as having a certain nature, i.e., being of a certain kind, then, as a matter of linguistic usage, we do this not as we might by saying that it is a 'waltz occurrence', but by using the word 'waltz' in one of its verb forms, e.g., waltzing, being waltzed, having been waltzed, etc.

That we are thus able to distinguish conceptually the fact of occurrence from the nature of the occurrence is what permits us to speak of dancing a waltz, although to speak in this way is redundant since merely 'waltzing' would have said just as much. But this possibility of distinguishing the fact of occurrence from the nature of the occurrence in no way permits us to suppose that a waltz might exist apart from any waltzing, i.e., apart from occurrence of any case of the kind 'waltz'. The only sort of existence, if we wish to call it that, that a waltz has apart from occurrence of it, i.e., apart from being waltzed, is logical existence, and this sort of existence is never in doubt about anything, for anything whatever that we might mention possesses it in virtue merely of its being mentionable. Even contradictions, such as 'round squares', possess logical existence, for to say this is only to say that the words have meaning, i.e., that when we say that round squares do not occur, we understand what it is that there are none of.

Let us now return to the question of the relation between smelling, or seeing (in the literal sense), and the smell that is smelled, or the colour that is seen. In the light of the distinction we have discerned between the fact of occurrence and the nature of what occurs, we are now able to perceive that 'smell', or 'colour', or more generally, 'sense quality', are the names by which we indicate merely the 'what', i.e., the class or kind, that constitutes certain logical entities about which we desire to speak; whereas 'smelling', 'seeing', or more generally 'sensing', or 'feeling', are the names by which we indicate *both* the fact of occurrence *and* the kind or nature of what occurs. This distinction, as in the other example, permits us to speak (although again redundantly) of the smelling of a smell, the seeing of a colour, the sensing of a sensation, or the feeling of a feeling; but it does not permit us to suppose that *what* is smelled, or seen, or sensed, or felt (in the literal sense), could exist (otherwise than merely logically) apart from any smelling, seeing, sensing, or feeling, since these are but the respective names for the *occurrence* of smell, colour, sensation, and feeling.

All this means in brief that the relation between smell and smelling, colour and seeing, sensation and sensing, is simply the relation between *kind* and *case*; and the relation between sensation and colour or smell or taste, etc., or between sensation and green or blue or pink, etc., is that of kind to narrower kind, i.e., genus to species. Obviously, when the terms 'seeing', etc., are used in the elliptical sense, we can similarly distinguish between the 'what', i.e., the nature or kind of the material thing (elliptically) seen, and the occurrence of a case of that kind. But 'occurrence of a case of that kind,' and 'seeing (elliptically) a case of that kind', are not here at all synonymous expressions, as on the contrary they were when literal seeing was in question. The difference is made obvious by the fact that the judgement 'I see green' (in which 'see' has the literal sense) cannot possibly be erroneous if I understand correctly the meaning of the word 'green'; whereas the judgement 'I see a tree' (in which 'see' has the elliptical sense) may very well be erroneous even if I know perfectly well the meaning of the word 'tree'. This is because the second judgement has an objective reference, i.e., the occurrence of a case of a material thing, e.g., of the kind 'tree', does not consist in the seeing (elliptical) of a tree; whereas the first judgement had no objective reference, i.e., the occurrence of a case of the kind 'green' does consist in the seeing, even if only in a dream, of green.

We may put the matter still more explicitly by saying that, when literal seeing is in question, *only* the relation of kind to case is involved, and it obtains between what is literally seen or smelled, viz., colour or odour, and the seeing or smelling of it; whereas when elliptical seeing (or smelling, etc.) is in question, *two* relations are involved. One of them obtains between the material thing elliptically seen, and the seeing of it, but it is the relation of *cause* to *effect* (and hence of signified to sign), and not that of kind to case. The other relation involved is indeed that of kind to case, but it obtains between the *kind* of material thing (of which a case is elliptically seen) and the *case* of that kind (which is elliptically seen) and not between what is seen and the seeing of it.

15. *Conclusion*

We are now in position to perceive that in including qualities as well as material things under the vague, question-begging heading of 'things' and treating as definitive of all 'things' the independence of observation which is true only of material things, Professor Perry[1] is himself guilty of the fallacy that he calls that of 'definition by initial predication', with which he justly taxes Berkeley when the latter does the exact opposite, viz., extends to material things the dependence on observation which is true only of qualities, through the initial inclusion of everything under the vague, question-begging term 'ideas'.

More generally, we can say that, where sense qualities are concerned, Berkeley is right; and all realists are wrong who claim it

---

[1] *Present Philosophical Tendencies,* Longmans, Green & Co., New York, 1916, p. 128.

possible that such qualities should, independently of their being sensed (or imagined), have any existence at all (other than purely logical). On the other hand, where material things are concerned the realists are right in asserting that they exist independently of their being perceived. And Berkeley is wrong in denying this, because a material thing cannot correctly be defined as a complex of sensations; nor even sufficiently as a permanent possibility of sensations; but only as a complex of *properties* (in some of which the defining effects are not sensations at all) possessed by a region of space during a time.

7.

'SUBSTANTS', CAPACITIES, AND TENDENCIES*

In this article, the writer will attempt to define in a manner both precise and non-arbitrary what a capacity, whether of the active or the passive kind, essentially is. Also, to make clear the relation between a possessor of capacities, as such—which is what he means by a Substant—and its capacities. Also to distinguish and define the six formal categories of capacities there are, and the respective functional statuses of the substants exercising them. And lastly, to make clear both what a tendency is, and how tendencies are related to capacities.

That an analysis of the meaning of a term is non-arbitrary means that it fits the data of the analytical problem; and these can consist only of a variety of expressions employing the term concerned, that together constitute a representative sample of the term's particular usage—whether standard or eccentric—which one desires to explicate. And that a particular account of the intension of the term, which one may have reached after scrutiny of the sample expressions, 'fits' the employment of the term made in them means that that account is substitutable in those expressions for the term concerned without thereby altering their logical properties or the truth-values of such propositions as those expressions formulate.[1]

1. Examples of capacities

Let us now therefore list various sentences illustrating the usage of the term capacity which we propose to analyse.

* The Review of Metaphysics, vol. XVIII, No. 1, 1964.
[1] cf. the writer's 'How does one discover what a term means?' Philosophical Review, vol. LXIII, No. 1. January 1954, pp. 88–91.

Examples of such sentences would be that glass has the capacity (termed 'brittleness') to break on very slight deformation; that rubber has the capacity (termed 'elasticity') to recover its shape and size after deformation; that various other substances have respectively the capacities designated 'combustibility', 'malleability', 'fusibility', 'plasticity', 'abrasiveness', 'corrosiveness', 'corrodibility', 'indigestibility', 'poisonousness', 'impermeability', etc.; that water has the capacity to take on the liquid state, the solid state, the gaseous state; that an ivory ball has the capacity to roll; that a rolling ivory ball has the capacity to cause another ivory ball it strikes to roll; that a glass bottle has the capacity to become broken; that a lump of glass has the capacity to become a bottle; that a blunt pencil has the capacity to become sharp; that a caterpillar has the capacity to become a butterfly; that a caterpillar, a vine, a tree have the capacity to die; that a given person has the capacity to distinguish red from green; the capacity to swim; the capacity to decide whether he will go to swim; the capacity to locate auditorily the direction from which a sound comes; the capacity to raise his arm; the capacity to raise a book; the capacity to perform arithmetical addition; to remember where he parked his car; the capacity to become a stenographer; or an engineer; or a carpenter; the capacity to become ill; to become crippled, etc.

2. *The possessors of capacities: 'substants'*

In each of the sample phrases just listed, something is mentioned that 'has' the particular capacity concerned. We need a general term whereby to refer to any possessor of capacities, and for this the term 'substance' would suggest itself. But the utility of it for this purpose is impaired by the fact that, in the history of philosophy, diverse senses have been assigned to it; and that, in ordinary language, it also has several senses. Because of this a different term, namely, *'a substant'*, which is free of the ambiguity of the term 'substance', will be used in these pages to designate that which, in expressions such as listed in section 1, has the particular capacity concerned.

That the notion of causality is implicit in that of capacity is obvious in many of these expressions; and the analysis of capacity to be presented further on will make evident that it is implicit also in all the others. Hence a substant will be anything that has capacities analysable in terms of causality relations, as distinguished from capacities, if there be any, not so analysable.

Contrary, however, to what the etymology of 'substant' would suggest, the relation between a substant and the capacities it 'has' is not analogous to the relation between, for example, a table and the objects it 'stands under' and supports. Rather, the relation between a substant and its capacities is analogous to that which obtains between, for instance, a week and its days; or an automobile and its wheels, engine, gears, etc.; or a living body and its organs; or more generally, between any *whole* and its *parts*. This is so irrespective of whether the nature, or the existence, of a substant and of its capacities is in view.

Thus, among substants would be those which ordinary language calls substances, stuffs, or materials. Examples of these would be paper, lead, water, air, etc. They are aggregates, and are 'divisive' or 'homeomerous' in the sense that and in so far as partition of given concrete instances of them yields portions that are themselves paper, lead, water, air, i.e., that have the same capacities as the wholes of which they are parts. Many other substants, on the other hand, which may be called structures, i.e., not aggregates but organizations or systems of parts, are 'indivisive' or 'heteromerous' in the sense that and in so far as their parts do *not* have the same capacities as the wholes of which they are parts. Examples would be an automobile, a tree, a dog, a man.

Each of the latter examples illustrates one of the four comprehensive kinds of observable (vs. only hypothetical) structured substants: the inanimate, the vegetable, the animal, the human. Substants of each of the last three of these kinds possess some of the capacities of each of the kinds of substants preceding them in the list: a human being, an animal, or a vegetable has, for example, weight, as does a rock; again, certain parts of the nervous system of a man, or of an animal, are, like the vegetative processes, autonomic, and hence are sometimes called the vegetative nervous system; and a man has, like some at least of the animals, capacity for sensory and perceptual consciousness and for voluntary movements.

In addition, however, he has certain specifically human capacities. Of these, the capacity called 'rationality' is the one traditionally mentioned, though commonly without being defined with precision. But probably the most distinctive is the capacity for what may comprehensively be termed 'self-consciousness': that is, capacity to become aware of some of the capacities he does or does not possess; capacity to appraise, i.e., to value positively or negatively, those he becomes aware of; and capacity, in the light of such appraisal, to attempt to eliminate, or correct, or develop, or acquire, or guard against acquiring, those he becomes aware that he has, or that he does not have.

3. The six formal categories of capacities, and the functional statuses of the substants exercising them

So much being now clear as to what will here be meant by a 'substant', attention may next be called to the fact that the capacities of substants fall into one or another of the following six formal categories; three being of capacities to 'do' and three of capacities to 'undergo'.

(1) Capacity for *activity* of some particular kind: The 'activity' or 'behaviour' of a given substant at a given time consists in exercise by it at that time of one or more of its intransitive, as distinguished from its transitive, capacities. For example, an ivory ball's rolling is exercise by it of an intransitive capacity; whereas its pushing another such ball by rolling against it would be exercise by the given ball of a transitive capacity.

In so far as the capacity which a given substant exercises at a given time is its capacity for activity of some kind, as defined above, the functional status of the substant at that time is that of *enactor* of activity of whatever particular kind is concerned.

(2) Capacity *to be in a state* of some particular kind. The 'state' of a given substant at a given time consists of such capacities as it actually possesses at that time, as distinguished from those which, at that time, it only has the capacity of acquiring. For example, that a given instance of the kind of substant called 'lead' is at a given time in the liquid state means that it actually possesses at that time the capacity to flow; whereas it does not at that time have the capacity called 'solidity' but only the capacity—called 'solidifiability'—of acquiring the capacity called 'solidity'.

In so far as the capacity which a given substant exercises at a given time is its capacity to be in a certain state, its functional status at that time is that of *tenant* of that state.

(3) Capacity of a substant S (by enacting activity of a particular

kind C in circumstances of kind K) to *affect* directly or indirectly a substant Z (which may either be the substant S itself or be a distinct substant).

In so far as a substant S is exercising a capacity it has, to affect a substant Z, the functional status of S at the time is that of *agent*, i.e., of *operator on* Z. Agency is thus essentially transitive; whereas activity, considered simply in itself (e.g., rolling, vibrating, waltzing, twitching, etc.) is intransitive. And what an agent, as such, 'does' is an *action*, i.e., an operation; not, as in the case of an enactor, an activity, i.e., a behaviour.

When, however, an agent is a *purposive* agent, then the behaviour through the instrumentality of which he causes the effect he intends is termed specifically *an act*; and the effect intentionally caused by that act is termed specifically *a deed*.

Examples of capacities of some substant S to affect some substant Z would be the capacities called 'abrasiveness', 'corrosiveness', 'toxicity', 'dangerousness', 'persuasiveness', 'subversiveness', etc. And the substants possessing them would respectively be termed an abrasive agent, a corrosive agent, a toxic agent, and a dangerous, a persuasive, a subversive, etc., agent (and more specifically, as the case may be, a thing, or a person).

Capacity of a substant S to affect a substant Z, however, is more specifically capacity to cause, or capacity to prevent, or capacity to facilitate, or capacity to hinder, under circumstances of kind K, occurrence of an event of kind E in Z.

Capacity to *facilitate* occurrence of E in Z under circumstances K is capacity to satisfy some of the conditions, satisfaction of which is (under circumstances K) necessary to occurrence of E in Z; that is, capacity to increase the then possibility of occurrence of E in Z. Evidently, such increasing of its possibility would include the case of necessitating occurrence of E in Z; that is, of satisfying all the conditions necessary to occurrence of E in Z under circumstances K.

On the other hand, capacity to *hinder* occurrence of E in Z under circumstances K is capacity to introduce impediments to its occurrence; that is, capacity to introduce additional conditions, satisfaction of which will, under circumstances K, be necessary to occurrence of E in Z; the introducing of them automatically decreasing the then possibility of occurrence of E in Z. And obviously, such decreasing of it would include the case of decreasing it to nothing; i.e., of preventing, i.e., of making impossible, occurrence of E in Z under the circumstances K.

'Possible', as predicated of occurrence of an event E, is therefore ambiguous; meaning sometimes that occurrence of E is not necessitated, but sometimes that it is not impossibilitated, by occurrence of an event C under the circumstances then existing. Indeed, that occurrence of E is 'possible' sometimes means that it is neither necessitated nor impossibilitated in the then existing circumstances by occurrence or non-occurrence of an event C; this being the most that can be meant by saying that on the given occasion, occurrence of E is 'contingent'. Another way of saying that, on a given occasion, occurrence of E is neither necessitated nor impossibilitated by occurrence or non-occurrence of C would be by saying that, on the given occasion, occurrence of E is independent of occurrence or non-occurrence of C and, conversely, that occurrence or non-occurrence of C is irrelevant to occurrence of E.

The remarks which precede, concerning what it means to say of a substant S that it has the capacity to affect a substant Z, make it appropriate to emphasize at this point a fact not infrequently overlooked; namely, that the terms 'necessary', and 'contingent', as predicated of events are as inherently relational as the term 'sufficient' obviously is relational even when employed in the expression 'self-sufficient'. Self-sufficiency, however, would not be congruously predicable of an event but only of some substant; and would then mean that exercise by that substant of any of its capacities is dependent on nothing but exercise of some others of them.

In the present connection, it is essential to realize that there are *four* relational statuses in respect of causality which one event may have to another event; namely, (a) causally sufficient to (i.e., cause of), and the other event then (b) causally necessitated by (i.e., effect of), (c) causally necessary to (i.e., condition of), and the other event then (d) causally contingent on (i.e., resultant of). It is especially important to keep in mind the ambiguity of the term 'necessary', for that a given event is 'necessary' sometimes means that occurrence of it is *necessary to* occurrence of a certain later other, but sometimes that occurrence of it is *necessitated by* occurrence of a certain earlier other.

From the fact that sufficiency is an inherently relational status, it follows that to say of an event that it is 'absolutely' sufficient could only mean that occurrence of it is sufficient to occurrence of no matter what other event.

Similarly, to say of an event that it is 'absolutely' necessary could only mean either that occurrence of it is necessary to, or else that occurrence of it is necessitated by, occurrence of no matter what other event. And to say of an event that it is 'absolutely' contingent could only mean, similarly, that occurrence of it is contingent on occurrence of any other event whatever.

Patently, however, no event is 'absolutely' sufficient, necessary, necessitated, or contingent in the sense of 'absolutely' just mentioned; any more than any man is an absolute uncle in the sense of uncle to no matter which other human being.

The above remarks, concerning the inherently relational character of causal sufficiency, necessity, and contingency, apply equally to logical sufficiency, necessity, and contingency. For the three traditional 'laws of thought'—the law of excluded contradiction, the law of excluded tautology, and the law of excluded middle, i.e., of excluded incongruity (irrelevance)—are not themselves 'necessary truths' since they are not propositions at all but are rules; rules of the game called 'signalling': an utterance (whether vocal, graphic, or other) by a person U is intended by him as a 'signal' to a person(s) P if it is intentionally placed by U within what he believes to be the present or eventual field of perceptual attention of P (who may be U himself at a later time), and is intentionally so shaped by U that, by virtue of certain conventions familiar both to U and to P, the utterance concerned will, when perceived by P, cause him, according to what may have been U's particular intention, to believe, or disbelieve, or doubt a certain proposition; or to think of some particular subject; or to perform some particular act; or to desire some particular thing; or to experience some particular feeling: etc.—in short, to exercise to some particular effect some particular capacity P has.

On the other hand, something which a person P perceives is interpreted by him as a 'signal' to a person(s) Q (who may or may not be P himself) if perception of it causes P to believe that it is an utterance of some person U intentionally placed by U within Q's probable field of perceptual attention, and intentionally so shaped by U that, by virtue of certain conventions familiar both to U and to Q, perception by Q of that utterance shall cause Q to believe, or according to what may have been U's specific intention, to doubt, or disbelieve a certain proposition; or to think of some particular subject;—or in short, to exercise to some particular effect some particular capacity Q has.

The reason why the conventions, according to which a signal is shaped by the utterer of it and interpreted by the perceiver, are not themselves either true or false, nor either veracious or mendacious, is thus essentially of the same nature as the reason why the chess convention that the king shall move only one step at a time, not being itself a chess move, is neither a legal nor an illegal chess move.

(4) Let us now pass on to the fourth of the six formal categories of capacities of substants; namely, capacity of a substant Z, in circumstances of kind K, to be affected directly or indirectly in a manner E by a substant S's activity of a kind C; Z's capacity to be affected by S being more specifically either capacity to be caused to undergo E, or to be prevented from undergoing it; or to have the undergoing of it facilitated, or hindered, by S's activity of kind C in the circumstances K.

In so far as the substant Z exercises a capacity it has for being affected by some substant S, it is functioning at the time as *patient*: it suffers, i.e., undergoes, a 'treatment' by S resulting from exercise by S of a capacity it has to affect Z. Examples of capacity of a substant to be affected by, and more specifically to be directly operated on by some substant, would be abradability, corrodibility, intoxicability, vulnerability, irritability, etc.

(5) Capacity to *endure* changes; i.e., to continue generically the same notwithstanding gain or loss of some particular capacities. Examples would be the capacity of a given knife to become sharp, and perhaps eventually dull again, while continuing throughout to be a knife; the capacity of a person to become learned, or infirm, or healthy, without ceasing to be a person throughout; and so on. The changes involved would here be termed alterations or modifications; and the functional status of a substant, in so far as exercising a capacity it has to remain generically the same notwithstanding various particular changes, is the status of *continuant*.

(6) Capacity *to change into something generically different*. Examples would be the capacity of a bottle to cease to be a bottle and change into fragments of glass; the capacity of a caterpillar to change into a butterfly; the capacity of a living being to cease to be this, i.e.,

its capacity to die; the capacity of water to cease to be water and change into uncombined oxygen and hydrogen; etc.

Change of the type concerned in all such cases is termed transmutation, metamorphosis, or transformation. In the occurrence of it, the given substant 'submerges' and the substant that replaces it 'emerges'. A substant, in so far as exercising a capacity it has to change into something generically different, has the functional status of *mutant*.

4. *Analysis of the notion of capacity*

The analysis of the generic notion of Capacity has to be formulated in terms of variables that will make it applicable to examples of no matter which of the six formal types of capacities distinguished in section 3. The following analysis is submitted as satisfying this requirement.

That, in circumstances of kind K, a substant S has a capacity X means that S is such that occurrence then of an event of kind C in a relation Q to S causes occurrence of an event of kind E in a relation R to a substant Z, which may be the substant S itself or may be a distinct substant.

The conception of Causation in terms of which this definition is framed cannot be set forth here in detail. In essentials, however, it is that (proximate) causation is the triadic relation which obtains between a strict experiment's three terms; namely, (1) a given state of affairs K, (2) an only change C in K at a time T_1, and (3) an only other change E in K at the immediately sequent time T_2. This conception of causation does not require that K and such a sequence of E after C in K ever occurred before or ever will occur again; but it entails that if K and C in K ever recurs, E then recurs. Thus, causal *laws* are empirical generalizations of observed concrete sequences each of which is, in its own individual right, a causation sequence defined as the kind of sequence which a strict experiment exhibits to observation.[1]

---

[1] A first account of this conception of causation may be found in Chaps. VI and VII of the writer's *Causation and the Types of Necessity* (Seattle, 1924); and a fuller account in Chap. 8 of his *Nature, Mind, and Death* (LaSalle, Illinois, 1951), where, in Chap. 7, Hume's conception of causality is shown to be untenable. Various objections that had been raised to the definition of causation as the species of sequence a strict experiment exhibits are considered

The following illustrations will make evident that the analysis of the notion of capacity given at the beginning of the present section fits each of the six categories of capacities distinguished in section 3.

(1) Capacity of a substant for *activity* of some stated kind: That an ivory ball, at rest on a smooth, level, unencumbered surface, has the capacity to roll means that the ball is such that occurrence then, e.g., of a tilting of that surface, or of a side blow on the ball, etc., causes occurrence of rolling activity in the given ball.

(2) Capacity of a substant *to take on a state* of some stated kind: That a piece of lead, at a time when it is cold, has the capacity to take on the liquid state means that the lead is such that occurrence then of increase of its temperature to 621°F. causes the lead to take on the liquid state.

(3) Capacity of a substant *to affect* some substant: That an ivory ball *I,* in circumstances where both it and another ivory ball *J* are at rest on a smooth, level, unencumbered surface, has the capacity to make ball *J* roll means that occurrence then of exercise by ball *I* of its capacity to roll in such a direction as to strike ball *J* causes ball *J* to roll.

(4) Capacity of a substant *to be affected by* some substant: The preceding example illustrates also possession by ball *J* of capacity to be made to roll by ball *I.*

(5) Capacity of a substant *to continue generically the same* notwithstanding acquisition or loss of particular capacities: That a knife has the capacity to continue to be a knife notwithstanding loss by it of the capacity called 'dullness' and acquisition of that called

and shown to be without force in the following papers: 'Of the Spurious Mystery in Causal Connections', *Philosophical Review,* vol. XXXIX (1930), pp. 398–403; 'On the Nature and Efficacy of Causes', *Philosophical Review,* vol. XLI (1932), pp. 395–9; 'On the Analysis of Causality', *Journal of Philosophy,* vol. LIV (1957), pp. 422–6; and 'Concerning the Uniformity of Causality', *Philosophy and Phenomenological Research,* vol. XXII (1961), pp. 97–101. See also the biologist H. S. Jennings' 'radically experimental determinism', which conceives causality similarly as the type of sequence an experiment constitutes, presented in his 1926 address, 'Some Implications of Emergent Evolution', *Science,* Jan. 1927; and later in his *The Universe and Life* (New Haven, 1933). Also the following statement by H. W. B. Joseph (*Introduction to Logic* [London, 1916], p. 404): 'We mean by the causal relation something that might hold between terms that were unique, and does hold between terms that are individual even though there are other individuals of the same nature.'

'sharpness' means that honing the blade causes such loss and such acquisition without the knife's ceasing to be a knife.

(6) Capacity of a substant *to change into a generically different* substant: That a sheet of paper has the capacity, called 'combustibility', to cease to be paper and change into something generically different, to wit, ashes, smoke, and gases, means that, in circumstances where the paper is dry, where air is present, etc., application of a flame such as that of a match to the sheet of paper causes it to cease to be paper and change into ashes, gases, and smoke.

5. *'Can', and the synonyms of 'capacity'*

The submitted analysis of what it means, to say of a substant that it has some particular capacity is, let it be noticed, equally an analysis of the meaning of 'can' when one says of a substant that it can enact some particular activity, or can perform a particular operation, or can endure some particular alteration; or as the case may be, that it can 'undergo' some particular state, or treatment, or transmutation.

Moreover, the analysis given of the meaning of 'capacity' is likewise an analysis of the essence of the meaning of a number of terms which are virtual synonyms of 'capacity', namely, the terms 'ability', 'capability', 'power', 'faculty', 'susceptibility', 'disposition'; and also of 'property' in the sense this term has when, for instance, combustibility is said to be a property of paper, or liquidity a property of lead at certain temperatures.[1]

The term 'disposition' is at present rather more fashionable among philosophers than is 'capacity'. Yet 'disposition' is in fact a less satisfactory term since, in some contexts, what it designates is specifically a *tendency* rather than generically a capacity; and in some other contexts, what it designates is neither a capacity nor more particularly a tendency, but an *episode*—specifically, occurrence of an impulse. This is what 'disposition' would designate for instance in the statement: 'When John realized the stress under which James had been labouring, his disposition was to forgive the injury James had done him.' Evidently, this statement does not mean that John has or had a forgiving disposition. Rather, it implies the opposite kind of tendency in him, and explains why

---

[1] 'Property' in this sense is to be sharply distinguished both from 'quality' and from 'property' as designating one of the five 'predicables'.

John's disposition at the moment, that is, his impulse at the moment, came to be to forgive.

6. *Tendencies, and their relation to capacities*

These remarks bring us to the question as to what is a tendency, and how tendencies are related to capacities.

The first thing to notice is that the analysis of the notion of capacity in terms of causality, formulated in section 4, entails that the event E occurs *regularly*; that is, as *often or as seldom as,* in circumstances of kind K, an event of kind C occurs in a particular relation Q to the substant S that has the capacity concerned.

Now, that a substant S has a *tendency*—proclivity, proneness, propensity—to exercise a particular capacity it possesses (no matter of which one of the six types distinguished in section 3) means not only (a) that S has that particular capacity, but in addition (b) that, in circumstances of the kind K specified in the definition of the particular capacity concerned, occurrence of an event of the kind C in the relation Q to S is frequent; or in a given case is facile, i.e., easily occurs, is likely to occur.

This analysis of the notion of Tendency implies that tendency admits of degrees. For example, the tendency of a ball to roll is great; that of a regular icosahedron solid is less than that of a ball; that of a regular dodecahedron still less; and that of a cube to roll, still less.

8.

SYMBOLS, SIGNS, AND SIGNALS*

In this address, no attempt to deal with any problem of symbolic technique will be made, for even if a problem of this kind should be found that was suitable to the present occasion, I should probably lack sufficient competence in the handling of symbols to deal with it satisfactorily. It occurred to me, however, that it might be interesting to consider the nature of symbols in general, to point out certain characteristics peculiar to the symbols used by logicians and mathematicians, and to say something concerning the relations of these symbols to the knowledge of Nature. Although developments in the science of logic are not dependent on such an inquiry, it yet provides us with a perspective on the nature and importance of that science which we cannot gain so long as we attend only to the problems arising inside its field.

1. *The symbolic relation*

Our attempt to gain this perspective may well begin with the trite remark that nothing is intrinsically a symbol, but that anything is a symbol if and only if it symbolizes. Moreover, the relation called symbolizing is not a dyadic but rather a tetradic relation. That is, in order for something A to be a symbol of something B, there must be in addition C, a mind trained in a special way, and D, a certain manner in which that mind is occupied at the time. For although we do say, for instance, that a mark consisting of a little cross is the symbol of addition, the fact is of course that at times when that mark is not present to a mind, it does not symbolize addition or anything else. Moreover, even when it is present to a

* *The Journal of Symbolic Logic*, vol. 4, No. 2, 1939.

mind, it does not symbolize addition unless that mind has been trained in a certain manner; for obviously such a mark does not symbolize addition to the mind of a Hottentot or other wholly illiterate person. And further, even when the mind to which that mark is present is one trained as our own minds have been, the mark does not symbolize addition unless the mental context in that mind at the time is of a certain kind, viz., mathematical; in a religious context, for instance, that mark obviously symbolizes for us something very different from addition.

Thus, to describe with some degree of precision the fact only roughly expressed by the statement that a little cross is the symbol of addition, what we must say is that *when* minds have been trained as ours have been, *and* are thinking about mathematics, *and* perceive or think of a mark consisting of a little cross, *then and then only*, (for these minds) that mark symbolizes addition. Nothing less than this adequately states the fact. Even this, of course, does not say what symbolizing consists in. Yet it makes clear at least that the relation called symbolizing is a four-term relation, and that it is not a physical but a psychological relation. As we shall see, it is in addition in certain cases a logical relation.

2. *Interpretation*

To reach a positive account of the nature of symbolization, it will be useful to turn our attention for a moment to a certain truly basic kind of mental event which—in accordance, I believe, with ordinary usage—I shall call Interpretation and define as follows: *Interpretation is the kind of mental event consisting in this, that consciousness of something causes us to become conscious of something else.* That which we are 'conscious of' sometimes is and sometimes is not itself a state of consciousness, but this does not affect the definition of interpretive activity in general. I may state in passing, however, that my reason for defining interpretation as a relation between consciousness of something and consciousness of something else, rather than as a relation between certain physical events and certain others, is that I believe the notion of physical event is one ultimately itself definable only in terms of interpretation of certain states of consciousness. This, however, is a question that cannot be gone into now, and I therefore return to the definition of interpretation as already given.

74

When in it I speak of consciousness of something *causing* consciousness of something else, I use the word 'cause' in the sense which I believe it always has in experimental situations, namely, to mean such change as is introduced in an otherwise unchanging state of things—the 'effect' then being the further change in that state of things immediately following the change introduced. Causation as so defined is a relation essentially between individual changes in an individual state of things, and is thus independent of the notion of law, since laws are never concerned with individuals but always with kinds.[1] But of course the individual changes and states of things which enter into several cases of causation may happen to exhibit resemblances, each to each—that is, fall into kinds—and if so we shall then be able to say that a change *of kind C* occurring in a state *of kind S* of something *of kind T,* causes *regularly* in it a change *of kind E.* That is, we shall then have not only causation, but a causal law.

Now, the definition of interpretation given a moment ago was framed in terms of causation simply. But if we substitute in it regularity of causation for causation simply, we then have something I shall call *semeiotic interpretation,* which is what we are really concerned with in most of the cases when we talk about interpretation. And because semeiotic interpretation is a case of regularity of causation, we shall in any case of it find not only that four terms are involved, but also that they are of the following kinds, which I shall call respectively:

(a) The *interpreter,* namely, the set of mental habits possessed by the person concerned. These constitute the kind of mind he has.

(b) The *context of interpretation,* namely, the kinds of things of which at a given time he is conscious, whether clearly or unclearly.

(c) The *interpretandum,* namely, a kind of change supervening in the context of interpretation and thus functioning as cause.

(d) The *interpretans,* namely, another kind of change immediately following it and thus functioning as effect.

3. *Signs and symbols*

With these distinctions in mind, we are now in a position to define the word 'sign'. Nowadays, this word seems often to be used to

---

[1] For the defence I would give of this view of causation, see 'On the nature and the observability of the causal relation', the first paper in the present collection.

designate something much the same as what I have called a semeiotic interpretandum. But such usage of it clashes needlessly with
its most common ordinary usage—the one, namely, according to
which the approach of black clouds is said to be a sign of rain, the
presence of wrinkles on a man's face a sign that he is ageing, the
ringing of the doorbell a sign that someone is at the door, etc. In
any case, it is the word 'sign' as used in statements such as those
just mentioned, that I now wish to define. It seems to me that a
sign is a semeiotic interpretandum which is in addition *opinative*;
that is, it begets opinion: what it causes us to think of is always a
proposition, and it always causes us to believe, or to incline to believe, the proposition it makes us think of.

For example, to say that the approach of black clouds is a sign of
rain is to say that perceiving or being otherwise informed that
black clouds are approaching, regularly causes us to think of rain
occurring soon, and in addition regularly causes in us some degree
of positive inclination to believe that rain will occur soon—provided, of course, that our mental context at the time does not consist of intense preoccupation with concerns other than meteoro-
logical. But to the definition just given of the word 'sign' it must
immediately be added that to be a sign is not necessarily to be a
reliable sign. Thus, to many persons, occurrence of the number 13
is a sign of the occurrence of misfortune. That is, it both makes
them think of its occurrence and makes them believe it will occur.
But it could be said to be a reliable sign of misfortune only if the
misfortune it causes people to think of and to expect did regularly
then occur.[1]

Now symbols, as distinguished from signs, may I think be

---

[1] When that which a semeiotic interpretandum makes us 'conscious of'
is not something objective but on the contrary is itself a state of consciousness
(as when in some persons perception of wavy motion causes the feeling of
nausea), the relation is still that of sign to signified as just described, but what
we then have is a limiting case of it. That is, the person is made conscious of
the feeling, not in the sense of being made to think of it, but in the sense of
being made to experience that feeling itself; and that it is at the time occurring
in him is something then impossible for him to doubt, i.e., it is something
he completely believes, even if tacitly. Of course, in the majority of cases
what we are said to believe is something not itself present to our observation
at the time; but the common remark, 'Seeing is believing', indicates that
ordinary usage permits us to say that we believe even what we are actually
experiencing.

defined as semeiotic interpretanda which are not opinative; that is, what they cause us to become conscious of either is not a proposition, or if it is, they do not cause in us any inclination to believe it.

4. *Discursive entities*

The point has now been reached where we must make among semeiotic interpretanda a certain very important distinction, that, namely, between those which are discursive and those which are not. To do so, however, we must first state in general what is to be understood by a 'discursive entity', irrespective of whether or not it happens to be playing a rôle in interpretation. By 'discursive' entities I propose to mean any entities fulfilling the following conditions:

(1) They are entities susceptible of being readily 'uttered', whether vocally, graphically, or otherwise; that is, they are such that the perceptible existence of cases of them can in ordinary circumstances be caused by the mere wish.

(2) They are entities recognizable as the same in the various utterances of them.

(3) They are entities of which cases occur only as results of human utterance. That is, cases of them are always man-caused, artifactual; never, or virtually never, caused by Nature independently of the activity of a human body.

It may be remarked that the first of the conditions above, viz., readiness of utterability, is relative to the means of utterance happening to be at our disposal. The means of *vocal* utterance are virtually always at our disposal, but those of graphic or other utterance, less often. Hence, when utterance is mentioned, we are likely to think primarily of speech, and to regard other modes of utterance, such as writing, as substitutes for and equivalents of speech. But the priority of vocal over graphic or other modes of utterance is only practical, not theoretical, and we therefore need take no account of it here.

From what has now been said, it is evident that the entities we call words, phrases, and sentences, and also those commonly called mathematical, logical, heraldic, astronomical, and other 'symbols', would be discursive entities as described above, irrespective of whether or not they happen in addition to be symbols or signs in the senses I have defined. For convenience, I shall from this point on use the noun 'word', in the broad sense in which it is synonymous with 'discursive entity', and the adjective 'verbal' similarly as synonymous with 'discursive'.

Discursive and non-discursive interpretanda

Symbols and signs, evidently, may be either discursive or non-discursive, either verbal or, as we may say, 'real', if for the purposes of this paper we agree to mean by 'real' simply 'non-discursive'. For example, a cloud shaped more or less like a human head would be for us a real or non-discursive symbol of a human head; whereas the words 'human head' would be a verbal or discursive symbol of a human head for us. Again, the crepitant sound I hear at a certain time (such as ordinarily is caused by raindrops on the roof), is for me a sign, and a non-discursive sign, that it is raining. On the other hand, the declarative sentence, 'It is raining', uttered by someone within my hearing, is for me also a sign, but a discursive sign, that it is raining.

5. Signals

In terms of discursive symbols and signs as defined, we are now able to define signals. A signal is an utterance of a discursive symbol or sign, deliberately placed by the utterer within what he believes to be the field of sensuous attention of another person, to the end that the other person shall thereby be caused to think of, or to think of and believe, that which the discursive symbol or sign symbolizes or signifies for the utterer. Of course, the person to whom the signal is addressed may be the utterer himself as existing at a later time. The utterance of discursive symbols or signs constitutes almost always, but not invariably, a case of signalling. The exceptions would be constituted by such a case as that of the use of Chinese characters by a Chinese artist merely for the decoration of articles intended by him for persons who cannot read the characters; or again by the case of a person who writes something which he does not intend either to read later or to have others read, but which he writes solely because the process of writing helps him to reflect.

6. *Technical and non-technical terms*

Let us next consider the distinction between terms which are technical, and those which are not. It turns on the way in which a discursive symbol has acquired its meaning. A technical term is a discursive symbol which acquired its meaning as the result of a stipulation, i.e., of an explicit convention made or accepted by us to fit the term to be an instrument of precision for symbolizing. In consequence, a technical term is very often at the same time an *esoteric* term—one, namely, which is used and understood by only a limited group of persons and constitutes a part of what we call the jargon, or lingo, or cant, of their particular field of endeavour. But a jargon term is not automatically also technical, for many jargon terms do not owe their meaning to an explicitly stated convention and lack the precision which seldom arises otherwise.

A non-technical term, on the other hand—whether it be a jargon term or be 'vulgar' in the sense of being a part of common language—is a discursive symbol the meaning of which is not traceable to an explicit convention but only to associations gradually established in our minds as a result of repeatedly hearing or seeing the term employed in certain situations and not in others, by persons who themselves learned its meaning in the same way. This is of course the way in which we first learn to understand the words of our mother tongue. The meaning a word acquires for us in this way is usually more or less indefinite, and this is a fatal defect if one attempts to use the word for technical purposes, e.g., as an instrument to remote inferences. Yet it is very important to remember that there can be technical language at all only by grace of our possessing to begin with a non-technical, unprecise language wherewith to formulate the stipulations by which technical language is created. The situation is here as with the highly accurate machine-tools industry makes today: they, or the tools with which they were made, or these tools themselves, originally were made with the weak and inaccurate tools consisting of man's two hands.

7. *Meanings, discursive and non-discursive*

Let us now turn from semeiotic interpretanda to semeiotic interpretants. It may first be remarked that just as in ordinary language we call as the case may be 'a symbol' or 'a sign,' that which I have analytically described as a semeiotic interpretandum, so do we in ordinary language call 'a meaning' that which, analytically, is describable as a semeiotic interpretant. Thus, nothing is intrinsically a meaning or intrinsically a symbol or sign, any more than a man is intrinsically an uncle or a nephew. These words are not the names of kinds of things, but of kinds of relational statuses which things can acquire or relinquish. In particular, being a meaning is the relational status which accrues to or is lost by anything which respectively is functioning or ceases to function as semeiotic interpretant.

It is obvious, then, that the meaning of a symbol or a sign may, like the symbol or sign itself, either consist of a word or words, or else of something other than words.

8. *The symbols and meanings of mathematics and logic*

The distinctions that have been made now enable us to say just what distinguishes from other things the entities commonly called logical and mathematical symbols. They are, namely, symbols which are discursive, and whose interpretants not only have been fixed by stipulation but also are themselves discursive. They constitute the cases, mentioned but not described earlier, in which the relation called symbolizing is not only a psychological but in addition a logical relation.

9. *Indicative versus quiddative symbols*

To what has already been said concerning the meaning of the word 'meaning' must be added something on which I do not propose to base anything that follows, but without which the assertion that a meaning is nothing more and nothing less than a semeiotic interpretant is very likely to be misunderstood. It is that among other distinctions possible among symbols, an indispensable one is that between indicative and quiddative symbols. An indicative (or demonstrative or denotative) symbol is one of which the distinctive property is to orient our attention to some *place* in an order system, no matter what in particular may or may not be occupying that place. On the other hand a quiddative (or descriptive or connotative) symbol is one of which the distinctive property is to make us conceive a certain *kind* of thing—a certain 'what'—no matter where in any order system it may or may not be existing. The same entity may function both as indicative and as quiddative symbol: or one part of a complex symbol may be quiddative and another indicative. I believe that having both those functions at once is the distinctive character of the symbols which are symbols of propositions, and I believe it can be shown, although I cannot attempt to do so here, that the difference between the two roles is irreducible: the indicative is not a species of the quiddative, nor vice versa. But Ogden and Richards, in their otherwise valuable work, *The Meaning of Meaning,* appear to assume that thinking, which they call reference, consists solely in responding to an indicative symbol, that is, in becoming oriented by something to something; and that that which is thought of, which they call the referent, is accordingly always an indicable, and indeed a physical indicable. This I believe to be a fatal error, and that it leads them to invalid conclusions from their otherwise sound contention that the relation between symbol and meaning is analysable in terms of causation. But I cannot go into this further on the present occasion, and will only add that if as I contend there are not only indicative but also quiddative symbols, then among meanings or referents we must likewise distinguish between those consisting of something to which attention is being orientated by the symbol, namely, of *places* in one or another order-system; and those consisting of something for which the mind is being prepared by the symbol, namely *characters* of groups of characters.

10. *Four kinds of interpretation*

Leaving now aside the distinction between indicative and quiddative symbols, let us notice next that since both interpretanda and their meanings may be either verbal or real, i.e., either discursive or non-discursive, cases of interpretation will necessarily be of one or another of four kinds, which we may conveniently describe as, respectively,

(1) rei-real interpretation,
(2) rei-verbal interpretation,
(3) verbo-real interpretation,
(4) verbo-verbal interpretation.

11. *Formulating and deciphering*

Concerning the first of these I shall on this occasion say nothing. The second, however, namely, rei-verbal interpretation, is the activity which would commonly be called formulating, or as we might also say, ciphering, or coding. It is what occurs when consciousness of a non-discursive entity causes us in accordance with a rule to become conscious of a certain discursive entity. How important is this kind of semeiotic interpretation becomes obvious if we notice that it constitutes what occurs not only on the occasions when we are said to be thinking of the name of, or to be describing something concretely present, but also on the occasions when we are said to be counting things or to be measuring them. For measuring instruments, e.g., a yardstick, a balance, a clock, etc., are devices for bringing to our minds —although indirectly instead of directly—the same discursive entity, viz., specifically, the same numeral, whenever we perceive a particular kind of non-discursive fact having a certain magnitude which we could not directly distinguish from certain other magnitudes.

But no less important than formulating is the converse operation, viz., verbo-real interpretation. The word in common use which best describes its nature in general is deciphering. But when the discursive symbols or signs deciphered happen to be written rather than spoken, the operation is called more particularly *reading*.

12. *Postulating, defining, and calculating*

The remaining species of interpretation, viz., verbo-verbal interpretation, is of particular interest in connection with symbolic logic and mathematics, for I believe these sciences are exclusively concerned with interpretations of this kind. More explicitly, it seems to me that, for one thing, these sciences take as their primitive facts, that is, as the facts to which they always ultimately appeal and from which they never appeal, certain stipulations as to the discursive interpretants of certain discursive entities—stipulations of this kind being what are commonly called bi-verbal definitions, and defining postulates. The latter may be regarded as in effect including the various rules of construction and of transformation for the discursive system one creates by stipulation, since these rules are statements of the discursive properties stipulated for the discursive entities entering into the system.

Further, what we ordinarily call calculating, in the sense of developing a calculus, consists in discursive interpretation according to the stipulated rules, of the primitive verbal facts created by stipulation. Such verbal interpretation of them is what we should ordinarily call making their implications verbally explicit.

13. *Example of a set of logico-mathematical entities*

What seems to me to be the nature of the entities of pure logic and mathematics will be made clearer if we consider an example. I therefore propose to set forth, although only in outline and without any attempt at formal rigor, what—largely following Norman Campbell—I conceive a cardinal number to be.

Let us first take a certain set of utterable entities, i.e., of words, of one utterance of which the following are a part: 0, 1, 2, 3, 4, 5, 6, 7, 8, 9. The rule for constructing other entities of the set out of these may be assumed to have been already laid down.

We then stipulate that the utterable entities constituting that set shall be called 'the numerals'.

We next stipulate that the numerals shall have a standard serial order, viz., the order: 0, 1, 2, 3, 4, 5, 6, 7, 8, 9, . . . The rule for ordering the remaining ones in the standard manner may be assumed to have been already laid down.

We then select from among the numerals in their standard order the following standard sets:

> 0
> 0, 1
> 0, 1, 2
> 0, 1, 2, 3
> 0, 1, 2, 3, 4
> etc.

These sets, we next stipulate, shall be called 'the cardinal numbers'.

But now, since each of the numerals is an utterably entity, i.e., a word, we can stipulate finally that the *last* numeral of each standard set shall be used as the *name of* the set.

Now the point of special interest for us in connection with this sketch of the nature of cardinal numbers is not that in it they consist of collections each of which has to all a unique relation in respect of including and included, but much rather the fact that the collections concerned are collections *of words*; so that a cardinal number was exhibited as consisting of certain words related to a certain one of them, which is used as its name, in a manner fixed by stipulation. This, I say, is of special interest here for I believe that just this general character is the one distinctive of logical and mathematical entities in general. That is, any such entity consists of *certain words related to a certain one of them, which is used as the name of the entity, in a manner fixed by stipulation: the other words being each itself similarly the name of some other logico-mathematical entity.*

14. *Have pure logic and mathematics importance?*

If logic and mathematics are thus concerned exclusively with verbal entities and the relations established between them by stipulation, the question arises what importance these sciences can then have for knowledge concerning entities other than words, which are what both the natural sciences and the plain man are interested in. As to this, it must be said first of all that logic and mathematics can be and largely are developed without any regard whatever for the possibility of their being useful in the study of Nature. If any of their researches should happen to have no possible utility, then those particular researches would have to be described as constituting simply an intellectual form of sport, like chess, and therefore as neither less important nor more important than other intellectual games. But then it would be appropriate to recall the fact discerned by William James that, in ultimate analysis, the importance of anything consists only in the fact of somebody's being interested in it either directly or indirectly; so that even if logic or mathematics never had indirect importance for persons not directly interested in them, their development would still be important to the mathematicians or logicians who find it intrinsically interesting. When we find ourselves inclined to worship utility too blindly, it is well to remember that what the useful is useful to is always ultimately something useless, and that useless is not synonymous with worthless.

However, what is in need of being made clear in connection with the verbal constructions and operations of logic and mathenatics is much rather in what way, and under what conditions, they can be important to persons who are not directly interested in them. What I can say as to this is nothing particularly new, for everyone knows that mathematics, at least, is useful—indeed indispensable—to the sciences which study Nature. But the specific nature of this utility, and especially the conditions under which alone it can be present, seem very often not to be realized. Examination of a simple concrete example of such utility will perhaps be the best way to make the matter clear.

15. *The example of numerical addition*

Let us examine, for instance, the nature and conditions of the utility of the addition of numerals for the solution of a simple problem concerning empirical facts, the problem, let us say, whether the bricks in two given heaps will be enough and no more than enough to build a brick pillar of the same size as one already erected at one side of a proposed gateway. Solution of the problem requires counting the bricks in each heap, adding the numerals so obtained, and counting the bricks in the pillar already built.

Now, of what nature are these various operations? Counting, as already pointed out, is a species of rei-verbal interpretation. It is, namely, a passage from a fact in Nature (here consisting of a certain set of bricks) to a certain word, namely, to the numeral which, by stipulation, is the name of a certain set of numerals. The general kind of operation of which counting is a case is the one we earlier proposed to call the formulating, or ciphering, or coding of a fact in Nature.

The next operation we perform consists in passage from the two numerals obtained by counting the two heaps of bricks, to a certain other numeral called their numerical sum. Such passage constitutes the operation called numerical addition. It is a case of verbo-verbal interpretation, of the general kind called calculation.

We next compare the numeral obtained by addition and the numeral obtained by counting the bricks in the pillar already built. And lastly, we perform an act of verbo-real interpretation, namely, we decipher or decode the verbal fact consisting of sameness, or, as it may be, difference, of the two numerals compared. This deciphering consists, specifically, in passage from that verbal fact to the physical fact that, if another pillar is built with the bricks in the two heaps, it will be of the same size as (or, if the two numeral were different, of a different size from) the pillar already built What we have done may be represented by a simple diagram in which the operations performed are symbolized by line arrows and the physical operation rendered unnecessary and therefore no performed, by an arrow of dashes.

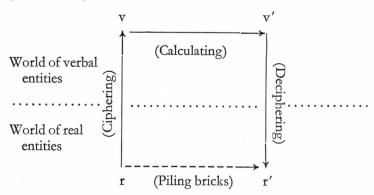

16. *Nature of the utility of verbal constructs and operations*

Thus, through performance of three kinds of operations in which words entered either in part or exclusively, but in all three of which words were essential elements, we have learned quickly and easily what would be the outcome of a certain wholly physical operation which we did not perform, namely, the slow and laborious one of piling bricks into a pillar. This illustrates the kind of utility susceptible of being possessed by the verbal constructions of mathematics and logic: *They sometimes possess predictiveness*; that is, they sometimes enable us to discover, by means of relatively easy and rapid verbal operations, what would be the result of certain other operations which would consume much more time and energy, and which indeed would sometimes be impracticable for economic or other empirical reasons. Predictiveness in this sense may of course be not only of the future, but equally of the past, or of the present but spatially far away, or of things too minute or too large for direct observation, and so on. Moreover, the operations among entities of Nature, of which we can predict the outcome by means of verbal operations, are very often not even human operations at all but purely automatic natural processes.

But that verbal constructions and operations sometimes have predictiveness is obvious enough. What is less so is the nature of the conditions that they must satisfy in order to be predictive. These conditions are essentially two, and their nature will appear if we return to our example.

7. *Conditions of the predictiveness of verbal operations*

Let us note first that when, in the ciphering operation, we chose a word to use as verbal symbol of the bricks in the given heap, we did not have to pick it from among those called the numerals. We could instead have picked any other word, even one invented at the moment; for if we had resolved to use it as symbol of that collection of bricks, it would have symbolized it as genuinely as any other word could. Moreover, even if we had decided to use one of the numerals, we did not have to choose it by means of the operation called counting. We could have chosen it by some other method, or at random. Why then did we choose a numeral rather than some other word, and choose it by counting rather than otherwise?

The answer is that, unless we had done so, the first of the two conditions of the possession of predictiveness by words would not have been satisfied. This condition is that the word used must already be the name of a logico-mathematical entity *formally similar* to the entity in Nature which is to be verbally symbolized. In our example, this formal similarity exists between a cardinal number and a heap of bricks. The cardinal number, as we have seen, is a certain collection of numerals, having as its name a certain one of them. Formal similarity of this collection of numerals and of a collection of bricks consists (for the purposes of prediction about bricks through addition of numerals) in *sameness of numerousness* of the two collections. And in turn, sameness of two collections in the respect to be called numerousness consists in the existence of some way of matching, one-to-one, all the members of the two collections. But this matching operation, as between bricks and numerals, is the very one called counting the bricks.

Accordingly, when the numeral we shall use to symbolize the bricks is selected by means of the operation called counting, we get automatically a numeral which is not only (by prior stipulation) the *name* of a certain collection of numerals, but also (because selected by counting) an *adjective* of our collection of bricks. And to say that it is an adjective of it is to say that it is not simply a verbal symbol of it, but one having in common with it certain formal properties. These remarks incidentally bring out the fact that formal similarity between one thing and another is not, as sometimes asserted, a necessary condition of the one's being a symbol of the other, but a necessary condition only of its being a symbol *useful for purposes of prediction* about the other.

The second of the two conditions for predictiveness is again a matter of formal similarity, but this time between the verbo-verbal *operation* performed—in our example, the operation called addition of the numerals—and the rei-real *operation* of which the outcome is predicted without its being performed—in our example the operation of piling the bricks into a pillar. The respect of resemblance which, in the instance, constitutes the 'formal similarity' of the two operations is the possession by both of the familiar set of characters, viz., associativeness, commutativeness, etc., which jointly define addition in general—whether of numerals, of bricks, or of anything else. What formal similarity in general itself is is another question, not answered by merely giving illustrations of it as above. I venture to suggest that, in ultimate analysis, the respects of similarity to be called formal in any given sort of case are those which happen to be necessary and sufficient for predictions of the sort one desires to be able to make.

The foregoing discussion has pointed out how it is that a set of words which have been systematically related to one another by means of stipulations sometimes makes prediction possible concerning things other than words; and we all know that some such set is virtually indispensable if prediction is going to be exact and far-reaching. But that a given such set, and given operations within it, will meet the two conditions necessary to its having predictiveness for a given species of natural facts cannot be guaranteed in advance. And therefore we have today more mathematical and logical constructions than we yet can utilize. On the other hand, we know today many kinds of natural facts for the prediction of which we still lack the needed logic or mathematics; and often we find ourselves unable to invent it to order. Under the circumstances, it is obvious that the larger the variety of mathematical and logical instruments we have at hand for trial or aid in such cases, the greater is the chance that some one of them will fit or help us to invent one that fits. And although the construction of logico-mathematical instruments is undertaken by mathematicians and logicians in most cases for its intrinsic interest without regard to their possible utility, construction of an abundance of them is nevertheless something very important to the rest of us in the indirect way just stated.

In what precedes, I have spoken of mathematics and logic always together. The reason for this is that the symbols and meanings employed by them are of the same kind, namely, discursive and generated by stipulations. The two sciences are thus very closely related. But their exact relation is a matter not yet settled and I cannot here attempt to analyse it. A last remark about to be made has perhaps some bearing on the question, but is in any case needed to qualify the assumption seemingly made in what precedes, that such predictiveness as verbal operations may possess is always and directly predictiveness of the outcome of operations *in Nature*. This is, of course, not so. Indeed, perhaps most often, the slower and more laborious operations of which a given verbal operation directly enables us to predict the outcome are themselves also verbal operations, though of lesser generality. In such cases, the capacity of the new and more highly abstract verbal entities and operations to predict facts *in Nature* is, when they have it at all, indirect but correspondingly more sweeping. And when they do have it, we then vividly realize that the most highly abstract things, although in appearance wholly devoid of connection with the practical tasks of man, nevertheless do sometimes turn out to have practical value, and of the farthest-reaching kind.

9.

OBJECTIVITY, OBJECTIVE REFERENCE, AND PERCEPTION*

CONTENTS

* *Philosophy and Phenomenological Research*, vol. II, No. 1, 1941.

1. *Some statements of the problem of objective reference*

That many of our thoughts and sensations 'refer to objects' is generally accepted; but it seems to many philosophers that this objective reference is paradoxical. *How* it is possible is therefore a question often regarded as perhaps the most fundamental in the theory of knowledge. What the paradox is conceived to be may be shown by two illustrations.

Savery, for instance,[1] describes the problem as that 'of the mystery of how a state in experience can report what lies beyond experience. . . . How can anything be the thought of something else? How can a mental state report not what it is, but what it is not?' And Lovejoy[2] formulates the problem by saying that it 'consists in that peculiarity of knowing which philosophers call "meaning" or "transcendent reference"; that is, in the fact that when we know we appear somehow to have within the field of our experience at a given moment objects which we must at the same time conceive as existing entirely outside that field—for example, as having their being at a time other than the time of the knowing of them.'

The paradox is put most briefly by Cunningham[3] in the question 'If objects are outside of mind, how can they ever be known by it?' He goes on to remark, however, that the paradox 'is based upon the assumption that the mind is sharply sundered from objects' and that 'when once this separation between mind and objects is made, the question concerning the possibility of knowledge of objects becomes inevitable', but also unanswerable. He believes he avoids it by maintaining that 'the objective reference of judgement means that, in the act of knowing, mind and object are bound together and are not separate and distinct. Knowledge, then, is primarily a relation between mind and objects, and exists only when that relation exists. No object, then no judgement; no judgement, then no knowledge. How can the mind know objects? is a question which thus seems to be meaningless; it is impossible for the mind to know anything else but objects.'

---

[1] 'On the Nature of Objective Reference,' *Journal of Philosophy*, July 22, 1936.

[2] In a paper entitled 'The Anomaly of Knowledge', *Univ. of California Publications in Philosophy*, vol. IV (1923).

[3] *Problems of Philosophy,* Henry Holt and Co., New York, 1924, p. 102.

The comment suggests itself here, however, that if with Cunningham we say that whatever the mind knows is an object, then we are forced to distinguish between what might be called 'subjective objects' (viz., states of mind, such as our feelings called pain, or nausea, or *our conception of* Julius Caesar, or of the seventh decimal of π, etc.) and 'objective objects' (such as Julius Caesar himself, or the seventh decimal of π itself, etc.). The relation of the mind to 'subjective objects' perhaps constitutes no problem, but the mind's relation to 'objective objects' is in any case a radically different one and is the one specifically in view when 'objective reference' is discussed. But Cunningham's quoted denial that mind and object are 'sundered' when knowledge of an object is occurring, is only an assertion that at such times there *is* a relation, called knowing, between the mind and 'objective objects'. This may well be granted, but to have asserted it or granted it is not in the least to have described the specific nature of that relation. And elucidation of its nature and of the nature of its 'objective object' term is the very task with which the problem of 'objective reference' confronts us. On the other hand, if the problem is formulated as Lovejoy and Savery suggest, it is truly insoluble; for it then amounts to that of explaining how something *ex hypothesis* impossible nevertheless does occur.

2. *What I conceive the problem to be*

Proper formulation of the problem of objective reference is perhaps best approached in terms of the case of reference presented by our perception of physical objects, such as a book, a coin, etc. It will be useful in this connection to consider certain important passages in G. E. Moore's paper on 'The Status of Sense Data',[1] of which the following is a paraphrased summary. Moore there supposes himself to be looking at two coins flat on the ground at a distance from him, one of them a half-crown and the other a florin, and the half-crown so much farther away than the florin that the half-crown's visual image (its 'visual sensible') is visibly smaller. Under these circumstances he, or anyone else similarly situated, would ordinarily assume that he knows—more specifically, perceives,—certain objective facts, e.g., that he is really seeing two coins, that although their sensible appearances

---

[1] *Philosophical Studies*, pp. 185–90.

are elliptical the coins are really circular, that the coins have another side and an inside, that the half-crown is really larger than the florin, and that both coins continue to exist if he ceases to look at them. To know such facts under such circumstances is to 'see', i.e., to perceive visually, a physical object; and this is obviously 'seeing' in a sense different from that in which 'seeing' means merely to apprehend directly a 'visual sensible', i.e., a visual sensum.

In a case such as this, the knowledge Moore has of the objective facts mentioned is, he states, certainly 'based, in the last resort, on experiences of mine consisting in the direct apprehension of sensibles and in the perception of relations between directly apprehended sensibles. It is *based* on these, in at least this sense, that I should never have known any of these propositions (i.e., any of these objective facts) if I had never directly apprehended any sensibles nor perceived any relations between them.'

The fact pointed out by Moore in the last quoted sentence is, I believe, the one from which a right formulation of the problem of objective reference in perception must start. Borrowing for the time being his term, 'sensibles', I would state what I conceive to be that problem as follows: That apprehension of sensibles and of their relations is necessary to perception—and indeed even ultimately to conception—of 'objective' facts of the kind mentioned implies that such 'objective' facts are some *function* (in the logical sense) of sensibles and the relations of sensibles. The problem is then which *specific* function of them are they? Or we may put it otherwise as follows: 'Objective' facts of the kind mentioned have to sensibles a relation R, such that unless sensibles were apprehended 'objective' facts of that kind would not be known at all. The problem then is, what *specifically* is that relation R? When we are in position to specify it, we shall then be in position to say that, in cases of the kind mentioned, to be 'objective' is to have to sensibles the relation R.

This statement of the problem, however, directly concerns only such objective reference as enters into perception. A comprehensive statement of the problem must therefore be formulated in terms of the genus of which sensibles are but one species. This genus I propose to label 'intuitions'. But since 'intuitions' will play a fundamental role in the analysis of objective reference to follow, it is necessary to make clear to begin with the sense in

94

which that term will be used, and in which I am using it when I class sensibles as a species of intuitions.

3. *Intuitions*

This sense is defined in terms of the distinction between what I have elsewhere proposed to call the 'connate' *cognitum* and the 'alien' *cognitum* of a given act of cognizing.[1] The difference distinguished by these terms may first be illustrated. It is the difference between, for instance, the hearing of a tone—e.g., middle *C*—and the hearing of a bell, or between the smelling of a smell and the smelling of a rose, or between the tasting of a taste—e.g., of the taste called 'bitter'—and the tasting of a substance—e.g., of the substance called 'quinine'.

Although it is, I take it, obvious in each such case that there is an important difference, discernment of its exact nature and of its epistemological implications is possible only if certain easy confusions are carefully guarded against. For one, we must throughout keep in mind clearly the difference between, e.g., *sound* (i.e., sound-experience), *sound-stimulus* (viz., air vibrations), and *sounding-object* (e.g., a bell); or again between *smell, smell-stimulus* (air laden with molecules of certain substances), and *smelly object* (e.g., a rose); and so on. And it must be remembered throughout that when I speak here of hearing a sound, smelling a smell, tasting a taste, etc., it is the sound, smell, or taste *itself* that I am speaking of, and *not* the stimulus *nor* the object generating the stimulus.

Secondly, we must differentiate sharply throughout also between *smelling* in the sense of smelling some smell (whether or not a smell-stimulus be present at the time) and *sniffing*, which consists in drawing air through the olfactory apparatus in an attempt to respond to whatever smell-stimulus might happen to be present. Similarly, when I speak here of *hearing*, what I mean is hearing sound (irrespective of whether or not a sound-stimulus be present at the time); and *not* hearing in the sense of *listening* to, or listening for—which is the sense it has for instance in the exclamation

---

[1] In an article entitled 'Introspection, Mental Acts, and Sensa', *Mind*, N.S., vol. XLV (1936), No. 178. This epistemologically fundamental distinction being there set forth and argued in detail, I give here only a brief and more or less dogmatic account of the aspects of it needed to make clear what I mean by 'intuitions'.

'Hear! Hear!'—and which consists in orienting or attuning the auditory apparatus. Again, by *tasting* I mean here tasting some taste (whether or not a taste-stimulus be present at the time), and not the rolling about of the tongue, or other buccal adjustment, performed in the attempt to respond to whatever taste-stimulus might happen to be present.

If these confusions are successfully avoided, I submit it then becomes evident that smelling, and smelling some smell, are one and the same thing, and therefore that the *esse* of a smell consists in its being smelled just as the *esse* of a waltz consists in its being waltzed, the *esse* of a stroke in its being struck, etc. (But this is *not* to say that the *esse* of a smell stimulus consists in its being responded to, nor that the *esse* of a smell-stimulus-generator—e.g., a rose—consists in response by us to the stimuli it generates).

Similarly, hearing is identically the same thing with hearing some sound, and therefore no hearing exists which is not the hearing of some sound nor does there exist any sound (as distinguished from sound-stimulus and sound-stimulus-generator) which is not being heard: the *esse* of sound consists in its being heard. The same thing holds for tasting and the other modes of sensing; the *esse* of a taste, e.g., of the taste called 'bitter', consists in its being tasted, etc.

The foregoing remarks exhibit the reason for my proposal to describe, for example, the *cognitum* called 'sound' as *connate with*—that is, as automatically born with or coming to existence with—the cognizing activity called 'hearing'; and likewise the *cognitum* 'smell' as connate with the cognizing activity 'smelling', etc. It is necessary, however, to distinguish between being *co-ordinately* and being *subordinately* connate with a given cognitive activity. For example, taste is the *cognitum* co-ordinately connate with tasting; but bitter taste is a *cognitum* subordinately connate with tasting. This entails that although no bitter taste exists which is not being tasted, yet some tasting does exist which is not the tasting of bitter taste. This fact has been misinterpreted by the philosophers who have thought themselves able to conclude from it that 'bitter' is an *object* of tasting in more or less the same sense that quinine, for instance, is an object of tasting. But the truth is that tasting bitter is a species *of tasting*, not the tasting of a species *of object*; whereas tasting quinine is not a species of tasting but on the contrary the tasting of a species of object—and in a sense of 'tasting' radically different from the sense it has when one speaks of tasting bitter taste; for to 'taste' quinine is to place quinine on the tongue and to notice which taste if any then occurs. But obviously to taste bitter taste is not similarly to place bitter taste on the tongue (!) and to notice whether bitter taste then occurs.

But now, just as bitter taste is a (subordinately) connate *cognitum* of the cognitive activity, tasting; so are taste, smell, sound, etc., themselves in turn subordinately connate *cognita* of the generic cognitive activity, sensing. Again, to fear and to experience fear are one and the same thing; and so is to wonder and to experience wonder, or to sorrow and to experience sorrow, etc. Fear, wonder, sorrow, etc., are thus not *objects* of experience (the dark, on the other hand, would be an *object* of the experience called 'fear' or 'fearing') but *species* of experience, and are thus (subordinately) connate *cognita* of 'experiencing', which may be taken in this connection as the *summum genus* of cognitive activities.

In terms of the considerations of which a summary has just been presented, 'intuiting' and 'intuitions' may now be precisely defined. I call 'intuiting' any cognizing *qua* cognitive of its connate *cognitum,* and I call 'an intuition' the connate *cognitum* of any given cognizing act. Further, I use 'an intuition' and 'a phenomenon' as synonyms; and I would say that the 'mental' or 'psychical' consists (primitively) of intuitions and (derivatively) of whatever is analytically or synthetically implicit in intuitions.[1] The peculiarity of the *cognita* described above as 'intuitions', which fits them for their basic role in epistemology, and which I have attempted to point out, is that in their case *the cognitum is identical with the cognizing*: intuitions are those acts of cognition in the case of which what is cognized by the act is *its own specific nature*.

A *cognitum* connate with the act cognitive thereof I shall call a *content* of consciousness; and I shall on the contrary call *object* of consciousness a *cognitum* 'alien to' the act cognitive of it. The cases of cognition in which 'objective reference' is involved are then those in which the *cognitum* is of the 'alien' sort. Alien *cognita*, however, have so far been characterized for the most part only negatively, as those which are not connate. The problem of 'objective

---

[1] For the distinction here intended between 'primitive' and 'derivative', see the writer's 'Philosophy and Natural Science', *Philosophical Review,* vol. XLIX (1940), pp. 127-9, or Chap. VIII of his *Philosophy as a Science,* New York, 1941.

reference' is that of stating in positive terms what it is to be an 'alien' *cognitum*, and what specifically is the relation of such *cognita* to intuitions. To this I now turn.

4. *Removal of some possible sources of confusion*

Not a little of the difficulty presented by the problem of objective reference arises from the fact that, in the cases one takes as examples, certain questions, other than and additional to that of the nature of objective reference, easily inject themselves without being recognized as other. This both greatly complicates the task one then actually attempts, and obscures the true nature of the task one believes oneself to be attempting. To avoid such complications and confusions, it is necessary at the outset to point out the principal of these other questions. Only thus can we isolate adequately for examination the problem of objective reference.

(a) *The question of the nature of objectivity is distinct from that whether cases of a given kind of object exist.* One of these other questions is whether the kind of object one perceives or thinks of exists. For objectivity in kind is one thing, and existence of cases of a given objective kind is another thing. For example, when I think of a centaur, my thought is not thought of a mental, subjective sort of entity, but is on the contrary thought of an objective, and a physical, kind of entity just as truly as when a horse is what I think of. Only, in the instance of the centaur cases of that kind of object do not exist, whereas in the instance of the horse cases of the kind do exist. On the other hand, *thinking of* something is a species of subjective activity, and a case of that activity exists at the moment I perform it whether what I think of be horse or centaur. Thus cases exist of kinds (e.g., of the kind 'thinking') which are not objective but subjective kinds; and on the other hand no cases exist of some kinds (e.g., of the kind 'centaur') which are objective kinds.

Where perceiving instead of conceiving or imagining is concerned, the situation is similar. When, for example, the dipsomaniac 'perceives' a pink elephant, his *perceiving*, i.e., his act of interpreting as appearances of a physical object the pink colour and shape he intuits, is a mental activity and exists at the time he performs it. His perceiving, however, is not of a mental activity but of a species of entity just as truly both objective and physical as the kind he perceives when he watches the circus parade. Only, in the instance of the pink elephant, a case of the kind of physical object he perceives does not exist there and then, and his perceiving is therefore classed as hallucinatory; whereas in the instance of the circus, cases of the kind of object he perceives do exist there and then, and his perceiving is therefore classed as veridical.

(b) *The question of the nature of objectivity is distinct from that of how we know whether cases of a given kind of object exist.* Another question, distinct from that of what it means to class the kind of entities called elephants (whether pink or grey) as *objective*, and distinct also from that of what it means for cases of an objective kind to *exist*, is the question *how we discover* whether a case of a kind of object we perceive does or does not there and then exist—for instance, how we discover that the pink elephants perceived do not exist, and the grey ones do. This question is not specially difficult to answer, for we need but observe how we actually proceed to remove such doubts as we may have on a given occasion as to the existence of the kind of object we perceive. At this point, however, we are not attempting to answer that question but only to make clear that it is distinct from that of the nature of objectivity.

(c) *The question of the nature of objectivity is distinct from that of the difference between physical and mental objects.* Another question also distinct from that of the nature of objectivity is the question whether a given kind of object is a kind of physical or of mental object. For although whatever kind is physical is objective, the converse is not universally true. Entities of a mental kind sometimes have subjective status and sometimes objective status: subjective always at the time of their occurrence for the mind of which they are part; but objective for that mind at all other times, viz., when they are remembered, anticipated, or otherwise thought of; and objective also at all times for other minds thinking of them. For example, if I now remember having felt fear yesterday, my past fear-experience is *object* of my present (and subjective) remembering activity. The fear, *at the time of its occurrence,* is *subjective,* for it is (subordinately) connate with the experiencing thereof; but when at a later time I am remembering it, I cannot at that later time say of the fear remembered that it *is now* subjective, but only that it *was at its time* subjective. Thus something which earlier had subjective status now has objective status, viz., is object of present remembrance. But there are kinds of entities, classed by us now as objective, which never had nor ever will have subjective status. This is the case with all the kinds of entities called physical.

(d) *Not substances only can be objective, but also events and properties.* When objectivity is discussed in connection with perception, it is natural to take as examples of objective kinds of entities books, or pieces of iron, or trees, i.e., cases of some kind of substance. But *objectivity must not be confused with substantiality or with physical substantiality.* For the realm of the objective includes not only kinds of substances but also kinds of *events* and of *properties.*

(e) *The basic problem is that of the nature of objectivity in the case of events.* Substantiality, as distinguished from existence of it, is conjunctiveness of some set of properties. Considering for instance the substance called 'gold', its *what*, i.e., gold-ness, consists in malleability *and* ductility *and* fusibility *and* electrical conductivity, etc. (each in a specific degree). Some pieces of metal do and others do not have all the properties comprised in this set. Those which do are cases of gold, i.e., of gold-ness; and those which do not are not cases of it. Thus *what* gold is is a question distinct from the question whether any of it exists.

Substantiality being thus analysable in terms of the notion of 'property', the latter is logically prior. Properties, however, themselves analyse into laws concerning kinds of events. The property called 'fusibility' or 'being fusible', for instance, analyses as follows: To be fusible is to be such that if subjected to heat (under circumstances of kind K), liquidity replaces solidity. And 'being heated', 'becoming liquid', 'ceasing to be solid', are kinds of events. The notion of 'event' thus seems to be the basic and minimal one, and what we must now discover is what exactly it means to speak of an *event* as objective; for when we have discovered this we shall then immediately be able also to define objectiveness of properties and substances.

Events are the sorts of entities susceptible of extending through some segment of time or both some segment of time and some region of space. To say this, however, is not to say what an *objective* event is, for the question as to objectivity can be asked concerning times and places themselves also. It appears, therefore, that the nature of time and space and the relation of objective to subjective time and space are the first questions we must consider.

5. *Time*

(a) *The intuition of times.* If we intuit a given *quale* at a given place, and also do not intuit it at that very place, we are intuiting *two times*.[1] Time, thus, is the possibility of one quale both being and not being at one place. We intuit two times under the condition stated no matter whether the quale concerned is an objective or a subjective one, but since we have for present purposes no right to use as part of our *definiens* anything objective, we shall take the quale concerned to be a subjective one. The *place* concerned will likewise, therefore, be not an objective place, but a place-intuition, which, as was contended in Section 3, is the same thing as an intuited place. (Although the so-called 'inner sense' is often assumed to have only the time dimension, this is certainly not true of some parts of it—for instance, of the intuitions of colour, sound, the tactual intuitions, etc.)

(b) *Minimum clocks.* The being and not being at one place, of a quale, constitutes a *minimum clock*—one, namely, having *two beats*, one *positive* (the quale is at the given place) and the other *negative* (the quale is not there). In clocks which have more than two beats the positive beats may or may not be quiddatively alike, and likewise with the negative beats (for the negative beats usually have some sort of quiddative content of their own and are 'negative' only in that their quiddative content is *other* than the quiddative content of the beat taken as 'positive').

---

[1] I use the term 'a *quale*' as synonymous with the awkward term 'a what' (as contrasted with 'a that'). My use of 'quale' is thus broader than that of C. I. Lewis, who means by it 'sense quale' (*Mind and the World Order*, p. 60); and is more or less the same, I believe, as the use made nowadays of the term 'essence'. Lewis criticizes 'essence' on the ground that it is made to cover not only sense qualia but also universal concepts which, however, he says, differ from sense qualia in that 'the object of the concept must always have a time-span which extends beyond the specious present' whereas 'the qualia of sense as something given do not, in the nature of the case, have such temporal spread.' This criticism, however, seems to me to rest on confusion between the 'object of the concept' and the concept itself. The objects of the concept represented by the word 'tree', for instance, that is, the individual trees, do have temporal spread; but the concept itself of the specific 'what' called 'tree-ness' is like sense qualia in having no time spread beyond the specious present.

(c) *Natural psychological clocks*. The successions of positive and negative intuitions which are correlated with physiological processes like breathing and heartbeat constitute natural psychological clocks which beat for us throughout life.

(d) *Time-succession*. The relation of any two times intuited at any one place where any one quale both is and is not is *succession*.

(e) *Earlier-later*. Of two times which are intuited as in the relation of succession, one is called *earlier*, or *past relatively to the other*, and the other *later*, or *future relatively to the other*. Of the two, the one whose quiddative content is the 'clearer' is called *later*, and the other *earlier*.

The respect of difference here called clearness, between qualia at intuited successive times, is *sui generis* and therefore not further describable. All that can be done is to take a situation in which difference in that respect is observable, and describe that situation in a manner that will call attention to the character meant by 'clearness' and thus aid one to discern which one it is, among those observable in that situation. For example, let us assume that the word 'relatively' is being heard. Then we can say that the character of which the syllable 'rel' has least, and the syllable 'ly' has most, at the time the syllable 'ly' is being heard (no matter with what intensity either of them is uttered) is the character meant by 'clearness'. A few such examples, with different words uttered in a diversity of manners, would suffice to identify beyond reasonable doubt the character to which the name 'clearness' is being applied. The field of visual space exhibits differences in respect of an analogous character, which we shall consider later and call 'distinctness'.

(f) *The present time, and past times*. Of several times intuited as in the relation of succession, the one whose quiddative content is intuited *most clearly* is called *now*, or the present time; and the others are called *past* relatively to it.

(g) *Simultaneity*. If two intuited qualia are intuited as not in the relation of succession, they are said to be intuited simultaneously, or *at the same time*.

(h) *Contiguousness of times*. If two times are intuited by us as being one later than the other, and no third time is intuited by us as both later than the first and earlier than the second, then the two times are called *contiguous* or *immediately successive*. Otherwise they are said to be *separated by an interval of time*.

(i) *Persistence*. If a given quale is intuited as simultaneous with every one of several other qualia, which are themselves intuited as at contiguously successive times, then the given quale is said to *persist, last, continue,* or *endure,* from the time of the first to the time of the last of these others; or *throughout the time between* that of the first and that of the last.

(j) *Times as instants and as durations*. If a given quale is intuited as simultaneous with everyone of several other qualia themselves intuited as at contiguously successive times, then intuition of the time of the given quale is said to be intuition of *a duration,* or a *segment of time,* or a *quantity of time,* or *some* (vs. *a*) *time.*

If on the contrary at the time at which we intuit a given quale we *do not* intuit simultaneously with it any two or more other qualia as at successive times, then intuition of the time of the given quale is said to be intuition of *an instant,* or *a* (vs. some) time, or (if assigned a proper name) a determinate *date*. Intuition of an instant, that is to say, is intuition of the time of a quale not simultaneous with any intuited succession of other qualia.[1]

Although the distinction between intuition of *a* time and of *some* time, i.e., of an instant and of a duration, is indispensable and perfectly definite, it is nevertheless essentially *relational*. That is, the time at which a given quale is intuited is intuition either of a duration or of an instant, according as, respectively, a succession of other qualia is, or on the contrary is not, intuited simultaneously with the given quale.

(k) *Equality of durations*. Duration is neither intuitable nor definable otherwise than as simultaneity of some given quale with several beats of some 'clock'. The question whether the beats of a given clock are of equal duration therefore cannot be either defined or decided otherwise than in terms of the beats of *another clock beating either faster or slower*. The beats of the given clock are said to be *of equal duration* if the same number of beats of a faster clock are simultaneous with each one of the beats of the given clock; or if the same number of beats of the given clock are simultaneous with each beat of a slower clock.

The objection naturally suggests itself that this establishes equality of duration of the beats of the given clock only if the beats

---

[1] A *mathematical instant* is the time of any quale which, *by stipulation,* is not simultaneous with any succession of other qualia.

of the other (faster or slower) clock are themselves of equal duration. But this could be ascertained (or even given any meaning) only in terms of some third and still faster or slower clock, in the same manner, etc., *ad infinitum*—the question thus remaining forever unsettled. The objection, however, is without force because among the clocks available to us there is always a fastest and a slowest, and because the question whether the beats of the *fastest* clock have equal duration is ultimately definable and decidable in terms of comparison of the number of them simultaneous with each beat of the slowest clock (in which case the question whether the beats of the slowest clock have equal duration becomes absurd since it then postulates another clock slower than the slowest). Or if on the contrary the question with which we start is whether the beats of the *slowest* clock have equal duration, this is ultimately a matter of whether an equal number of beats of the fastest clock are simultaneous with each (in which case the question whether the beats of the fastest clock have equal duration is analogously absurd). These reflections lead to the conclusion that, theoretically, we can take as *standard* clock any clock we choose, and then define and decide the equality or inequality of duration of the beats of other clocks by comparison with the standard clock. But with regard to the standard clock itself, the question of equality or inequality of duration of its beats is absurd (as implicitly denying that it is the standard clock).

(1) *Intrinsic direction of time.* The fact that the 'earlier-later' relation as it was defined is *unsymmetrical* is what gives *intuited* time an intrinsic direction. Although we have not yet defined physical time, we may here state parenthetically that physical time has no intrinsic direction. A non-arbitrary direction can be specified in it only by correlating it with intuited time, i.e., only insofar as physical time is *perceived*. Thus, inasmuch as 'now' or 'the present time' is definable only in terms of a certain intuition (viz., that of maximum 'clearness'), these words have no applicability to physical time apart from correlation of it with intuited time. In physical time, there is no past, present, or future. Indeed, there is an earlier or later only in terms of some arbitrarily selected pair of times A and B, with reference to which it is then true of a third time C that either: C is beyond B from A

or C is beyond A from B

or C is between A and B.

We can then assign a meaning to 'earlier' and 'later' in physical time by specifying, arbitrarily, e.g., that any time C shall be called 'later' than A if it is beyond A *from* B, (or if we prefer, no less arbitrarily, if it is beyond B *from* A), and otherwise 'earlier'.

5. Objective reference in the remembrance or expectation of mental events

The articles of Section 5 provide a meaning in terms of intuition for the principal time terms. Additional ones could be defined on the basis so laid but this is unnecessary for present purposes. We shall instead pass now to the question of objective times. It divides into two: one the question of what exactly it is to *think of*, or to think of and know, some mental event of our own as past or future; and the other the question of the nature of physical time and of our perception of it. Answer to the second question will be postponed until after space has been discussed.

Examples of reference to mental events of our own other than those occurring at the moment would be *remembering having worried*, or *expecting that one will worry*. To analyse rightly such instances of objective reference, we must realize first the falsity of the assumption sometimes made that we are able to intuit (or in the case of physical events, to perceive) only 'present' events. The fact on the contrary is that *we are able to intuit the successiveness of a number of events*, although their number is always small. This, rather small, range of our intuition of successiveness (or in the case of physical events, of our perception of successiveness) is what is often called our 'specious present'. Now the distinction between earlier and later and between strict present and past, can be made and is first made, on the basis of degree of clearness, *within the specious present*, i.e., among the events comprised *within the range of our intuition of successiveness*. And it is the relation of 'before-after', exhibited by the elements of our intuitive experience within that range, and abstracted from it by us, which enables us to 'refer' to mental events outside that range: *past* (i.e., past not within that range) means *before the earliest part of the specious present*; and *future* (i.e., future to the strict present) means *after the latest part of the specious present*.

Thus, to *remember having worried* is (with a qualification to be mentioned later) to have, towards the proposition 'worry by me, before (specious) now', the epistemic attitude called belief.[1] Or, in greater detail, to remember having worried is a complex mental act analysable as follows:

(*a*) intuiting the determinable relation 'earlier than',

(*b*) having as first term for it a certain determinate of the determinable quale 'worry'—this determinate worry being at the moment intuited only faintly, i.e., with imaginal rather than with sensuous intensity,

(*c*) having as second term of the 'earlier than' relation the earliest quale intuited in the 'specious now',

(*d*) having the attitude 'belief' towards the proposition we intuit in doing together (*a*), (*b*), and (*c*).[2]

To this account certain objections suggest themselves. The first would be that there is a difference between *believing* that one has worried, and *remembering* that one has worried, and that it is of the first, not of the second, that an account has been given above. This is true, but the difference is only that in the case of remembering, the quiddative intuition concerned would be not merely that of some determinate of the determinable 'worry', but, together with it, certain others (which were the simultaneous specific quiddative mental context of the worry). The proposition believed, in the cases of remembering, has for its quale-element this *total* quiddative intuition, and for its time-element the intuition of the same time-function, viz., 'before now'. (Or more often, a more specific one such as 'before-now and after . . .' viz., after some other event

---

[1] In a paper entitled 'Propositions, Opinions, Sentences, and Facts' (*Journal of Philosophy*, vol. XXXVII (1940), No. 26), I have proposed to call belief, disbelief, doubt, and the various degrees of inclination to believe, the 'epistemic attitudes', and I have contended that in declarative sentences the words 'is' or 'is not' or, more generally, the affirmative or negative form of the verb (whether or not modalized by 'possibly', 'probably', etc.) symbolizes no part of the proposition itself, but the particular epistemic attitude taken towards the proposition. Therefore, to state the proposition only, that is the proposition without any epistemic attitude towards it, the affirmative or negative form of the verb must be left out of the sentence; e.g., 'Napoleon, tall' formulates the *proposition* belief of which is formulated by 'Napoleon is tall', and disbelief of which by 'Napoleon is not tall'. Similarly 'here now, rain', or (as in the text) 'before now, worry', formulate propositions but no epistemic attitude towards them.

[2] The terms 'determinable' and 'determinate' are used here in W. E. Johnson's sense as set forth in his *Logic*, vol. I, ch. XI. It should be kept in mind that a 'determinate' is an *infima species,* not an individual.

before-now, also believed. For we seldom if ever remember an event wholly by itself, but usually rather some limited succession of events. That is, the event remembered usually has a remembered temporal context, as well as a remembered simultaneous context.)

A second objection that might be advanced is that, even granting the correctness of the account offered, it is an account only of what *remembering* having worried consists in, but that objective reference is involved even in merely *thinking of*, as distinguished from remembering, having worried. What then does the mere thinking of having worried consist in? The answer, I submit, is that elements (*a*), (*b*), and (*c*) above, without element (*d*), that is, without the belief attitude, would constitute merely thinking of, as distinguished from remembering, having worried.

Finally, it might be vaguely objected that even what has been said above still somehow does not seem to show how it is possible for a present mental act to refer to past mental events. If such a vague objection were made, I could say only that very often, in what is offered as constituting an analysis of a given thing, it is very hard to recognize the thing which was to be analysed: The corpse of even the person we know best would hardly be recognized by us as such if presented to us by an anatomist in thoroughly dissected form. For to recognize it, we should have to put together in imagination the parts offered to our sight, *in the relations also offered* (but to our understanding rather than our sight) by the anatomist; for these relations are, just as genuinely as the visible organs, a part of what the anatomical process offers to us. But such synthesis is a psychological act difficult in proportion to the complexity revealed by the analysis. And inability to perform it adequately at the moment is no evidence that the analysis is invalid. Thus, the implausibility of a proposed real definition is no sign that it is unsound: The definition of a point, for instance, by extensive abstraction as by Whitehead, is very implausible, but its validity or invalidity is solely a question of whether all and none but the properties of points are deducible from it.

If that which analysis places before us were indistinguishable from that which was to be analysed, no analysis at all could be said to have taken place. On the other hand, unless we are willing to say that a certain thing *was to be* analysed, and that *that very thing* now *has been* analysed, we are in effect saying that no such thing as analysis is ever possible—indeed, we are robbing the word of its very meaning.

With regard to my analysis—whether prima facie plausible or unplausible—of the nature of objective reference in the case of remembrance of past events, all I can add is then this: If I have given a true account (i) of what it means to call something an 'event', (ii) of what it means to call an event 'past', and (iii) of the specific kind of mental act one is performing at the time one is said to be 'remembering', then I have in so doing given not only a true account, but also a complete account of what 'objective reference' consists of in the sort of case considered. For what else then remains yet unknown about it? The feeling, if one has it, that something—the very essence of 'objective reference'—has been left out is, I venture to say, then due only to the fact commented upon above, that the dissected corpse does not have the familiar appearance it had undissected. That feeling, that is to say, does not impeach the adequacy of the account I have offered. Of course my account may be inadequate, but if it is, this is not because it is incomplete, but because it is *erroneous* in respect to one or more of the three constituent parts just mentioned, which any account of the matter must have.

7. *Legitimacy of using certain terms merely as names where their use as descriptive would be illegitimate*

At this point the following remarks concerning method, which have especial bearing on the conduct of the discussion of place-intuition to follow, need to be introduced.

Since in this paper the *ignotum* to be elucidated is the nature of objectiveness, it is obvious that any proposed definition of it using objects as part of its *definiens* would be definition *per ipsum ignotum* and futile. Definition here must therefore be in terms of intuitions and of functions of intuitions. But it might seem that this requirement is at times violated in what follows. The situation at such times, however, is really this: Among the many species of intuition, only a few have names of their own—warmth, thirst, fear, lust, pain, bitter, etc. Because of this, when the species of intuition we are concerned with at a given moment happens to be one of the many nameless ones, the only way for us to enable someone else to identify it is to use either a phrase descriptive of the kind of *object* in the presence of which a normal person experiences an intuition of that species (e.g., the odour 'of roses', the taste 'of cinnamon', etc.), or a phrase descriptive of the kind of *objective* action in which normally eventuates an intuition of the species concerned (e.g., feeling 'about to sneeze', feeling 'like taking a walk in the woods', etc.).

What must be emphasized, however, is that the use of such phrases *merely as practical devices for the identification by someone else* of the species of intuition we desire him to consider, is in what follows perfectly legitimate, for *as so used* these phrases are virtual proper names. Such phrases would be illegitimate for the purposes of this chapter only if they were being used in it *to define* kinds of intuition, viz., to define them as effects of, or as causes of, certain objective situations or events; that is, if they were used to define kinds of intuition as functions of what here is the *definiendum*.

But the fact that the nature of objectivity in general is here the *definiendum*, and that we therefore cannot define it in terms of anything objective, does not require us to pretend that we cannot in practice identify objective things of the kind called 'roses', or objective actions of the kind called 'smelling a rose' or 'sneezing'; or that we do not know what kind of odour-intuition occurs in us when we smell a rose, etc. Nor are we debarred from making of such knowledge the sort of use here contemplated, since that use is other than definitional. This being now clear, let us address ourselves to the problem of space.

8. *Space in terms of tactual intuitions*

That space and time are indissolubly connected is shown by the fact that the notion of place figured in the account given above of the intuition of two times; and that the notion of time similarly figures in an account of our intuition of two places: If we intuit a given quale at a given time, and also do not intuit it at that very time, we are at that time intuiting *two places*.

The problem of the nature of objective space, and of the relation of place-intuition to the perception of objective space, is so difficult that we can hope to deal with it successfully only if we consider it first at the simplest imaginable level. Accordingly, we shall for the time being leave out of consideration altogether what is doubtless the favourite example of space-intuition and space-perception for all of us, viz., the visual; and shall first consider instead and by itself the tactual.

Let us then place ourselves in imagination in the position of a person blind from birth—indeed, to simplify matters still more, devoid not only of visual sensations, but also of all others except those *called* 'pressure' sensations and 'kinaesthetic' sensations.[1] And let us consider how, out of these intuitive experiences, the conception and perception by him of an 'objective' and 'physical' world would emerge.

(a) *Intuition of 'absolute' place.* Let us suppose that the pressure intuition occurring at a given time is of the kind we may call 'right-index-finger-tip-pressure'.[2] Simultaneously with this intuition, we would be experiencing also an equally specific kinaesthetic intuition-complex; and what we must now note is that from *the two together* emerges an intuition *of particular place* as being at the time occupied by a pressure intuition of that specific sort. If the kinaesthetic intuition-complex remained the same, but the particular quality of pressure intuition experienced were some other than the right-index-finger-tip one—say, the right-elbow-tip one—the particular place-intuition we should then experience would also be a different one. And likewise, if the quality of pressure sensation remained the right-index-finger-tip one, but certain changes occurred in the kinaesthetic intuition-complex—say, it included the 'raised-right-arm' quality of kinaesthetic intuition, instead of the 'hanging-right-arm' one—then the place-intuition we should experience would again be a different one.[3] Thus place-

---

[1] This is the first case of the use—vindicated in the preceding section as legitimate here—of certain words (in this case 'pressure' and 'kinaesthetic') merely *as names* of certain species of sensation, instead of, as ordinarily, as descriptive of the kinds of stimuli causative of them.

[2] These words are here used only as, again, the *name* of a certain species of pressure intuition and not as descriptive of the sort of conditions under which it is experienced. All that is assumed here is the introspectively verifiable fact that 'pressure' intuitions are somewhat unlike, as well as somewhat alike. For instance, if the tip of my nose, and the tip of my right-hand index finger, are both pressed in the same manner, the two sensations I get are introspectively alike enough to be both called by the same generic name (viz., 'pressure' sensations), but they are nevertheless qualitatively distinguishable just as a sensation of 'red' is distinguishable from one of 'blue', although both are sensations of 'colour'.

[3] The distinction between place 'on the body' and place 'relatively to the body' will be analysed in due course.

intuition does not consist of kinaesthetic intuition nor of pressure intuition; rather, it is an 'emergent' of the simultaneity of the two, and is *sui generis*.

Place-intuition, let it be noted, is thus *originally absolute* in the sense that, conceivably, a person might intuit one place, and his consciousness then be extinguished without its ever having included intuition of any other place and, *a fortiori*, without its ever having included intuition of the relation of the one place he intuits to any other. Intuition of *space* is intuition of the relation of one place to other places, and is thus essentially relational; but intuition of a *place* is independent of intuition of any other place, and is in this sense *absolute* although to it may be added intuition of its relation to some other intuited place. Tactual intuition of the place which at a given moment we call 'there' is *prior* not posterior to intuition of the relation of it to the place of our body at the moment. What is said below concerning the discovery of 'our own body' will make this evident.

(b) *Intuition of place as empty*. Intuition of a place as *empty* emerges when we have the same kinaesthetic intuition-complex as when it is intuited as occupied, but intuition of the specific quality of pressure intuition concerned has the inferior degree of intensity which gives it the status of 'image' instead of that of 'sensation'.

If *both* the pressure and the kinaesthetic intuitions have only imaginal status, then we are *imagining* the place they jointly determine.

(c) *Contiguity of intuited places, and motion-intuition*. If, e.g., the right-index-finger-tip pressure intuition persists while certain alterations are occurring in, e.g., the right-index-finger kinaesthetic intuition-complex, then the place first intuited after the original one is said to be *contiguous* with it.[1] And what is intuited *while* these alterations are occurring is said to be *motion* of the right-index-finger-tip-pressure intuition.

(d) *Three-dimensionality of the relation of places to one another*. The places to which that right-index-finger-tip-pressure intuition is found susceptible of moving are classifiable, on the basis of particular species of intuited alterations in the kinaesthetic sensation-

---

[1] Contiguity may also be defined in terms of a supposition somewhat different from the one made above: If pressure intuition persists but alters gradually in quality while the kinaesthetic intuition-complex remains unaltered, the place intuited first after the original one also is said to be contiguous with it.

complex, as being 'above' or 'below', or/and 'to the right' or 'to the left', or/and 'nearer than' or 'farther than', the original place.[1] Space, which is the relation of each place to every other place, is in this manner discovered to be three-dimensional.

(e) *Reference to places intuitable but not at the moment intuited.* The nature of the relations just named thus becomes known to us within what we may call the 'specious-here', that is, known to us as between places intuited within the duration of the already discussed specious-now; and—just as the before-after relation which becomes known to us within the specious-now enables us to think of times 'objective' in the sense of being times before or after the specious-now—so the above-below, nearer-farther, contiguous with, etc., relations (once they have been abstracted by us from the specious-here where we discovered them) enable us to think of places that are objective in a similar sense, viz., are (for instance) *farther than* the place being intuited at the moment. The thought 'place farther than there' is thus a complex of the following three factors: (a) the *determinable* place-relatum 'place', (b) the determinable relation 'farther than', and (c) the *determinate* place-relatum 'there'. To combine these three intuitions is what 'thinking of' unspecified places farther than there, that are not now determinately intuited, consists in.

(f) *Comments on W. James' criticism of Wundt's theory of space perception.* The theory of our intuition of space that has been outlined is in certain respects similar to Wundt's view (which, however, he states in terms of visual perception of space) that 'we can ascribe a spatial constitution only to *combinations* of retinal sensations with those of movement. . . . In its psychological nature this is a process of associative synthesis: it consists in the fusion of both groups of sensations into a product, whose elementary components are no longer separable from each other in idea.'[2]

James dismisses this view on the ground that the 'associative synthesis' or 'psychic fusion' or 'combination' in which its essence lies is 'an unmeaning phrase'. Yet the sort of process to which the phrase refers is well recognized today under the technical name of *emergence*. James' off-hand dismissal of it as mythical appears espe-

---

[1] These relations, *originally*, are dyadic, not triadic. That is, the intuited relation of a place A to a place B is first *simply* (for instance) *nearer than* . . . and only later if at all, nearer *to the place of my body* than. . . .

[2] Quoted by James in his *Principles of Psychology*, vol. II, pp. 277–8.

cially blind in view of the fact that, according to his own view of the emotions, an emotion would not itself be anything but the emergent of a complex of visceral and other sensations, none of which, admittedly, contain it. If he were to adhere to the logic of his statement that 'Retinal sensations *are* spatial; and were they not, no amount of "synthesis" with equally spaceless motor sensations could intelligibly make them so,' that logic would then compel him to say also that visceral sensations must have anger as an element of them, for had they not, no amount of synthesis with pectoral and other angerless sensations could beget the feeling of anger. Indeed, by that logic, James would be forced to say also that some of the parts of an automobile must have the character of automobility for otherwise no amount of synthesis with other parts equally lacking it could beget it!

James' own view was that in each and every sensation, though more developed in some than in others, there is discernible, beside the element of intensity, also an 'element of voluminousness', and that this element is *'the original sensation of space,* out of which all the exact knowledge about space that we afterwards come to have is woven by processes of discrimination, association, and selection'.[1] The first comment this suggests is, of course, that if there is no such thing as a 'psychic synthesis' by which the intuition of voluminousness could arise out of other intuitions, then psychic analysis must be equally mythical, and no process of 'discrimination', can be called upon by James to explain how the intuition of, e.g., place, could arise out of an intuition of voluminousness which is distinctly *other* than that of place.

Again, when the word 'volume' is used literally, it refers to something always susceptible of three-dimensional analysis. But when I have for example a sensation of sound, I find it as impossible to discriminate in it an upper and a lower part, a near and a far, a right and a left, as I would to discriminate such parts in the feeling of anxiety, in the beauty of poetry, or in the science of logic. What is susceptible of such space-dimension analysis is always a set of contiguous places. Sound-sensations have places, and a set of sound-sensations at contiguous places would be susceptible of space-dimension analysis. But it is only if, while I intuit a sound, I *move* forward and backward, up and down, right

---

[1] *Principles of Psychology*, vol. II, p. 135.

and left, that I get the intuition of three-dimensionality of the sound. Similarly, if I am enveloped by a uniform mist or smoke, or if, in the laboratory, I look at 'film colour', I do *not* get the intuition of voluminousness—three-dimensionality—*unless* I alter the convergence, accommodation, and direction of my eyes, the colour sensation remaining the while unaltered.

A sensation has extensity, whether one-, two-, or three-dimensional, only when it is intuited *at several contiguous places simultaneously* or within the specious present.[1] The sound-sensation, apart from intuition of motions back and forth, etc., by myself, does not, I submit, have voluminousness in any literal sense, any more than a so-called 'high' tone is literally farther from the centre of the earth than a 'low' tone. In both cases, those terms are applicable only in some elliptical sense, involving, in the case of the greater so-called 'voluminousness' of low tones, some sort of association with greater volume in the literal sense, just as in the case of the 'height' and 'lowness' of tones there is association with the fact that, in uttering them, the head is naturally tilted up, and down, respectively.

According to the view I have offered, the intuitions of place, of extensity, of volume, etc., that we have are genuinely *novel* in the sense that the intuitions out of which they emerge are not themselves, *individually*, intuitions of place, extensity, etc. But although novel, those intuitions are *not elementary but emergent*. That is, their occurrence is strictly dependent upon the presence of certain other intuitions, whereas such intuitions as those of blue, of bitter, of pressure, etc., are not similarly dependent upon the presence of others and are in this sense elementary.

9. *Physical objectivity, in tactual terms*

Physical objectivity, like objectivity of, e.g., our own past mental states, is to be defined in terms of a relation to certain of our intuitions. These, in the situation we have assumed to be ours, would necessarily be pressure intuitions. But the relation concerned in

---

[1] That pressure is intuited at several contiguous places *at one time* implies that the kinaesthetic intuition-complex which is a factor in the intuition of these places is not at that time altering. The intuition notwithstanding this of *several* places at which pressure is at that time is then possible only if the pressure intuited is itself several, that is, of several qualities or intensities.

the case of *physical* objectivity is the *causal* relation. It too, however, like the 'earlier-later' relation, is one the nature of which is already known to us through instances of it found among our intuitions in the specious present.

(a) *The causal relation does not require that its terms be intuitive qualia.* But—and this is the all-important point here—*there is no reason why the causal relation should be regarded as capable of existing only among our intuitions.* Use of the causal relation in defining physical objectivity would be illegitimate only if, with Hume, we were to define causation as a relation *among our impressions and images*, or, with Kant, as a form of synthesis the employment of which is valid *only within experience.*[1] But so to define it is only to restrict its possible scope gratuitously. All that the causal relation presupposes concerning the nature of its terms is that they be *events*—that they be entities of the kind susceptible of taking place in time, or in both time and space—but not that the times and places concerned be subjective rather than objective ones, nor that what occurs at them be intuitive qualia rather than not intuitive. For, let it be recalled, we found ourselves able to define 'objective times' and 'objective places' without making use of the causal relation, viz., in terms of certain other relations (abstracted by us from the specious present) to certain intuitions. And as regards the quale-content that may occur at these objective times and places, there is no reason why it should have to be itself intuitive rather than not intuitive.

It may be asked, however, what conception (if we start as we have with intuitions only) we can possibly have of any quale other than an intuitive quale. It is in the answer to this question that the causal relation—itself abstracted by us from among our intuitions—enters.

(b) *Physical events.* Still proceeding under the supposition that we are limited to pressure and kinaesthetic intuitions, we may now develop in terms of it the account of the nature of physical objectivity just suggested.

Among our pressure sensations, there would be some which

---

[1] Kant's own view that things in themselves *cause* our sensations (e.g., *Critique of Pure Reason*, Max Müller's trans., p. 403) was early objected to on this ground by Jacobi and Schulze. And, as Höffding remarks (*History of Philosophy*, vol. II, p. 61), 'From Kant's standpoint, this objection admits of no answer.'

could not be traced by us wholly or even in part to a cause consisting of some other of our intuitions (such, perhaps, as a volition). And basically a 'physical' event would then be for us an event conceived by us as *other than intuitive* (or at least as other than any intuited by us) *and as having to these otherwise unexplained pressure intuitions the relation of cause to effect*. Neither more nor less than that is what, under our assumed limitation, we should mean by 'being pressed by something', or 'undergoing physical pressure'. Thus, far from defining 'pressure' intuition as the kind of intuition caused by the kind of physical event called 'pressure', *we are here on the contrary defining 'physical pressure' as the kind of non-intuited event which causes intuition of the kind called 'pressure' intuition.*

Our basic notion of a physical event is thus in part positive and in part purely negative: *positive* in that it is framed in terms of a relation already familiar to us, viz., the causal relation, which is a relation between events; and in terms also of an effect-relatum consisting of an intuition, viz., here a 'pressure' intuition; but *negative* in that the event functioning as the other relatum, viz., the cause-relatum, is conceived by us *only negatively,* viz., only as being an event *other than* any intuition of ours.[1]

It may be asked how we can then ever know that there are events other than intuitive, or what their nature is. As regards the second question, the answer is that basically, the *generic* nature of 'physical' events is the very one we have just been describing; and that to be a *specific* kind of 'physical' event similarly consists in being such specific kind of non-intuited event as is capable of causing a given specific sort of intuitive event.

As regards the other question, viz., how we can ever know that physical events as defined exist, the answer is that strictly speaking their existence always retains the same status as that of the universality of causation, viz., the status of *a postulate only*. It might be urged that postulation of a cause *ad hoc* for each intuition for which no cause is discoverable among our other intuitions is entirely

---

[1] Although intuitions for which we find no cause among other intuitions are what first leads us to postulate non-intuited events as causes for them, postulation of such events is extended to some other cases. If, for instance, intuition of a certain place causes pressure sensation at a given time, but does not do so at another time, we postulate a difference in non-intuited conditions between the two, to account for the fact that the same effect does not both times result from intuition of the same place.

futile if no other effect than the given intuition is predictable from the postulated cause. The answer to this objection will appear further on in some detail but is essentially to the effect that only in terms of physical events in the sense defined can physical properties and physical substances be defined, and that property and substance are predictive notions.

(c) *Perception of a physical event.* In any case 'perception of physical pressure', as distinguished from intuition of the kind called 'pressure' intuition, consists in *belief* (unformulated) *that an occurring pressure-intuition is being caused by an event which is not being intuited by us.*[1]

(d) *Perception of physical motion.* If 'pressure' intuition is persisting through a given time, but alters gradually in quality while the kinaesthetic intuition-complex is persisting unchanged, *and* we believe that the pressure intuition is throughout being caused by a non-intuited event, then we are said to be *perceiving* (whether 'veridically' or 'hallucinatorily') *change of place, i.e., motion, of physical pressure.*

(e) *Perception of physical properties and substances.* What we have so far defined (in terms only of the two kinds of sensations to which we have assumed ourselves restricted) has been physical events rather than physical properties or substances. We may now turn to the latter two. Let us bear in mind, however, that what we are here concerned with in the case of substance is *substantial-ness,* i.e., the nature, as distinguished from the existence, of substances.

As stated earlier, to be a substance is to be a *conjunct of properties,* or it may be better to say, a *system of properties* since the constituent properties are not all related to one another simply as conjuncts, but some depend on some others.[2] A property, as already pointed out, is essentially a law; and, where 'real' as distinguished from 'logical' properties are concerned, a law relating *events* of given

---

[1] Whether perception of physical pressure, as so defined, is in a given case 'veridical' or 'hallucinatory', or what meaning is to be assigned to these terms, is a further question; but one that need not be considered at this point. By an 'unformulated' belief, I mean a belief not put—either overtly or in imagination—into words or other discursive symbols. I have defended elsewhere the contention that many of our beliefs are unformulated. See 'Propositions, Opinions, Sentences, and Facts', *Journal of Philosophy,* vol. XXXVII (1940), p. 703.

[2] e.g. Being hot is a property, and being liquid is a property; and being wax is (in part) being such that whenever hot, then liquid.

kinds. Thus, 'to have property P' is 'to be such that if . . . under circumstances . . . , then . . .'; the relation between the 'if . . .' and the 'then . . .' being either one of necessary sequence or one of necessary coexistence of events of the kinds concerned.

It is important, however, in this connection to be quite clear as to the nature of the relation symbolized by 'of' when we speak of a property 'of' a substance. The property is *implied* by the *nature* (the 'what') of the substance, but (at least where the property is one of the kind I shall describe later as physico-physical) is *possessed* or had only by the *cases* of that nature. For example, gold-ness implies malleability, i.e., consists in part of it, but does not possess it in the sense that gold-ness could be said to be malleable. The adjective, malleable, is applicable only to goldness-existing, i.e., to cases of gold-ness—pieces of gold.

But what is it then that possesses the complex property, gold-ness, or likewise the complex property, metal-ness, which stands to gold-ness as genus to species? It is, I submit, simply *a place during a time*. I can see no need whatever to postulate some mysterious 'substance' which is neither a place-time, nor a complex property, nor such a property at a place-time, but something additional to all that and conceived only as 'support', in some vague sense, of the property. I submit that all which 'gold-ness' needs as 'support' or possessor of it is a region of space during a time. This will do all that the occult 'support' classically called 'substance' is needlessly postulated to do. If we knew, for example, just what properties together define 'glass-ness' and also knew every (if any) 'where' and 'when' that set of properties is present, then we would know absolutely all there is to glass. 'Substance' as the word is used in ordinary language is the name not of the support or possessor of gold-ness, glass-ness, metal-ness, etc., but of the *summum genus* of which all these are subordinate *genera* or *species*. On the other hand, if one insists on using 'substance' as name of their support or possessor, then substance is nothing other than space-time.[1]

One remark, however, needs to be added. It is that some properties, e.g., malleability, fusibility, etc., viz., the properties I shall

---

[1] For a fuller defence of this contention, see the writer's 'On Our Knowledge of Existents', *Proceedings of Seventh International Congress of Philosophy*, pp. 163–7.

describe in the sequel as physico-physical properties, cannot by their very nature exist or be conceived to exist alone but only conjointly with others. In the case of such a property, the corresponding adjective, e.g., malleable, cannot be applied to a place-time simply, that is, to a place-time empty of any other property, but only to an *existing* substance, that is, to something consisting of, *together,* a complex of other properties and a region of space-time at which the complex is present. But there are properties which, unlike these, are conceivable as existing separately from any others; and in the case of each of them the corresponding adjective is applicable directly to a region of space-time. For example, we cannot properly speak of a malleable place or a ductile place, but we do speak without any feeling of impropriety of a warm place, a cold place, a noisy place, a smelly place. And if we do not quite so readily speak likewise of, e.g., a hard place or a soft place or a tangible place, it is only because, even cutaneously only, we hardly experience hardness or softness or tangibility without experiencing at least some temperature also, that is, without experiencing a conjunct of properties. But even then no absurdity is involved in speaking of a place as tangible or soft or hard as on the contrary one would be involved in speaking of a place as, e.g., ductile or fragile, etc.

Returning now to the perception of physical substance, it should be clear in the light of these remarks that, under the restriction to pressure and kinaesthetic sensations we have been assuming, perception of *physical substance* and perception of *tangible physical substance* will be one and the same thing. That is, perception of physical substance will be perception of a system of properties consisting of only one property, viz., tangibility; and in such a case no occasion arises for distinction between substance (composite property) and (elementary) property. Under the assumed restriction, then, perception of tangibility, or equivalently of substance, (i.e., of 'body') will consist in (unformulated) *belief that at an objective place contiguous with a certain intuited place at which pressure is at the moment intuited by us, there is occurring throughout a certain period a non-intuited event which is such as to cause in us a pressure intuition whenever we intuit that certain place during that period.* That is, that objective place is believed by us to have during that period the property of causing pressure intuition in us if we intuit the certain place with which it is contiguous. A property of this kind may be called a *physico-psychical property*. And the description just given of what is being believed by us in such a case is a description of what, under the restrictions assumed, would be for us the whole meaning of 'tangibility', or '(tangible) substance', or 'physical thing', or 'body'.

(f) *Perception of change of physico-psychical property*. Perception of hardness and softness can be analysed in terms of a basis of pressure and kinaesthetic intuitions, and of quantitative variations in them. In terms of hardness and softness, we can then define change of property, or at least of degree of a property (viz., of tangibility) at a given place, as what is perceived when perception of, e.g., hardness at that place is gradually replaced by perception of softness there.

(g) *Perception of a physico-physical property*. If a given sort of change A in the physico-psychical property at one place is observed to cause regularly a certain sort of change B in the physico-psychical property at another place, then what is being observed is a *physico-physical property*. Namely, the first place, through a given period, has this property: it is such that occurrence of a change of kind A in the physico-psychical property there causes occurrence of a change of kind B in the physico-psychical property at the other place (and the other place has the converse property).[1] This, at least, is our *basic* conception of physico-physical properties. But these in turn may be conceived to be related to other physico-physical properties by other such laws; and a law concerning the relation of a physico-physical property to another physico-physical property may be called a *derivative* physico-physical property (whether the two physico-physical properties it relates be basic ones or themselves also derivative). In this way, physico-physical properties may be conceived in the case of which the physico-psychical properties at the basis of the conception are quite lost sight of and forgotten; or deliberately abstracted from. But ultimate analysis of a physico-physical property can always exhibit them.

(h) *The distinction between perception of 'our own' body, and of other bodies*. Having now an account of the nature of tangible body, and of the nature of (tactual) perception of a body, we may next

---

[1] A physico-physical property may concern one place only, the law constituting the property then being a law of coexistence (instead of a law of succession) of the two (or more) physico-psychical properties involved.

pass to an account of the distinction between 'our own' body and other bodies. A body perceived is said to be 'our own' if occurrence of the kinaesthetic intuition-complex presupposed by the perceiving results automatically in occurrence of a *double* instead of a *single* pressure sensation, e.g., in occurrence not of only a right-index-finger-tip-pressure sensation, but also of, let us say, a middle-of-forehead-pressure one.

(i) *Shape.* A shape is a set of places each of which is contiguous with some of the others. Intuition, within the specious present, of the variations (in, for instance, the 'arm-and-hand' kinaesthetic sensation-complex) which yield uninterruptedly, say, the right-index-finger-tip-pressure sensation, yields to us the intuition of touch-shape; and this touch-shape intuition is the intuitive basis of perception (in the sense already defined) of tangible physical shape, i.e., of the shape of a (tangible) body.

Any given one of these intuited variations in the kinaesthetic sensation-complex constitutes the intuitive basis of perception of the spatial relation (i.e., distance plus direction) of the initially perceived place on the body touched to the place on it terminally perceived. It is in this way that (tactually) we discover the shape of, in particular, the body we call 'our own', and the spatial relation to each other of any two or more places on it.

(j) *Places of physical origin, natural and conventional.* Some place or set of places on our own body is the basic or absolute physical 'here', and is for each of us the *natural place of physical origin*. That is, it is the place each of us actually used as origin in developing knowledge of the places, and of the spatial relations of the places, of physical objects other than our own body. Of course, some origin other than this could be used; for instance, I could use the place now perceived by me of a certain corner of a certain desk as origin. That is, I could inquire *only* into the spatial relations to the *place of that corner*, of the places of physical bodies *other than my own*; thus, let us suppose, never even discovering the body called my own. When our purposes are purely natural-scientific we often use such conventional origins, e.g., the pole star, the Greenwich meridian, etc. But it is to be noted that knowledge of the place of an object relatively to such conventional origins is wholly useless to us for any *practical* purpose unless supplemented by knowledge of the spatial relation of the place of origin used *to the place of our own body at the time*. For example we could make no practical use whatever of a knowledge that an escaped tiger is a the moment in a clump of bushes 952 feet due north of th northernmost point of the city limits of New York unless w knew in addition the place of New York, and of the north *relatively to the place of our own body at the moment.*

(k) *Enrichment of the perceived physical world on the basis of intuition other than tactual.* Our assumed restriction to pressure and kin aesthetic intuitions having served its purpose, may now be aban doned. This will enrich for us the content of the perceived physica world, but will not in any way alter the nature of the genera relation—described above specifically in terms of the minima equipment we had assumed—of the world we call physical to th world of our intuitions.

Admission of the other 'cutaneous' sensations and their com binations, and of 'olfactory', 'gustatory', 'auditory', and 'visual sensations will furnish the basis for perceptual additions whicl will together supply its familiar richness and complexity to th content of our perception of the physical world. Physical sub stances, for example, will then be perceived by us no longer merel as tangible, but also as having temperature, odour, sapidity, sound colour.

The manner in which the additional kinds of sensations furnisl the basis for perception of such additional physical properties i essentially identical with that already considered in the case o pressure sensations and the perception of (tangible) substance But, since our ordinary perception of the physical world is so largely visual, it will be appropriate to take now visual instead o pressure sensations as starting point, and to sketch again, bu this time in terms of the former and more briefly, the relation o intuition to the perception of physical properties and substances and also to make clear in what sense a physical substance tactuall perceived and one visually perceived, or a place tactually intuitec and one visually intuited, can be said to be 'the same'. Here again the problem has two parts: first, we must give an account of spac in terms of visual intuitions, i.e., more specifically, an account o the nature of visual place, direction, and distance, and of colour shape both two- and three-dimensional; and second, we mus give an account, still in terms of intuitions and of relation to intuitions, of the nature of physical events, physical properties and physical substances as visually perceived.

10. *Space in terms of visual intuitions*

Here again the basic intuition is not vaguely of 'space', but of *place*, and of place absolute in the sense already considered. As before it is the emergent of two factors, one of them consisting of kinaesthetic intuitions. For colour-intuitions (including under colour also white, black, and the greys), no less than pressure intuitions, are always accompanied by kinaesthetic intuitions of certain characteristic kinds—specifically those we may call 'eye-convergence' intuitions, 'eye-direction' intuitions, and 'eye-accommodation' intuitions.

(a) *Superior distinctness of some of the constituents of the colour-complex intuited at any moment.* The second factor, however, is one peculiar to visual intuitions: There is a certain character, admitting of degrees, which is possessed in superior degree by some of the constituents of the complex of colour-intuitions at any given moment, and in various inferior degrees by the other constituents. This peculiar character we may call *distinctness*. Identification of it will be easy if we state that in the case of colour constituents that have it in superior degrees we are able more readily and confidently to decide whether they are alike or unlike, to identify them or their parts, etc., than in the case of constituents that have it in inferior degree.[1]

(b) *The intuition of visual place.* Now the basic intuition of visual place—the visual there-intuition—is the emergent of these two factors together: it emerges from, together, intuition of this superior distinctness of certain of the constituents of the colour-complex intuited at the moment, and intuition of a complex of kinaesthetic sensations of the kinds mentioned. That is, the colour-constituents which are distinct are intuited *as at a specific place*; or as we may equally say, *a specific place is intuited* as occupied by the colour-constituents which are distinct at the moment.

If the given kinaesthetic intuition-complex is replaced by a different one, then from the latter, together with the intuition of superior distinctness (no matter what colour-intuitions it may attach to at the moment) there emerges intuition of a different visual place.

---

[1] Subsequently acquired knowledge of the eye and its structure permits us to say that the colour-intuitions possessing this superior distinctness at a given moment are those resulting from stimulation of the part of the retina called the fovea.

(c) *Intuition of direction and distance*. Intuition of the *nature and quantity of the change* in the given kinaesthetic intuition-complex through which is reached a certain other such complex, yields (as conjoined with intuition of superior distinctness) intuition of the specific 'spatial relation' between the visual place initially intuited and that terminally intuited—that is, intuition of a 'direction' and 'distance' of the second from the first.

On the basis of the various kinds of changes found possible in a given kinaesthetic intuition-complex, the *directions* from the place intuited are classifiable as 'above' or 'below', or/and 'to the right' or 'to the left' or/and 'nearer' and 'farther'.

(d) *Intuition of extent, and of colour-shape*. Intuition within the specious present of a number of contiguous places in one, two, or all three, of these dimensions yields to us the general intuition of *extent* and (in conjunction with intuition of the colours at the places intuited), intuition of one-, two-, or three-dimensional *colour-shape*.

(e) *Intuition of colour without place or extent*. Absolute place was defined above as emergent of, together, any given kinaesthetic intuition-complex (of the kinds mentioned) and the character of superior distinctness attaching to some of the constituents of the colour complex intuited at the moment. It may be asked, how then about the places of the colour-constituents that are *indistinct* at the moment? As to this I believe that originally, and even now in some measure, these indistinct colour-constituents are intuited *without any place-intuition, or therefore any extent-intuition, attaching to them*. This contention may appear paradoxical since we are now usually so conscious of the places, relatively to the place of the superiorly distinct colour-constituents, of some at least of the inferiorly distinct ones. Moreover, to some persons it appears obvious that if colour is intuited at all it is intuited as extended.

To deal with the latter allegation first, I submit that it is possible to intuit colour at a place within which we are unable to discriminate different places. Such a place, which constitutes a psychological *point*, is psychologically extentionless.

As regards the other objection, I believe that, when we intuit simultaneously a number of places as having certain relations to a given one, what takes place is that, within the specious present, there occurs in the kinaesthetic complex the variety of alterations which are the bases for the intuition of the relations of those other places to the given one—these alterations in the kinaesthesia being susceptible of having either the degree of intensity that would determine us to call them 'sensory', or the inferior intensity that would lead us rather to call them 'imaginal'. At least, this is what I believe occurs when the other places concerned are places in the 'spread-out' dimensions as distinguished from the 'third' or 'nearer-farther' dimension.

In the case of the latter the quantities of change in the 'convergence' and 'accommodation' intuitions (which are the kinds at the basis of our intuitions of 'nearer' and 'farther') very early become associated with changes in the *degree of doubleness* of the 'nearer' and 'farther' colour-shapes (and with kinds of disparity of portions of certain colour-shapes in depth); and these are therefore capable of arousing the intuitions of 'nearer' and 'farther' without actual occurrence of the changes in the 'convergence' and 'accommodation' kinaesthesia that constitutes the original bases of those intuitions.

That the intuition of depth, and even the intuition of spread-outness, although indeed each *sui generis*, are emergent rather than primitive may I believe be shown by performing a simple experiment, which for the sake of simplicity I shall describe in physical terms rather than in the basic intuitional terms. If, while looking at a given thing at some distance from us, we shut one eye (thus eliminating double images), we are immediately aware of a marked weakening of our intuition of the distances (in the third dimension) of other things relatively to the thing looked at. If we are careful to avoid moving the head or eyeball (so that no slightly disparate view arises that we could synthesize with the given one), and, by prolonging the contemplation, allow time for the fading of our consciousness of the nature of the objects having the colour-appearances we intuit, then very soon we find that all intuition of relative distances in the third dimension ceases. And now, if we prolong the contemplation, and are especially careful to *avoid attending to things in the periphery* (for attention to them is cheating since it involves, if not actual motions of the eyeball, at least alterations in the relative tensions of the eye muscles, and corresponding changes in the kinaesthetic intuitions), then we find that even the intuition of place-in-spread-out-ness relatively to the place of the thing fixated ceases. Complete unchange of eye-muscle tensions for more than a very short time is quite difficult to achieve, and the experiment is therefore not easy to perform with full success; but a measure of success sufficient to give considerable support to the contention the experiment is intended to test is reasonably attainable. It is especially necessary to bear in mind, however, that when we reach the point in the experiment where we ask ourselves whether the intuition of place-in-spread-out-ness has really ceased, what we find ourselves automatically doing in order to make sure is to attend to something peripheral—which means moving the eye or at least altering eye-muscle tensions—*and this is cheating*; for of course doing this does bring it back (as the theory predicts it should).

11. *Physical objectivity, in visual and other terms*

What now is the difference between intuiting colour-shape—even three-dimensional colour-shape—and perceiving a coloured physical thing? Here as before, introduction of the relation of cause and effect is the first step towards the answer.

(a) *Visual perception of physical events, properties, and substances.* Among our intuitions of colour just as among those of pressure, there are very many for which we are unable to find a cause among our other intuitions.[1] In these cases we postulate as cause for them an event, conceived by us only negatively as non-intuited, occurring (as the causal proximate relation demands) at a place contiguous with that at which the colour is intuited.[2] Then, in a manner exactly similar to that considered in the case of pressure intuitions and therefore in no need of being described again here, we pass from these non-intuited causal events to *properties* of the physico-psychical sort; and then to physical *substances* conceived first only as systems of physico-psychical properties, and later of physico-physical properties also. This passage depends only on the general relation between event, property, and substance, and not at all on whether the events concerned be causes of intuitions

---

[1] cf. Berkeley's statement in the *Principles of Human Knowledge*: 'When in broad daylight I open my eyes, it is not in my power to choose whether I shall see or no, or to determine what particular objects shall present themselves to my view; and so likewise as to the hearing and other senses; the ideas imprinted on them are not creatures of my will'.

[2] It is hardly necessary to state that the place at which a colour is intuited is not 'in one's head'.

of the pressure kind, or of the colour kind, or some other. Thus perception of the physical property 'being green' or (equivalently so long as physical substance is perceived solely in terms of colour) perception of 'green substance', will consist in (unformulated) belief that at an objective place contiguous with a certain intuited place at which we are at the moment intuiting green, there is occurring throughout a certain period a non-intuited event which is such as to cause in us an intuition of green whenever we intuit that certain place during that period.

(b) *The occult entities of physics.* The difference between various such non-intuited events are eventually described by us in terms of occult entities such as 'molecules', 'atoms', or 'sub-atomic particles' postulated for the very purpose of accounting for (ultimately) the specific intuitions we do have on a given occasion and especially of enabling us to predict from them the intuitions we should have on certain other occasions. The definitions specifying the properties of the occult physical entities we postulate are at least—to use Karl Pearson's term—'conceptual shorthand'. But if postulation that entities having these properties exist does enable us to make regularly true predictions, this is evidence that such entities *really* exist. For we may well ask in what else could consist the difference between existing only in imagination and existing 'really'. I submit that if the hypothesis, for instance, that a given man is a scoundrel invariably enables us (in circumstances to which it is relevant) to predict successfully how he will behave, then he *really* is a scoundrel.

(c) *Visual identification of 'our own body'.* Among the variety of physical substances we perceive visually, we distinguish one of them as being 'our own body' and the next question is on what basis we do so, for in the case of visual perception no such mark is available to us as was provided by doubleness of 'pressure' sensations (when tactual differentiation of 'our own body' from other substances was the problem).

For visual identification of a perceived substance as being 'our own body', we are fortunately able to lean on tactual identification of it. The manner in which we do so may be formulated in the following rules:

(i) If, simultaneously with visually perceived contact between two visually perceived physical substances, there occurs regularly a *double* touch sensation, then *both* of the visually perceived contacting substances are said to be (parts of) 'our own body'.

(ii) If, simultaneously with visually perceived contact between two visually perceived substances, there occurs regularly a *single* touch sensation, then *only one* of the two substances is said to be 'our own body'.

(iii) Which one it is is determined by noting which one is such that, when contact of it with a third substance is visually perceived, a touch sensation (whether single or double) regularly occurs simultaneously.[1]

(d) *'Sameness' of something visually perceived and something tactually perceived.* Perception of regular simultaneity of tactual perception of a substance, and of visual perception of contact between a part of our own body and a substance, is what constitutes perception of 'sameness' of the tactually perceived substance and the visually perceived substance; and of 'sameness' of the place of each. A similar criterion is used for identification as 'the same' of substances perceived also otherwise than tactually and visually.

(e) *Natural and conventional places of visual origin.* Our own body as visually perceived by ourselves, and in particular the part of it which (except when it is 'in the dark') is seen by us whenever we see anything else, viz., our nose and orbital arch, is the physical object the place of which is used by us as natural place of visual origin, to which we refer directly or indirectly the visually perceived or conceived places of all other physical objects. The remarks already made concerning conventional origins, however, apply here also.

(f) *Externality to our body and externality to our mind.* When we speak of trees, houses, mountains, and other physical objects we perceive, as being 'out there' or 'external to us', this means, then, *at a distance from a certain other physical object we also perceive, viz., the one called 'our own body'.* This sense of being 'external to us' is obviously wholly different from that in which the physical world, *including our own body* can be said to be 'external to us', for in the

---

[1] These are the sorts of experiments we spontaneously make and the sorts of criteria we spontaneously use in learning to distinguish the body we call 'our own' from other visually perceived substances. But obviously, at the time we learn it, which is very early, the experiments are not undertaken by us deliberately. They just happen to occur. Nor are the criteria we use formulated at the time. They merely are the sorts of differences there are to be observed between a certain physical body and all others.

latter case these words mean *other than psychical*. Yet many philosophical discussions of 'the external world' appear based on a failure to distinguish these two radically different senses of 'externality'.

(g) *Substantial objects in the natural sciences.* It has been pointed out above that our first and basic conception of physical substances is in terms of their physico-psychical properties; and that it is only on the basis of a conception of physical substance so obtained that physico-physical properties can be conceived by us and can further enrich our conception of a given physical substance. The natural sciences, however, abstract just as far as they can from physico-psychical properties and seek to include in their accounts of the nature of physical substances only physico-physical properties. This is a perfectly legitimate aim, but it should be clearly recognized for what it is, viz., for the manifestation of the fact that natural scientists, as such, interest themselves in none but the physico-physical properties of physical substances. But that only these properties are of concern to natural science does not imply that physical substances do not also have physico-psychical properties; nor that, without the latter, neither the physical substances themselves nor their physico-physical properties could ever be perceived or conceived by us.[1]

(h) *Fourfold classification of 'real' properties.* In the course of the foregoing account of the nature of the 'physical' world and of its relation to the 'psychical' world that our intuitions constitute, two sorts of properties have been distinguished, viz., physico-psychical and physico-physical. Our discussion may now be brought to a close with a brief notice that, on the same basis of classification, two other kinds of properties have to be mentioned, yielding a fourfold classification.

Recalling that a property is in all cases a law—an 'if . . . then . . .' relation between events of given kinds—we may name and briefly describe the nature of each of the four types of real properties as follows:

(i) *Physico-psychical properties,* viz., those in the case of which

---

[1] In a paper 'On the Attributes of Material Things', *Journal of Philosophy*, vol. XXXI, (1934), pp. 60–1, I have suggested that the distinction between physico-psychical and physico-physical properties, as defined, is the one which Locke's untenable account of the difference between 'secondary' and 'primary' qualities was really groping for.

the 'if' term is a physical event and the 'then' term a psychical event. Examples of such properties would be being odorous, being sapid, being bitter, being green, being tangible, etc.

(ii) *Physico-physical properties*, viz., those in the case of which both the 'if' and the 'then' term are physical events. Examples would be being malleable, being waterproof, being elastic, being ductile, having affinity for oxygen, having a density of so much, being a good conductor of electricity, etc.

(iii) *Psychico-psychical properties*, viz., those in the case of which both the 'if' and the 'then' terms are psychical. My mind, for example, happens to possess the property describable by saying that if I intuit chloroform-odour of more than a certain intensity, then I also intuit nausea. This property was, and most other psychico-psychical properties are, acquired rather than native. The psychico-psychical properties that are most important in the case of human beings and the higher animals consist in the forms of 'interpretation', i.e., in the mental habits, they possess. Examples of psychico-psychical properties that have received names would be timidity, irascibility, patience, curiosity, etc. (whether acquired or innate).

(iv) *Psychico-physical* properties, viz., those in the case of which the 'if' is psychical and the 'then' physical. The physical event proximately concerned is always one in our own body—occurrences in other physical substances being causable psychically only remotely as effects of occurrences proximately caused in our own body. Noteworthy among psychico-physical properties are those we may call our *powers* over our own body, e.g., the power to move the arm, to hold the breath, to expel air in the manner called vocalization, etc., at will. In other psychico-physical properties, the 'if'-event may consist of imagination of some objective event, and the 'then'-event of circulatory or respiratory changes, or of secretory activity in some gland, etc.

Although this account of four kinds of properties was reached without acquaintance by me with W. E. Johnson's views as to four kinds of causation, described by the same adjectives (physico-psychical, etc.), in §§ 9 and 10 of the introduction to volume III of his *Logic,* it is, I believe, in complete agreement therewith. Both, indeed, are accounts of what Johnson calls the common-sense view. My defence of psychico-physical and physico-psychical causation is, however, on quite a different basis from that attempted by Johnson in his § 11, which seems to me unsound. Johnson anyway takes throughout the notions of physical event and physical object for granted, whereas I do not but have on the contrary attempted above to analyse them. The analyses, as we have seen, are partly in terms of postulation of a non-intuited cause of certain intuitions. But it should be noted that, once physical events and objects are perceived at all, then cases of physico-psychical causation additional to the one which according to our analysis is *postulated* in 'perception' are, not likewise postulated, but *observed* in the same sense of this term in which cases of physico-physical causation can be said to be observed. For example, I may have until now perceived a certain physical substance only visually and tactually. Then, however, I am in position to observe experimentally what kind of taste-intuition, if any, is *caused* by placing that substance on my tongue. If I discover in this way that the substance has the physico-psychical property, 'being bitter', I discover it by means of an experimental, i.e., cause-revealing, procedure of precisely the same nature as that by which I may have discovered that the substance has the physico-physical property of, e.g., being inflammable. For, as regards the nature of the terms that the causal relation can relate, the definition of that relation specifies nothing at all except that they be *events*. It leaves completely open the possibility that both the cause-event and the effect-event may be physical, or that both may be psychical, or that either may be physical and the other psychical, or indeed that they be events of whatever other kinds might be conceivable.

10.

A LIBERALISTIC VIEW
OF TRUTH*

In two previous articles[1] the writer has endeavoured to defend what may be called a liberalistic interpretation of the predicates Real, and Right. The present paper attempts a similar task with regard to the predicate True. Attention must first of all be called to some of the characters of the situations where questions of truth or falsity arise.

1. *Datum and Dubitatum*

When actual doubt exists concerning the truth of a proposition, it attaches in most cases only to some one element of the situation which the proposition sets forth. Thus, if, wishing to avail myself of the mails to send a gift to a friend, I present myself at the post-office window and formulate a doubt concerning the truth of the proposition 'This package weighs 1 lb.', there is no doubt either in the postmaster's mind or in mine, of the concrete presence of something, nor of its being a package, nor of its having weight. These are *data*, i.e., facts assumed or already admitted as self-evident to observation then and there. What is doubted, on the other hand, is whether the weight of the object concretely present (and sufficiently distinguished from the rest of the environment by the characterization 'package'), *is* 1 *lb., or not*. That is the *dubitatum*, i.e., the assertion ventured.[2] Sometimes indeed, more

---

* *Philosophical Review*, vol. XXXIV, No. 6, 1925.

[1] 'A Defence of Ontological Liberalism,' *Journal of Philosophy*, vol. XXI, 13; 'Liberalism in Ethics', *International Journal of Ethics,* April, 1925.

[2] To say that what the proposition asserts is that the object present is a member jointly of the two classes 'packages' and 'things weighing 1 lb.', would be wholly to misrepresent its import. The membership of the object

than one point is at issue at once; but what we then have is really not one but several doubtful propositions, with some common *datum* and diverse *dubitata* (which latter may or may not be logically independent of one another). But in every case of a proposition actually doubted there is distinguishable something given and something ventured;[1] and the two are best separated by stating explicitly the question to which the proposition is intended to be an answer. For we can then say that such elements of the proposition as figure in the question indicate the given; while the element which figures in the proposition but not in the question, constitutes the ventured—the *dubitatum*. Thus if the proposition 'This package weighs 1 lb.' is intended as an answer to the question, 'How much does this package weigh?', the given is then a

---

in the class 'packages' is not asserted but assumed, not doubted but admitted. An important instance of a misrepresentation of this sort is furnished by the statement often heard nowadays, that the contradictory of 'All men are mortal' is not the traditional 'Some men are not mortal', but instead, 'Either there are no men, or some men are not mortal.' This statement constitutes a grave error, which rests on the failure to distinguish between assertion and assumption. In this instance, the usual assumption is that there are men, and under this assumption, the traditional contradictory is the correct one. Of course, we do not have to assume that there are men. But not to assume that, does not mean that no assumption is made. For to say that 'Either there are no men, or some men are not mortal' is the contradictory of 'All men are mortal' is correct only under the assumption that the existence of men is not taken for granted. This assumption, indeed, is an assumption about assumptions about men, instead of about men, but it is an assumption just the same, and one which is no less arbitrary than the other. It is very desirable, of course, to make our assumptions as clear and explicit as possible, but this can be done without traversing the fundamentally important distinction between assumption and assertion.

[1] Such a proposition as 'The nightingale now perched on the end of my pen is singing', appears to constitute an exception to the assertion just made. However, the form 'The ... which now ...', is relevant only if what is presupposed by it, viz., that there is a nightingale there, is admitted. But if on the contrary this is not admitted, then the use of that form gives rise to a self-irrelevant (not self-contradictory) subject; just as, in the proposition 'You have not quit beating your mother', we have (if the person referred to is not admitted to have been doing it), a self-irrelevant predicate. And if, in either case, the presupposition is not only not admitted, but false, then we have a fallacy of false insinuation in subject or predicate. In such a case the proposition about the nightingale would really then be a false existential proposition, viz., there is a singing nightingale now perched on my pen—in which *datum* and *dubitatum* can be distinguished. See below, section 3.

package and its weight *in concreto*; and the *dubitatum* is the particular weight 1 lb.

2. *Truth a function of three factors*

The writer being firmly convinced that the proper method of philosophical investigation is inductive, the present inquiry will begin with the analysis of a concrete case of a proposition, e.g., that already used as an example, 'This package weighs 1 lb.'.

 1. It is evident that the question whether or not that proposition is true is insoluble unless some one definite meaning is attached to the term '1 lb.', for otherwise no question has really been asked. Obviously, then, the truth or falsity of the proposition is functionally dependent upon, among other things, a definition of the term '1 lb.'.[1] And any definition of it that can be offered is essentially of the nature of a verbal convention, and therefore theoretically quite arbitrary; that is to say, theoretically, any one such definition is as good as any other, if it be but clear and free from contradictions. What is theoretically important is that there be such a convention, but not what particular one it shall be, provided it be known.[2] The meaning, which, in these United States, belongs 'officially' to the term '1 lb.' was fixed by Act of Congress, and may be changed by Act of Congress. This is to say that an

---

 [1] Were it objected that what we have with each such definition is a different proposition, the reply would be that this is to confuse a proposition with the import of a proposition. There is between them a useful and well established distinction, and no occasion to traverse it arises. What we do have is one proposition, but an ambiguous one. cf. 'A Criticism of Scepticism and Relativism' by R. M. Blake, *Journal of Philosophy*, vol. XXI, 10, pp. 269–70; and the writer's article already referred to, in the *International Journal of Ethics*.

 [2] What the convention shall be is, as Whewell has pointed out (*Novum Organon Renovatum*, pp. 36–7), often a matter of certain propositions which we desire to *make true* by the definition. However, such definitions *ad hoc* are permissible only when, or so far as, the terms defined do not already possess an established meaning in the language, for otherwise nothing but confusion results. The meaning of most terms is obviously a much more ancient affair than that of the term '1 lb.', but it is not on that account any less essentially of the nature of a verbal convention. The convention in their case is tacit and passively inherited, instead of explicit and actively entered into; it is of those which most essentially constitute the particular tongue to which the word belongs. And to accept it, i.e., to speak that tongue as already made, is the most convenient thing for us to do. But no such convention is logically binding, since, if we but specify another, we shall be equally intelligible.

Act of Congress can make false tomorrow a proposition which was true yesterday, since the truth of falsity of the proposition is dependent, among other things, upon the meaning of its predicate, and Congress can change that meaning. But, obviously, it is not to say that Congress can, by an Act passed today, bring it about that yesterday's true proposition shall no longer have been true yesterday.

The first of the factors, then, of which the truth of the proposition considered is a function, is some definition of the term '1 lb.' e.g., '1 lb. means the weight of this piece of metal'; this definition specifying what we may call the standard with which the package is to be compared, and agreement or disagreement with which determines the truth or falsity of the proposition.

2. At once, however, the question arises as to just what 'agreeing with' is to be taken to mean; and to this question no such sweeping and at the same time determinate answer as 'correspondence' theories of truth have often attempted, is possible. For the particular meaning of 'agreeing with' is, once more, a matter of convention in each case or sort of case. What can be said in general terms is that 'agreeing with' the standard means being 'equal to' it in the desired respect, i.e., having to it in that respect— here that of weight—a symmetrical and transitive relation. But whether such a relation obtains, or does not, between the object and the standard, depends on the *manner of comparison* selected; that is, in the case of weight, on the particular scales used, e.g., on whether the chemist's or the postmaster's. For there is no such thing as equality or its absence apart from some at least definable test. The test may not be practicable—in which case the truth or falsity of the proposition remains unknown; but unless a test is definable the assertion or denial of equality as between the object and the standard is meaningless; and until one is defined it remains ambiguous.[1]

---

[1] An illustration of a proposition in the case of which a test is, if not perhaps undefinable, at least difficult to define, would be the proposition that in the 'Bohr steady state' of the hydrogen atom, the electron is in motion. The 'Bohr steady state' is a state of perfect equilibrium of energy in the atom, and this means that the atom does not then radiate and is therefore not merely too small to be seen, but essentially unseeable, untouchable, etc.; in short, unobservable even supposititiously, because the supposition that it is observed contradicts the supposition of the perfect equilibrium of energy in it. But how else than in terms of a supposititious observation can a meaning be

But which scales are used is, once more, something theoretically quite arbitrary, and a matter chiefly of the purposes of the occasion. This means, in the instance, that the weight of the package is not more truly ascertained by the use of the very sensitive scales at the jeweller's or the chemist's, than by the less sensitive scales at the postmaster's; but only more usefully for certain purposes, e.g., those of physics or chemistry. For when we weigh the package on the post-office scales, we give one meaning to the question we ask, and when we weigh it on the jeweller's scales we give it another, even though the same standard pound has been used, and the same words have formulated the question, in each case. For each meaning of the question there is one definite answer; not, one of them, truer than the other, but one better for such purposes as may be ours, than the other. On these purposes depends whether the more delicate or the coarser instrument shall be used: an axe is worthless in a barber shop, and so is a razor in a lumber mill. Thus, the use of the jeweller's scales does not in the least yield a 'correction' of the weight obtained by the post-office scales, nor at all a nearer approach to the 'true' weight of the package, if our purpose is to mail the package. Correction, and nearer approach to 'the truth', are expressions which have applicability only to cases where two *methods of comparison* are available, both of which are relevant to the purpose which actuates us. In such cases we can speak of one as being better than the other in the proper, quantitative sense of the term 'better'; e.g., if rapidity (within certain limits of accuracy) is part of our purpose, then, of two methods both of which yield results that fall within the desired limits of accuracy, one may be better than the other in the sense of more rapid. But there is a different sense of the word 'better', which is illustrated by the case of the man whose purpose is to mail the package. It is the sense in which A is said to be better than B because A (e.g., the use of the post-office scales) is perfectly satisfactory[1] and B is not merely less satisfactory, but not satis-

---

given to the question whether or not the electron is at the same place at different instants? Yet, unless it can be done, the proposition is meaningless; and until it is done, unintelligible. cf. W. S. Franklin, 'The Quantum Puzzle and Time', *Science*, Sept. 19, 1924. Also 'The Non-Existence of Time', by the writer, in the *Journal of Philosophy*, vol. XXII, 1.

[1] In such a case, the Absolute could not know the true weight of the package more perfectly than we do.

factory at all. The use of the jeweller's scales is perhaps not a very good illustration of the latter; a better illustration would be the use of scales (and such exist) sensitive enough to detect the weight of the graphite deposited by a pencil on a sheet of paper in writing one's name. It is safe to say that the answers returned by such a balance to the question, 'Does this weigh 1 lb. ?' would not correlate with the postmaster's answers any more closely than would answers based on the toss of a coin—and would therefore be as wholly worthless as the latter for the purpose of mailing the package.

It is, however, a great and insidious temptation when—as now —scientific purposes are those which animate us, to ascribe to them a superior validity in *all* cases—even in cases where not they but others actually rule. Utmost accuracy is a god to whom others than the scientist need not always sacrifice, for it is a god whose commands, to them, are often impertinent, i.e., irrelevant to their purposes.

It is apparent, then, that the meaning of the proposition 'This package weighs the same as the standard pound' is not unambiguously fixed until the balance to be used, and the environmental conditions under which it is to be used, have been specified. And therefore such specifications constitute another factor on which the truth or falsity of the proposition is no less functionally dependent than on the standard definition of the *dubitatum*. And that other factor is, as stated, again one that is theoretically arbitrary.

3. Whatever the manner of comparison specified, the comparison must actually be made and its outcome observed, if the truth or falsity of the proposition is to be not merely defined, but ascertained. It must be observed whether or not the pointer on the beam of the balance is at the zero mark on the quadrant—whether or not a difference is felt between the colour of an object and some standard colour which it was asserted to match, etc. And these are matters of immediate, individual, sensory intuition, which no instrument can ultimately eliminate. What instruments can do is only to translate, or magnify, differences not directly observable, into differences that are so. But the instrument furnishes no theoretical guarantee that the ultimately direct sensory intuitions of various observers, i.e., the several readings of the instrument (if an instrument has been specified) by these various observers, will

agree. And if they do not agree, then there is no one answer to the question whether, for instance, the package does or does not weigh 1 lb. It is true that it weighs 1 lb. if equality of weight is defined in terms of one man's intuition of the place of the pointer on the quadrant, and false if it is defined in terms of some other man's. That is to say, once more, the meaning of the proposition has not yet been unambiguously fixed. To remove the ambiguity, one more convention is needed, which will specify the particular observer whose intuition is finally to define the sameness or difference of the weights. And the specification of such a standard observer, including his circumstances, is the third factor on which the truth of a proposition is functionally dependent.

Even the greater sensitiveness of a particular observer, which enables him to perceive differences not detectable by others, and on the basis of them perhaps to predict facts that the others will eventually perceive—even this is a theoretically arbitrary ground for selecting him as standard observer. For this respect of superiority which he has may not be relevant to the purposes back of a given problem any more than, in the case of the instrument of comparison, was the greater sensitiveness of the jeweller's scales relevant to the purpose of mailing the package. This, however, obviously does not mean that the truth of a proposition is a matter of the success of our purposes. Whether the purposes that animate us succeed or fail is wholly irrelevant to the truth of the proposition. What is relevant to it is, not their success or failure, but their nature. That nature determines the test in terms of which equality to standard shall be defined in the instance, i.e., what the proposition considered shall mean; but not whether the proposition shall, by that test, be true rather than false. That is something to be settled only by observation.

It may seem far-fetched to suppose that two observers, looking at the position of the pointer of a balance through the same peephole in turn, should perceive that position diversely. Every person whose eyes are normal, we are convinced, must necessarily perceive it alike. But obviously this is only to say that everybody will perceive it alike, except people whose eyes are such that they perceive it otherwise. And all such terms as colour-blind, hard of hearing, abnormal, hypersensitive, crazy, stupid, feeble-minded, prejudiced, astigmatic, etc., but designate classes of observers whose reports are ruled out by other people in certain cases. A man who perceives no differences of colour where the rest of us do, is called by us colour-blind. But in a world of persons like him, persons like us would be charged with 'seeing things', and our reports ruled out for many purposes—although indeed, for certain other purposes our reports might, in such a world, be acknowledged as the only relevant ones.

4. Since purposes or interests determine not indeed the outcome of any proposed test,[1] but the relevancy of it to the question of the truth of a given proposition, the problem arises, what bearing conflicts of purposes would have on the truth of the proposition. And the answer obviously is, no bearing at all in theory. For as soon as a meaning has been unambiguously assigned to the proposition, there is an absolute answer to the question whether the proposition is true. But, in practice, other considerations enter. Our social system functions not so much on the basis of contents (meanings), as on the basis of labels (words). It is to words that men mainly react in society, and such reactions to labels are what confer or remove the values that they and others seek: What is of immediate practical importance to Tom Jones is whether it is commonly pronounced 'true' that Tom Jones is a sharper; and not what exactly 'sharper' means. So far as definitions come to be considered at all in such cases, then, the practical issue will for the most part be only whether any proposed definition is such as to make the proposition true, or false. Tom Jones will insist on one definition, and the man with whom he did business on another. And the outcome of such a conflict of definitions is purely a matter of the relative might possessed by, or at the command of, the parties to the dispute.[2] But since definitions themselves are neither true nor false, but only used or not used, the outcome of such a conflict has no theoretical bearing on the truth of the proposition. For all that victory in the conflict confers, is the power to attach penalties to the consequences in behaviour, of refusing to define a term in the particular way insisted upon by the victor.

5. Before we leave the example which we have been examining, close attention must be given to a point so far barely mentioned, but of great significance, and to illustrate which that example is

---

[1] Including in the meaning of 'test' both a method of comparison and an observer.

[2] cf. 'Liberalism in Ethics', *loc cit*.

particularly appropriate. It is this: The meaning of the proposition 'This package weighs 1 lb.' is not unambiguously fixed, as we have seen, without the specification of three things—standard, method, and observer. But ultimately, these factors are not themselves unambiguously specifiable otherwise than by being concretely denoted: this piece of metal, this balance, this observer, each of them under the conditions present here now. But then the truth or falsity of the proposition, although rendered absolute by such completely unambiguous specification, is also at the same time rendered useless. That is, the proposition loses all scientific or practical significance, and becomes of purely historical interest. On the other hand, however, what we sought was, in the instance, a proposition true not merely at the post-office where the package is mailed, but also at the post-office which is to deliver it. And this character of 'community' or 'over-individuality', in the truth we seek, is exactly what is involved by saying that the relation of 'equality' (e.g., of the package and the standard, as to weight) is not only a symmetrical but also a transitive relation.[1] That the verdict of the particular balance gives us 'equality' means, so far as symmetry is concerned, that if the object and the standard pound are each shifted to the opposite pan of the balance, the pointer remains at the same place. But so far as transitivity is concerned, it means that the outcome of the particular test at the mailing post-office will be the same as, e.g., the outcome of the test to be performed at the delivering post-office. And the only condition that will guarantee this is that the two tests shall be the same test—which is impossible as soon as either of them has been specified in the completely concrete, i.e., unique, manner mentioned above as needed to render the proposition wholly unambiguous. And we therefore find ourselves in this dilemma: If the test has been uniquely specified, then the other test will necessarily be a different test, and it then remains doubtful whether the two will have the same outcome. And if, on the contrary, the test specified is not an individual and unique one, but only a test of a certain kind, it then remains doubtful whether the two tests, although both of them of the prescribed kind, will not, owing to accidental circumstances, have different outcomes. Thus in either

---

[1] i.e. As the reader will recall, a relation such that if it exists between A and B, and also between B and C, then it exists also between A and C.

case the sameness of outcome, i.e., the transitivity of the relation, i.e., the 'equality' of the weights, i.e., the (other than purely historical) truth of the proposition, remains ultimately a postulate, that is, a fond hope only. That any generalization of the subject of a proposition rests upon some such postulate as that of the so-called 'Uniformity of Nature', is a commonplace. And the above remarks only point the fact—by no means novel, but not usually described in these terms—that the generalization of the predicate is no less of a sheer gamble than that of the subject. This, however, furnishes no occasion to throw up our epistemological hands in despair. To say that all knowledge rests upon certain postulates, i.e., fond hopes, does not imply that to weigh the package means the same thing as to guess at its weight. To *know* does not mean the same as to guess. And the distinction between the two amounts to a distinction between the guesses that we cannot avoid and the guesses that we can avoid. The guesses that we cannot avoid (the 'postulates') condition the ultimate meaning of the terms of the propositions about which we can avoid guessing (e.g., the proposition that the package weighs 1 lb.) no less if such propositions be put forward as the result of a guess or as articles of sheer faith, than if they be put forward as the result of a test actually performed. To guess, in the sense in which to guess can be contrasted with to know, is thus to guess where one could test, to guess *before* one needs begin to.

3. *The truth of Existential propositions*

So much for the analysis of the concrete example with which we began. The question may now well be asked whether the view of the nature of Truth formulated on the basis of the analysis of that example fits propositions of other sorts also. And if the inquiry is to continue to proceed inductively, that question can be answered only on the basis of an examination of, at least, cases of such sorts of propositions as might most easily appear not to fit in with the view of truth defined.

1. Propositions, or, if one prefers, interpretations of their imports, may be distinguished as Descriptive and Existential. In the Descriptive, the concrete existence of something is assumed given and the problem is, *What* is it?, i.e., does a certain proposed concept (the *dubitatum*) fit it or not? (in the sense of fitting, or

agreeing with, already indicated). The proposition analysed was of this sort. In Existential propositions, on the other hand, a certain nature, i.e., a certain description, a certain 'what', is assumed understood, and the problem is, Is it there?, i.e., is it discernible *in concreto* among the characters of any of the objects of a specified field? In Descriptive propositions the existent is the *datum* and the description is the *dubitatum*; in Existential propositions it is the description which is the *datum*, and the existence of something agreeing with it, which is the *dubitatum*.[1]

The word 'existence', however, is used in all sorts of ways, and it will therefore be conducive to clearness if, here again, we examine a concrete case. Thus, we may ask, 'Is there a copy of Hume's *Treatise* in this room?' Now this problem, at first sight, appears to differ from such problems as 'Does a God exist?', 'Are there mermaids?', 'Is there a number the square of which is 9?', etc., in being not so much a problem of existence as one of location. That is, one might say that the existence of copies of Hume's *Treatise* is, in the question, not doubted, but only the location of one of them in this room; while in the other cases suggested it is the very existence of the sorts of things mentioned, that is doubted. But I do not believe any essential distinction can be maintained between the two sets of cases. For in each of the other questions also, a *locus* of existence is essentially involved. If it is not in each case explicitly mentioned, it is either because it is assumed to be already clearly understood, or else because the proponent of the question is not himself clear as to just what he wants to know, i.e., the question is ambiguous. Thus, in the case of the existence of God, the question is ambiguous so long as it is not specified whether the existence which God is declared to have is that of physical objects, that of mathematical entities, that of beliefs without which men cannot live righteously, etc. And the matter is plainer still in the case of the other two examples: the intended *locus,* in the case of the mermaids, is the sea; and in the case of the number the square of which is 9, it is integers, etc. Thus, in every question of existence there is reference to a certain realm or class of entities to which 'objective' status is given to start with; and the question is whether, among the individuals

[1] cf. Royce, *The World and the Individual*, vol. I, p. 49; Coffey, *The Science of Logic,* vol. I, p. 101, *apud* Satolli; Aristotle, *Anal. Post.,* bk. II, chapters VII, VIII.

of that group one (or more) is to be found possessing, in addition to the characters which make it member of that group of 'objects', the *other* characters desired, viz. being a God, a copy of Hume's *Treatise,* a mermaid, a number the square of which is 9, etc.

And by speaking of 'objective status' I mean simply that the entity considered as having it, is, at the time, functioning for us as the terminus or limit of our thought, i.e., as meant but not as itself meaning; this being, I submit, the sole essential difference between an 'object' and a 'notion'—the latter being definable as that which not only is meant (by a name or by another notion) but also itself means (another notion or an object).[1] However, it is of the greatest importance to note here that to ask whether something exists, and to ask whether that thing is real, are two wholly distinct questions. Most anything one may be pleased to mention exists in some realm; but what we wish to know in every case where we raise the question of existence is whether what we mention has existence in the realm of real existence, i.e., in the realm of existence which is important to us at the time. The distinction between existence and reality is quite fundamental here if confusion is to be avoided, but it cannot, for lack of space, be now more than indicated.[2]

2. There is another consideration to which it is necessary to advert before a fair comparison can be made between Descriptive and Existential propositions, in respect of the elements upon which Truth was asserted to be functionally dependent. It is that of the distinction between problems of Proof and problems of Discovery, which, in the case of Descriptive propositions would be sufficiently illustrated by the two questions 'Does this package weigh 1 lb.?', and 'How many lbs. does this package weigh?', respectively. It is obvious that the second question cannot be solved except by the repeated formulation and solution of questions such as the first, each with the hypothesis of a different weight, until the correct hypothesis happens to be hit upon. Thus the direct problem is always one of proof. Now the same thing is true,

---

[1] I have elsewhere endeavoured to defend in detail these definitions of 'object' and 'notion'. See *Causation and the Types of Necessity,* Univ. of Washington Press, pp. 103–10.

[2] I have argued it at length in the paper on 'A Defence of Ontological Liberalism' already mentioned. Some comments on the views of Russell and Johnson on reality and existence will be found on pp. 345–6.

but not so evident, in the case of questions of Existence. Such questions as 'Is there something weighing 1 lb. in this room?', 'Is there a copy of Hume's *Treatise* on this shelf?', cannot be answered directly in most cases, but only on the basis of the repeated formulation and solution of questions such as 'Is a copy of Hume's *Treatise* this, that, the other . . . object on this shelf?'. In other words, to find out whether or not there is one, we have to examine in turn the various entities jointly constituting the realm of existence specified, and observe whether or not, in any of them, the characters understood by 'copy of Hume's *Treatise*' are concretely discernible. The direct existential problem also, is therefore always again a problem of proof—here one of the form 'Is X-ness present in this?'.

And now it is evident enough that, in a proposition of the form 'X-ness is present in this' the factors of which the truth of the proposition is a function are essentially the same as those already brought to light in the case of a proposition of the form 'This has X-ness'. The differences are only that, as already noted, what in the latter is a *datum* is in the former the *dubitatum*, and vice versa; and that what, in Descriptive propositions is naturally spoken of as a method of comparison for determining equality is, although not concretely a different thing at all, more naturally described in Existential propositions as a method of inspection for determining presence.

3. Some of the bearings of the analysis of Existential propositions just set forth may be illustrated by some remarks on the relation between mathematics and physics—a question which, since the advent of the theory of Relativity, is of greater interest than ever. That theory, it is sometimes said, gives us one all-embracing mathematical formula into which fit all the events of the physical world, and one from which the observer has been entirely eliminated; and this easily becomes an argument in support of a radical Realism.

However, as a distinguished exponent of the Theory of Relativity[1] has pointed out, to eliminate the observer is one thing, and to generalize him is another and a very different thing.

---

[1] Lyndon Bolton, in a lecture on 'Materialism and the Theory of Relativity', read at Sion College, London, Nov. 25, 1924, of which he has very kindly allowed me to see the manuscript. cf. His *Introduction to the Theory of Relativity*, ch. XXI.

And it is the latter, he maintains, which Relativity has really done —the observer, in his metrical status, being the reference system. Now, I could not agree that the observer can, even metrically, be identified with the reference system, for this, it seems to me, would be to identify, e.g., the clock with the person who reads the clock. But aside from this, I would agree both that it is very important to distinguish generalization from elimination, and that the observer has not been and cannot be eliminated.

However, a misunderstanding as to the sort of observation involved when this is said would be very easy, and, to avoid it, it is indispensable to distinguish sharply between two things that are easy to confuse and in practice often confused, viz., the mathematical and the physical import of equations or formulæ. In the present instance the distinction becomes one between what may respectively be referred to as the Principle of Relativity, or of Invariance, and the Theory of Relativity. The Principle is a proposition of pure mathematics: the truth which it claims—and which I am told it has rigidly been proved to have—is mathematical truth, i.e., truth in the sense of agreement of the assertion which it ventures with data belonging to the same sort of a realm as do such objects as integers, roots, powers, etc., viz., to the realm of entities that are strictly and solely creatures of definition. Thus, the Principle does not even so much as whisper or hint anything concerning the entities of the physical world.

But the Theory of Relativity, on the contrary, is essentially a proposition concerning the physical world, and it is made such by introducing the supposition that the quantities entering into the statement of the Principle represent measurements. Now, that the physical world and the processes of actual or conceivable measurement are such as to yield none but measurements that can be fitted into the formula of the Principle, is a physical hypothesis, to be tested like any other hypothesis about the physical world, on the basis of appropriate observations of that world, e.g., the now famous eclipse observations. By the outcome of such observations, the Theory stands or falls; while on the contrary their outcome has not even the remotest bearing upon the truth or falsity of the Principle. This, of course, is not to say that the truth of the Principle is definable independently of observation, for it is not; but the sort of observation relevant to it is not the observation of physical objects, but that of pure mathematical entities as such—it is the same sort of observation as that involved in establishing the truth of such a proposition, for instance, as that the cube of 4 is 64, namely the observation of the result of a mathematical computation.[1]

The above remarks, when generalized, turn out to mean something which, in the abstract, is obvious and commonplace enough, namely, that the truth of a proposition concerning entities (whether mathematical or logical) that are creatures of definition, is one thing; and the truth of a proposition concerning entities of some other realm, e.g., the physical, alleged to be cases of the former entities, is a very different thing and one that does not automatically follow from the former, but must on the contrary be certified by testing the truth of that allegation. But the overlooking of this in practice is easy and frequent, owing to the fact that the very same words (or symbols) are very often used to denote on the one hand pure mathematical or logical entities, and, on the other hand, physical entities.

4. *The meaning, the criterion, and the knowledge of truth*

We are now in a better position to formulate a general proposition concerning the meaning of truth. We may say that, in every case, *the truth of a proposition means the agreement, according to some definable test, between the notion and the object which the terms of the proposition stand for.* I say 'object' rather than 'fact', for 'a fact' means nothing but the import of a true proposition. And I use 'object' and 'notion' in the senses specified above. Also, I must here recall and stress the distinction already indicated between definable, defined, and performed; for that distinction marks the difference between the meaning, the criterion, and the knowledge of truth, of which much is often made.[2] But it should now be apparent that that difference does not avail to eliminate reference to a test from the account of the nature of truth.

---

[1] See below section 5, art. 4.

[2] In a very rough way it might perhaps be said that insistence upon either the first, or the second, or the third, wellnigh to the point of blindness to the others, is what most nearly characterizes the essential difference between the coherence, the pragmatic, and the self-evidence theories of truth. But each of these has been so variously stated, and withal usually with such ambiguity, that any unambiguous assertion concerning them would probably be foredoomed to futility.

5. *Analysis of cases of propositions of other sorts*

The case for the view of the nature of truth now set forth will be strengthened by the examination of some propositions differing in various respects from those already considered. We may take first the consecrated 'All men are mortal'.

1. It must be noted at the outset that this proposition might be intended either as real or as verbal. Let us examine it first in its verbal interpretation. It would then declare that 'Man' means, among other things, being mortal. And the assertion that 'Man' possesses such a meaning might be made either *a priori*, viz., as a (partial) definition laid down by the speaker; or *a posteriori*, as an inductive generalization from observations of the apparent intention of persons, on occasions where they used the term 'Man'. Since definitions are neither true nor false, but (if free from contradictions) only adopted or rejected, we need consider here only the second alternative. Now it is clear that the utterances of people, in which a given term is used[1] can be observed no less than can physical things; that hypotheses concerning the intension of the term in such actual good usage can be formulated no less than can hypotheses concerning the properties of things; and that such hypotheses concerning the meaning of terms as used can be strengthened or disproved, by checking against additional cases of actual good usage, no less than can hypotheses as to the properties of things by checking against additional cases of those things. And the agreement of the hypothesis ventured with the *data* about which it is, can, in the verbal proposition also, be precisely defined in terms of an appropriate test; and the test can be performed and its outcome observed. The matter is but slightly complicated in the example we are considering by the fact that two hypotheses are there ventured at once: one, that when the term 'Man' was used in this, that, and the other actual utterance, 'being mortal'

---

[1] To observe how people use a word is a very different thing from asking them to say what they mean by it. The definition they then attempt is their theory of what they mean by the word, but actual cases of their manner of using it are the facts which the theory must fit; and there is no *a priori* reason to believe that their theory is more likely to be correct than that of someone else. And by their actual usage of a word, is not meant the nature that the object to which they apply the word, has, but the nature which, all unanalysed, they believe that object to have.

was part of what the speaker intended by it; and the other, that these utterances constituted a 'fair sample' of utterances in which the term 'Man' is used, and therefore warrant a probable conclusion concerning all such utterances.

2. However, the proposition 'All men are mortal' will hardly in fact be regarded by anyone as a verbal proposition. And the analysis just made is therefore useful chiefly to show that the view of truth set forth applies to verbal no less than to real propositions. That it applies to the proposition 'All men are mortal' when it is regarded as a real proposition, is obvious: That proposition, under the assumption that there are men, again involves two hypotheses, viz., first that the men actually examined were mortal—which is a hypothesis of exactly the same type as that 'this package weighs 1 lb.'; and second that the men examined were a 'fair sample' of Men and therefore that what was true of them is probably true of all men.

3. We may next consider briefly a typically relational proposition, e.g., 'This man is brother of that man'. The truth or falsity of this proposition is a function of, first, a standard definition of the relation hypothetically asserted to exist between the two men, e.g., 'brother of, means child of the same parents as'; second, a method of comparison between the relation as defined and the relation concretely present between the men, e.g., 'a person A shall be said to be child of the same parents as a person B if the parents of B, on being asked whether A is their child, both answer affirmatively'; third, the immediate perception by a specified observer (e.g., ourselves) of what the answer has been.[1]

4. Lastly, we may examine a proposition similar to that just discussed, but concerned with mathematical instead of physical

---

[1] The temptation is strong here to say that even the supposition of an affirmative answer does not really define the truth of the proposition. The parents of B might be lying, one objects, and that would not change the fact that A either is, or is not, their child. But this objection only means that the particular test suggested above might have an outcome different from that of some other test, which other is perhaps the only one relevant to our purposes on the occasion; it does not mean that the truth of the proposition is independent of any test whatever. The test suggested above might, e.g., be relevant for legal purposes; but it would not be directly relevant to the purposes, e.g., of an investigation into the transmissibility of acquired characters; and vice versa. This amounts to saying that 'child of' may be interpreted to mean 'legally child of', or, no less, 'physiologically child of'.

entities, e.g., the proposition '64 is the cube of 4'. Here again are involved, first, a definition of the relation 'cube of'; second, a method of comparing the relation as defined with the relation concretely present between 64 and 4, e.g., putting the question to a trusted computer, possibly oneself, or to a calculating machine; and thirdly the immediate observation of the result of the performance of the comparison, e.g., the observation of the computer's 'yes' or 'no', if he be other than oneself; or, if oneself, of the identity of the number calculated with the number given, etc.

6. 'The true view of Truth'

According to the considerations that have now been set forth, Truth might, like Right, be said either to be something absolutely relative, or something relatively absolute. That is, the truth of a proposition is relative to the specification of the three factors already described—but how they shall be specified is something which is theoretically arbitrary, i.e., absolute in the same sense as verbal definitions. On the other hand, relatively to any one such arbitrary set of specifications, the truth of a proposition is absolute and final.

Such a view of Truth is perhaps best characterized as a liberalistic one. And it is obvious what would be involved if, instead of contenting oneself with describing or naming this view, one were to claim it to be the true view of Truth! The claim could of course be made without involving theoretical inconsistencies, but so far as settling it goes, the most that on that very view of Truth could be done, would be to settle it in a manner consistent, for instance with the use of terms, the interests, and the intuitive observations, of most of us. But the others, with their uses of terms, their interests, and their immediate intuitions, would continue to exist in spite of our calling them names meaning that they do not 'count' (when *we* do the counting). No such procedure will bully them into nonentity, and, in our very own sense of the word 'true', propositions true for us would not necessarily be true for them. The liberalistic position thus involves that if any man is to be brought to a conviction of his errors—whether in his view of Truth or of anything else—it needs must be by words out of his own mouth.

PROPOSITIONS, TRUTH, AND THE ULTIMATE CRITERION OF TRUTH*

The problem of the nature and criterion of truth is central in the theory of knowledge and has been studied by philosophers for centuries. For the most part, however, the terms in which it has been stated and discussed have been too vague to make definite solution of the problem possible. Before such a solution can be reached, certain preliminary questions must have been investigated and disposed of; but these are more technical, and by themselves no doubt less interesting. Accordingly, one is likely to be impatient of them until the repeated failures to solve the problem of truth have brought home the fact that it remains insoluble if these other questions have not first been answered. This situation, of course, parallels what one finds again and again in the natural sciences, where the immediately interesting problem which motivates some inquiry turns out to be soluble only on the basis of the results of other and highly technical inquiries.

The contribution towards solution of the problem of truth which I shall attempt to make in this paper cannot, for several obvious reasons, be more than a very modest one. I propose to indicate first what I believe to be the methodologically sound manner of stating the problem. Then I shall summarize and supplement the results of certain inquiries which have seemed to me indispensable if discussion of the problem is to be purged of the ambiguities that usually infect it. Next, I shall criticize briefly some of the more common opinions as to the nature and criteria

* *Philosophy and Phenomenological Research*, vol. IV, No. 3, 1944.

of truth. Finally, I shall submit a brief statement of the hypothesis which, in the light of all this, seems to me to recommend itself.

I

1. *The data of the problem of truth*

In conformity with the first principle of what seems to me sound method in philosophy, I must make clear to begin with the nature of the data of the problem of truth as I conceive it.

These data consist of ordinary statements in which the adjectives 'true' or 'false' enter as predicates. For example: 'It is true that 17 times 49 is 833', 'It is true that the Japanese bombed Pearl Harbor', 'It is true that Caesar crossed the Rubicon, but false that he crossed the Atlantic', 'It is true that water is a compound of hydrogen and oxygen', 'It is false that glass is malleable at ordinary temperatures', and so on.

Statements such as these are 'data' for the problem of the nature of truth not in the sense that they are themselves assumed as true beyond question, but in the sense that they are samples of the particular usage, among the several current usages of 'true' and 'false', with which I shall be concerned.

The problem itself of the nature of truth, as it concerns the kind of data just exemplified, is, if reduced to essentials, simply that of discovering a definition of the adjectives 'true' and 'false' that will 'fit' the sort of use made of them in statements of the type illustrated. Furthermore, to say that a given definition of, for instance, 'true' *fits* that use means that the *definiens* of that definition can be substituted for the word 'true' in all such statements without thereby altering the truth-value (whether it happen to be 'truth' or 'falsity') of those statements; and, conversely, that 'true' can similarly be substituted for that *definiens* in any statement where the latter happens to be predicate.

2. *What kind of thing is either true or false?*

The first of the preliminary questions that need to be answered is, what sort of thing, generically, is it, which, in such statements as those above, is introduced by the phrases 'It is true that . . .' or 'It is false that . . .'; and is the only sort of thing so introducible without incongruity.

Writers on the subject of truth seem not always to have realized the fundamental importance of this question. Therefore, instead of really facing it and dealing with it critically before passing to that of the nature of truth, they often have simply assumed some particular answer to it; speaking, for instance, of ideas, or of judgements, or perhaps of statements, or else of opinions, or of propositions, as true or false. Indeed, several of these terms have not seldom been used indifferently, as if they were essentially synonymous. But I believe that lack of discrimination at this point has probably been the greatest single source of confusion in discussion of the problem of truth.

I propose to align myself here with what has been the position prevalent on the whole among logicians, namely, that the sort of thing, and the only sort of thing, which either is true or is false is a *proposition*; and moreover that a proposition, and only a proposition, is the sort of thing capable of being believed, disbelieved, doubted, or supposed. The important thing, however, is not what one shall *call* that sort of thing, but that one shall discriminate sharply between it and the other sorts of things called respectively statements, opinions, and judgements; and that one shall perceive exactly how these four sorts of things are related to one another and to 'facts'. To analyse their mutual relations was the aim of an earlier paper of mine, and since the results arrived at in it are basic to the argument of the present essay, a summary of them must be introduced here.[1]

2

3. *Propositions, opinions, statements, judgements, and facts*

Those results supplemented at some points, are essentially as follows:

(a) 'Inclination to believe' is a psychological attitude towards propositions. It may be positive or negative inclination, and has degrees: the maximum degree of it, belief; the minimum, disbelief; the exactly intermediate, neutral degree 'dubitance'. (Such a phrase as: 'I doubt that . . .' ordinarily means: 'I am inclined to disbelieve that. . . .' That is, 'doubt' does not there refer to the exactly intermediate degree; as on the contrary it does in: 'I am in

---

[1] 'Propositions, Opinions, Sentences, and Facts,' *Journal of Philosophy*, vol. XXXVII, No. 26, December 19, 1940. Also, 'Is a Fact a True Proposition?' same journal, vol. XXXIX, No. 5, February 26, 1942.

doubt as to whether or not. . . .') The attitudes consisting of the various degrees of inclination to believe I propose to call the epistemic attitudes.

(b) An *opinion* is a proposition *plus* some 'opinative' attitude towards it, i.e., some degree of positive or of negative inclination to believe it. An opinion in the case of which the inclination is positive will be called, broadly, a belief; and one where the inclination is negative, a disbelief. To speak of an opinion O does not imply that any person holds it.

(c) An opinion consisting of a *true* proposition plus *negative* inclination to believe it, or of a false proposition plus positive inclination to believe it, is *erroneous*. On the other hand, an opinion consisting of a *true* proposition plus *positive* inclination to believe it, or of a false proposition plus negative inclination to believe it is *sound*.

The adjective 'true' is commonly used both as opposite of 'erroneous' and as opposite of 'false'; but since it is crucially important never to forget that the meaning of 'true' is radically different in the two cases, I propose to use 'true' exclusively as opposite of 'false'; and, for the opposite of 'erroneous', to use throughout the adjective 'sound'. Failure to discriminate sharply between falsity and error and between truth and soundness, and to bear in mind that only opinions are erroneous or sound, and only propositions, false or true, is responsible for many philosophical errors. Bertrand Russell, for instance, when considering the hypothesis that there are in the world objective 'falsehoods' not dependent on the existence of judgements, declares that 'this is in itself almost incredible: we feel that there could be no falsehood if there were no minds to make mistakes'[1]. But obviously, the incredibility really attaches not to the hypothesis that without minds there can be false propositions, but only to the very different hypothesis that without minds there can be erroneous opinions.[2]

(d) In an opinion, the proposition to which the positive or negative inclination to believe attaches will be called the *content* of the opinion.

---

[1] *Philosophical Essays*, p. 176.

[2] Falsehood is a treacherous word to use in such discussions, for it means sometimes falsity, sometimes a lie, sometimes a false proposition; although never an erroneous opinion: 'this man has erroneous opinions' cannot be replaced by 'this man has falsehoods'.

(e) We all have many opinions of which, at a given time, we are not conscious; but whenever any opinion we have is conscious, the constituents of the proposition which is content of the opinion are, at the time, apprehended by us (whether perceptually, conceptually, or imaginally). Our apprehending or being conscious of that proposition, however, is, in all but certain special cases, something distinct from the proposition itself which we are apprehending; and it is the proposition apprehended, not our apprehending of it, which is believed, disbelieved, or doubted by us, and which is true or false. That is, a proposition thought of is not ordinarily itself a thought.

(f) A *fact* is not something to which true propositions 'correspond' in some sense. A fact *is* a true proposition. What corresponds, or fails to correspond, to a fact can be only an epistemic attitude, e.g., disbelief; or else a set of words purported to represent or symbolize the fact. To speak of correspondence between propositions and facts is possible only if by a 'proposition' one means either a sentence or some sort of thought. But one cannot consistently mean either of these if one has committed oneself to the position that a proposition is the sort of thing which can be believed, disbelieved, or doubted; for what one believes, disbelieves, or doubts is not sentences but what the sentences signify; nor is it one's thoughts, but what they are thoughts of: If, for instance, I believe that the moon has another side, it is the moon itself not the word 'moon' nor my percept or thought of the moon, which I believe to have another side.[1]

(g) A proposition such as the one the asserting of which would be represented by the sentence 'Quadruplicity drinks procrastination' (an example of Russell's) is 'absurd'. That is absurd which cannot possibly be true, i.e., is necessarily false. Quadruplicity

---

[1] In the *Journal of Symbolic Logic,* vol. VII, No. 2, June, 1942, p. 96, E. J. Nelson states that 'it is not clear how general propositions such as (x) : (Ǝy) . $\sim$f (x, y) could be treated in this way', i.e., how one could hold that a true proposition of this type is a fact. If I read this formula correctly, it means: 'For every x, there is at least one y such that x is not f of y' i.e., if x = men, y = women, and f = husband of: 'For every man there is at least one woman such that he is not her husband'. This, in ordinary language means: 'No man is husband of every woman', or: 'A man husband of every woman exists nowhere'. If Nelson grants that some facts are general facts, I do not see why the identification of 'fact' and 'true proposition' is not as possible in this case as in any other.

does not drink procrastination because it does not drink anything, and not only does not actually drink, but, having no drinking apparatus, could not possibly drink. Moreover, procrastination not being any kind of a drink could not be drunk even by an entity capable of drinking. Therefore, 'quadruplicity drinks procrastination' is necessarily false. But if a proposition is necessarily false, it is false. Thus there is not, beside true propositions and false propositions, any third class of 'meaningless' propositions that are neither true nor false.

(h) A *sentence* is the discursive symbol of an opinion or a question.

(i) A *statement* is the kind of sentence (viz., declaratory) which formulates, i.e., is the discursive symbol of, an opinion. The converse of formulating is deciphering.

(j) Statements of the form 'Statement S is true' are elliptical. Their full meaning is 'The proposition, which is content of the belief formulated by statement S, is true', or 'The proposition, which is content of the disbelief formulated by statement S, is false.'

(k) A *judgement* is an opinion arrived at critically, i.e., as a result of attention to such evidence, *pro* and *contra*, as one has at the time concerning the truth-value of the proposition concerned. That is, a judgement is the consummation of an attempt to resolve a doubt.

(l) In any case of doubt there is something (the *datum*) which the doubt *is about*, and something else (the *dubitatum*) which is in doubt about it, i.e., which the doubt *is of*.

(m) In the judgement which resolves the doubt, that which the doubt was about is the *subject* of the judgement; and that which was in doubt about it but is now affirmed or negated of it is the *predicate*. Thus, every judgement has subject and predicate.

(n) Since 'subject' and 'predicate' are thus each the name of a *status* in respect to an antecedent doubt, and not of a constituent of the proposition which is content of the doubt and of the judgement, no *proposition* has subject or predicate; and the very same constituents of a proposition, which *functioned* respectively as subject and as predicate in a given judgement, might function instead respectively as predicate and subject in another judgement. For example, if the doubt resolved by the judgement expressed by the sentence 'here is a copy of Hume's Treatise' was 'What is here?' then the predicate of the judgement is 'a copy of Hume's Treatise'.

But if the doubt was instead 'Where is there a copy of Hume's Treatise?' then 'here' is predicate of the judgement.

3

4. *What is a proposition?*

What precedes puts us now in position to deal with the question, of what kinds are the essential constituents of a proposition. What has just been said concerning judgements already enables us to say at least that the constituents of a proposition must in every case be such as to be capable of serving as subject and predicate in a judgement, and that any pair of entities capable of being so used is a proposition. But the question remains, Of which two generic kinds are the entities constituting such a pair?

5. *Judgements are quiddative or existential*

To discern the answer, we must first attend to a familiar distinction, dating back at least to Aristotle,[1] which is of truly basic importance for the theory of knowledge. It is the distinction between the *what* (i.e., the nature, character, kind) of something, and the *that* (i.e., the existence) of it. To have some existing thing indicated to us is not automatically to know, or to know adequately, what it is; else there would never be occasion for the question 'What is it?' On the other hand, to know what something is, for instance, a dodo, or a black swan, or a sea serpent, or a brownie, is not automatically to know whether anything of the kind exists; else there never would be occasion for the question 'Are there any?'

A judgement may be called *quiddative* if it is *of* some 'what' *about* some 'that'; and on the contrary *existential* if it is *of* some 'that' *about* some 'what'. Moreover, every judgement is either quiddative or existential in this sense. This is true even of relational, of quantitative, and of operational judgements: what is judged in them is either the specific 'what'—whether relational, quantitative, or operational—of some given existent; or else that a relation, or a quantity, or an operation of some given kind exists.

---

[1] *Anal. Post.,* book II, ch. VII.

6. *Existential judgements*

But a little more explanation is needed here as to existential judgements. They are essentially *ubietive, locative*. This becomes evident if we bear in mind two things.

One is that where mathematical existence, for example, is concerned instead of physical existence, the *ubi* predicated is a place not in the space-time order system but in some other, e.g., in the series of the whole numbers when it is asserted that there is a square root of 4 but no square root of 2.

The other thing to notice is that existential judgements, like quiddative, may be of several degrees of determinateness. Existentially most indeterminate are those of the form '*A* exists' (or, synonymously, 'there is some *A*' or 'there are *A*'s'); that is, '*A* is somewhere'—at some place not specified. For example, 'Black swans exist', or 'There are black swans.' That '*A* exists' means '*A* is somewhere' is shown by the fact that, after a statement of this form has been made, the further question 'where?' is always possible.

Existentially less indeterminate are judgements of the form '*A* exists in . . .,' or, synonymously, 'there are *A*'s in . . . '. For example, 'Black swans exist in Australia', or 'There are black swans in Australia.'

Lastly, completely determinate existential judgements are of the form 'Here now is an *A*', or 'An *A* now exists right here' (for example, 'Here now is a black swan'); or, generically, 'An *A* is at, or exists at (*not*, within) place *P*' if *P* is the name of some completely determinate place, whether temporal, spatio-temporal, mathematical, or other.

7. *The ultimate constituents of a proposition*

In the light of the considerations set forth in what precedes, I now submit the conclusion that the ultimate, i.e., the essential, irreducible constituents of a proposition are some *ubi* and some *quid*— some *locus* and some *quale*. A proposition, then, is any pair consisting of at least a locus and a quale.

Moreover, it is of the essence of a locus to be occupiable by some 'what'; and of the essence of a quale to be capable of presence somewhere. This means that any locus and any quale are automatically in the propositional relation to each other: to constitute a propositional pair, they do not need any event external to both, such as somebody's affirmation or negation. A proposition, in itself, is neither affirmative nor negative. It is opinions, not propositions, which are affirmative or negative. But to say that any locus and any quale automatically constitute a propositional pair leaves, of course, wholly open the question whether the proposition they constitute is true or is false.

In the case of such a statement as 'this man is a philosopher', it may seem that the analysis just given does not fit the proposition which is content of the opinion that statement formulates. The constituents of that proposition seem to be an individual and a class. But 'this man is a philosopher' really states two propositions, one of which is assumed and the other asserted, viz., 'here is a man' and 'at this same place and time is a philosopher'. Again, a statement such as 'all men are mortal' explicates into 'at every place where a man is, there too, is a mortal'.

In connection with this account of the nature of propositions, many questions of course suggest themselves. They cannot, however, be gone into here, since that account is introduced only because of its relation to the problem as to what constitutes the truth or falsity of a proposition.

I should like to point out, however, that what has seemed to some critics of that account the paradoxical character of some of its implications is owing solely to the fact that 'proposition' is commonly used, uncritically, to mean sometimes an opinion, sometimes a judgement, sometimes a sentence, even by those who profess to distinguish propositions from these and to mean by a proposition solely that which is susceptible of being believed, disbelieved, doubted, or supposed; and is true or false. I have only brought out into the open what these professions imply. That a fact is a true proposition, for instance, is indeed paradoxical, if, in spite of having assigned to 'proposition' the meaning just mentioned, one nevertheless insists on calling 'propositions' entities which, according to one's own distinctions, one should be calling 'sentences', or perhaps 'opinions', or something else. One cannot, without generating paradoxes, *both* restrict a term to one of several meanings in which it is currently used without discrimination, *and also* hang on to the habit of using it indiscriminately for any one of them.

I turn now to some comments on the principal answers commonly proposed to the question as to the nature and the criterion of truth.

4

8. *The coherence theory of truth*

The greatest difficulty in the way of criticism of the coherence theory of truth is that of finding out exactly what the advocates of it conceive it to be. Blanshard, himself one of the most lucid of its exponents, quotes Ewing as saying that 'it is wrong to tie down the advocates of the coherence theory to a precise definition. What they are doing is to describe an ideal that has never yet been completely clarified but is nonetheless immanent in all our thinking.'[1] But, if the nature of this ideal is uncertain, is not the immanence of that ideal in all our thinking necessarily also uncertain in exactly the same degree?

Blanshard, however, states that 'fully coherent knowledge would be knowledge in which every judgement entailed, and was entailed by, the rest of the system';[2] and this, I take it, means definitely at least that, although our knowledge is not yet fully coherent, nevertheless coherence is essentially a matter of entailment: to say, for instance, that a proposition Q coheres with another proposition P means at least that P entails Q.

In Blanshard's usage coherence, and therefore entailment, is a relation that may obtain not only among propositions and judgements, but also among experiences, physical things, biological organs, etc.[3] Hence coherence would seem to be for him the name of a genus of relations, of which logical entailment, causality, the part-whole relation, the compound-component relation, etc., would be various species. The 'if . . . then . . . ' character is thus the generic one; and I see no objection to using the terms entailment or implication to designate it.

If so much is agreed, however, a comment then immediately suggests itself. To say that a proposition P entails a proposition Q

---

[1] A. C. Ewing, *Idealism*; *A Critical Survey*, p. 231, quoted in Brand Blanshard's *The Nature of Thought*, vol. II, p. 264.

[2] Op. cit., p. 264.

[3] Op. cit., pp. 265, 267.

means, in terms of truth-values, that truth of P would necessitate truth of Q; *but no less* that falsity of Q would necessitate falsity of P. Thus coherence of Q with P—entailment of Q by P—is compatible just as much with falsity of both P and Q as with truth of both. Hence it is not, by itself, a criterion of the truth of either.

But further, let us conceive a certain set S of propositions which is *perfectly* coherent (whatever perfectness of coherence of the propositions of a set may mean). Then, since any proposition P of S has a contradictory not-P excluded from S (since contradiction is negative of coherence), there will automatically be another set Z of propositions, consisting of the contradictories of the propositions constituting S. Hence, no coherent set of propositions can be comprehensive of *all* propositions.

Moreover, let P and Q be any two propositions of S, such that P entails Q. Then, automatically, there will be in Z two other propositions, not-P and not-Q, which will be such that not-Q entails not-P. Hence, the set Z will, automatically, be as perfectly coherent as the set S.

But if coherence is truth, or even a sufficient criterion of truth, then the propositions of Z, as well as those of S, are all true. Yet, by the law of contradiction, this is impossible since the propositions of each set are, one to one, the contradictories of those of the other. Hence coherence is not truth, nor, *by itself*, is it a criterion of truth.

One of the most eminent advocates of the coherence theory, F. H. Bradley, declares that judgements of perception and of memory are all fallible, and that the test of truth is system.[1] But, one may well ask, are not our judgements of system equally fallible? and what, anyway, is the criterion of *their* truth? How, for instance, can we tell whether or not a judgement that P entails Q is itself true? Must not this be something known to us, at least in some cases, as a matter not of coherence but of self-evidence?

Blanshard attempts to meet this crucial objection, but, as it seems to me, does not truly do so. He holds, as I understand him, that even presence of coherence is known through coherence as the test, but coherence of a somewhat different type, viz., 'coherence of a principle with the instances that exemplify it.'[2] But this,

---

[1] *Essays on Truth and Reality*, p. xi, and ch. VII.
[2] Op. cit., p. 258.

of course, does not answer the question asked above, for granting that something is not an instance of a principle unless it 'coheres' with that principle, the question remains *how* we can tell that something alleged to be an instance of a given principle *is* an example of it, i.e., 'coheres' with it. Blanshard perceives this, and his reply to the objection it constitutes is that the question is really illegitimate—that the demand for a criterion of the coherence of an alleged example of a principle with the principle 'is one that would be fatal to all criteria, for it would object to the criterion's having instances.'

But what exactly is then entailed by his statement that 'the whole demand is illicit'? Not, apparently, that we *cannot know* whether an alleged example coheres with a given principle. But, if we can and sometimes do know it, what can it then mean, to say that the question as to *how* we know it is illicit? Does it mean that although we know it, we do not know it *through* some other thing but simply 'see' it?

This is what Ewing, as quoted by Blanshard apparently with approval, holds. But, I then ask, is not this 'seeing' that something coheres with something else exactly what would ordinarily be meant by saying that the coherence is in such a case *self-evident*? And if so, how can Ewing assert that coherence might nevertheless be left 'in the position of the sole criterion'? I submit that the most Ewing could claim consistently with his admission of such 'seeing' would be that coherence is the only sort of thing which ever is so 'seen', i.e., is ever self-evident. But I see no reason to believe, *a priori,* that only coherence can be self-evident.

In this connection, it should be pointed out that if the contention of an adherent of the 'self-evidence' theory of truth should be (as it well can be) that the character called 'being true' *consists in* (not just is made known by) being evident (whether immediately or mediately) then the question 'whether it is self-evident that that which is self-evident is necessarily true,' which Blanshard quotes from Spaulding as an objection to the self-evidence theory of truth, would be obviously absurd.

The sound insight at the bottom of the coherence theory of truth seems to me to be only that, since there are many propositions the truth-value of which is not evident directly on the mere attending to them, we, therefore, cannot come to know it otherwise than *through* the fact that certain other propositions, the truth-value of which is somehow already known to us, entail the former. This, however, ultimately requires that both the truth-value of these other propositions, and also the presence of the entailment relation between them and the propositions considered, be directly evident in at least some cases.

9. *The pragmatic theory of truth*

A central thesis of contemporary pragmatism is that an idea is essentially a plan of action, and hence that to say an idea is true means that, when action is directed by the plan the idea constitutes, the action successfully brings about the result the plan envisaged.

Obviously, however, that an idea is a plan of action is true of only some of the things commonly called ideas; when pragmatists assert that an idea is a plan of action, they apparently mean by 'an idea' specifically a belief.

But a plan of action is simply a resolution by a person P to act in a certain manner M in a given situation. It is *based*, of course, on several things. One is that P desires a certain state of affairs S, not now existent, to come to exist. Another is belief by P that action by him in manner M would bring about S. But neither the believing of this, nor what is believed, viz., that a causal connection obtains between M and S, is a plan of action. Only the resolution to act in manner M is so. The belief, however, that action of kind M would cause state of affairs S, is potentially a basis not for just one plan of action, but for a variety of plans, according to what we desire; for instance, what we desire might be instead to prevent S. Thus, a *basis* for plans of action, viz., a belief as to causal connections, is one thing, and a plan of action itself quite another thing, for the first is to the second as a map is to an itinerary.[1] Confusion between the two is responsible for the error that a belief is a plan of action. Such surface plausibility as this error has arises from two solid facts. One of them, mentioned above, may be stated in a more general manner in terms of the notion of *property*, as follows.

Belief that a given substance is, for instance, gold, is belief that

---

[1] This point is clearly made and aptly illustrated in a study, entitled *An Examination of Dewey's Theory of Knowledge*, by W. M. Sibley of the University of Manitoba.

the substance has certain properties, $P, Q, R. \ldots$ But the properties of anything are the laws of its behaviour: to say that something G has property P means that *if*, when G is in circumstances of kind C, a change of kind E occurs in these circumstances, *then* G behaves in manner B. For example, that gold has the property called fusibility means that when heat is applied to gold, it melts; that a substance is poisonous means that when introduced into an organism, it causes the organism to sicken or die. Hence, in the case of things whose nature consists of some set of properties, belief that the thing has nature N is a potential basis for plans to deal with that thing in manners instrumental to ends of certain kinds.

The other solid fact which renders tempting the error that a belief is a plan of action is that, if we wish to know whether a given proposition is true or is false, we have in most cases to *do* something to discover this—we have to perform some operation.[1] The operation called for, however, may be of any one of many kinds. It may be an operation with words, i.e., a logical or mathematical operation—an inference. Or it may consist in counting physical objects (to find out, for instance, whether it is true or false that there are, say 25 cards in a given stack). Or it may consist in transporting ourselves to the Arctic and observing the birds (to discover whether is is true or false that penguins exist there). Or the operation may be that of putting a given key in a given lock and turning (to discover whether it is true or false that the key opens that lock); or that of putting a given book on one pan of a balance and a 1 lb. weight on the other (to discover whether it is true or false that the book weighs 1 lb.). Or, of course, it might be the very simple one of directly comparing the colour of one piece of paper with that of another piece, to discover whether it is true or false that one appears to us darker than the other.

In each case the operation, when performed, does or does not have the sort of result which the particular question we seek to decide describes; e.g., the number 25 as a result of counting the

---

[1] This fact, of course, slays at one stroke that famous myth, the 'spectator' theory of knowledge. But one must not confuse, as pragmatists are prone to do, the purpose, to discover the truth-value of a proposition (nor the operation by which this purpose is attained), with the purposes to the attainment of which knowledge of the proposition's truth-value, once attained (and the operations it suggests) can be made instrumental.

cards; or opening the lock as result of turning the key; or level-ness of the balance beam in the case of the weighing; etc.

If the operation does have the specified kind of result, the proposition is then pronounced true; if it does not, false. Moreover, that the operation is one that does have the specified result might then be claimed to be not a *sign* that the proposition is true, but to be what truth itself of the proposition *consists in*; and analogously with falsity.

The pragmatists who have conceived the pragmatic theory of truth most nearly in such terms are, I believe, the two Italians, Vailati and Calderoni. Leroux, who gives an account of their views, regards their conception as the one most faithful to the maxim of Peirce, but as 'much more precise and more comprehensive' than Peirce's conception.[1]

Peirce's maxim, of course, is: 'Consider what effects, that might conceivably have practical bearings, we conceive the object of our conception to have. Then, our conception of these effects is the whole of our conception of the object.' Peirce, however, restated this in French a year or so later, and in somewhat clearer form. An exact translation of this second version of the maxim would be: 'Consider what are the practical effects which we think capable of being produced by the object of our conception. The conception of all these effects is the complete conception of the object'.[2] Leroux states that Vailati and Calderoni 'respect the original sense of the maxim, but at once free it from all ambiguity by frankly sacrificing the term action to that of experience.' That is, they speak in terms of *prediction* rather than in terms of success of a plan of action.

But although this disposes of a number of difficulties, there remains even in this version of the pragmatic theory of truth a shortcoming inherent to any purely pragmatic definition of truth. For, if, in *all* cases, we can discover whether a proposition P is true or is false *only* by performing some operation, then, to discover whether it is true or false that the outcome of the operation we performed in a given case was the outcome specified, we must embark on a new operation. But to discover whether it is true or false

---

[1] E. Leroux, *Le Pragmatisme Américain et Anglais*, pp. 276–90.

[2] This amounts to saying that our conception of the nature of an object is our conception of the *properties* of the object, in the sense of 'property' stated above.

that this second operation has the outcome specified for *it,* a third operation has to be undertaken; and so on, *ad infinitum.*

Hence, a *purely* pragmatic theory of truth is unworkable for discovery of truth. To bring to a stop the infinite regress of verificatory operations such a theory implicitly requires before any truth at all can be discovered, it is necessary that, at *some* time, it should be *directly evident* that the outcome of an operation is, or is not, as specified. But this is to say that 'self-evidence' is then the *ultimate* criterion of truth.

Thus, what is sound in the pragmatic contention is only that there are many propositions whose truth-value is not directly evident; and that we can come to know *their* truth-value, if at all,only through the intermediary of some testing operation in the case of which it will be directly evident whether its outcome is or is not as specified.

The foregoing critcism obviously applies equally to any other form of the pragmatic theory of truth which ignores its own inescapable need to call in at the last the 'self-evidence' criterion of truth. For, that our plan of action has 'succeeded'; or that our demands are 'satisfied'; or that the consequences of a situation and those of our responses to it 'interlock', or 'interadjust'; or that our belief has 'worked'; and so on, either is sooner or later evident *directly*, i.e., without need of trying next whether it 'works' to believe that our belief did work, etc.; or else we have an infinite regress on our hands and therefore no verification at all, even partial, of anything.

10. *Truth as verifiability*

Let us now turn, however, to the somewhat different contention, at times put forward by pragmatists, that truth is verifiability.

Since 'verifiable' means 'capable of being made true', or 'shown true', to say that truth is verifiability means that a proposition is true if it is capable of being made true or shown true. But the question remains in what sense of 'true'? However, the contention that truth is verifiability seems to be essentially a proposal to identify truth with *performability* of some act of causation or of demonstration. The question still remains, of course, as to what specifically this act consists in. The answer would be that its nature varies with that of the proposition concerned; but that, generically, it would consist in 'successful' performance of some causative or demonstrative operation (such as counting, trying a key, looking for penguins, weighing a book, etc.)—'success' meaning that the operation turns out to have the particular result that had been envisaged for it.

I propose now to examine one by one the several more specific meanings which may be given to the contention that truth is 'verifiability' in the sense of performability of some specified operation with success.

First, it may mean that *we are in a position to perform at will* an appropriate *demonstrative* operation. If we are not in position to do it, the proposition concerned is unverifiable, and this means, one is then told, that it is *neither true nor false*—that it is *meaningless* to ask whether, or assert that, it is true or false. For example, Bridgman contends it is meaningless to say it is either true or false that 'somewhere in the decimal expansion of π there occurs the sequence of digits 0123456789', because nobody at present can prove it true or prove it false.[1]

The obvious comment, however, is that this contention rests on nothing more solid than confusion between truth and ability, and, indeed, known ability, at a given time, to demonstrate truth; or if not on confusion, then—which is worse—on a perfectly arbitrary demand that the established usage of terms shall be so violated as to make henceforth synonymous the two phrases: 'P is true' and: 'we know we are now able to prove that P is true'—a demand which would entail, for instance, that it is not true a rattlesnake is venomous, or the earth round, or a man tuberculous, etc., unless we can and know that we can at the moment prove it to be true; or indeed, that it is not true a man is deceiving us unless we are at the time able, and know we are able, to prove true that he is doing so!

A variant of the contention just discussed is that when we say a proposition is verifiable ('in principle' rather than actually), this means that we would be in position to perform at will the appropriate demonstrative operation if certain conditions, not at the moment fulfilled, were fulfilled—these conditions, however, being both specified and known not to imply violation of any law of

---

[1] P. W. Bridgman, *The Nature of Physical Theory*, p. 41.

nature, or, as the case may be, of logic; or contradiction of any fact.

This proviso is needed to rule out the sort of question-begging conditions which would make the contention mean only that we would be in position to perform the verificatory operation if we were in position to perform it. That is, the proviso entails, for example, that one could not specify, as one of the additional conditions needed, availability of a 'time-reversing machine' unless it were known that existence of such a machine would be consistent with all the laws and particular facts of nature; and this could not be known unless its materials, structure, and *modus operandi* were exactly described; or unless such a machine had already existed some time.

The variant we are considering implies that, if a proposition would not be verifiable under any conditions (conforming to that proviso) which one is at the time able to specify, then that proposition is again neither true nor false; and the criticism already set forth applies to this also.

But the variant, by substituting conditional performability of the demonstrative operation for categorical performability of it, escapes the absurdity of implying that it is not true a man is deceiving us unless we know we can prove true that he is doing so. For what is now implied is that it is not true unless, *if* the conditions specified were eventually fulfilled, we would then know that he *had been* deceiving us; and this implies no contradiction.

Even then, however, the objection mentioned earlier still remains, viz., that only appeal sooner or later to the 'self-evidence' criterion of truth could save us from an infinite regress of operations, and could reveal to us that our performance of the demonstrative operation had been successful.

Allied to the variant just discussed would be the contention that, to say that every proposition is either verifiable or confutable (i.e., either true or false) means that, for every proposition, there is some appropriate operation, possible in the sense defined by the proviso mentioned, and such that, if it were performed, its outcome would be the one or the other of two specified outcomes. Verifiability and confutability are then being conceived as properties of propositions in the same sense as that in which combustibility, or incombustibility, for instance, is said to be a property of any physical substance, or divisibility, or indivisibility by 5 a property of any whole number.[1] As before, however, the question remains as to how we could tell whether the operation had had the verificatory or the confutory outcome.

From this I turn now to the meaning given to the contention that truth is verifiability if the verificatory operation is conceived to be a creative rather than a demonstrative operation. The contention would then be that to say *P* is verifiable means *that we are in position to make P true if we will*.[2] This implies the famous contention that truth is something which happens to propositions, and that 'verification' is to be taken, in its etymological sense of 'making true', as the act or process which makes truth happen.

Ordinarily, if one should say that, on a certain day, verification happened to a proposition *P*, one would mean not that on this day truth was *conferred* on *P*, but that on this day somebody *discovered* that *P* is true. But sometimes there are made also statements such as that *facts* make propositions true or false; or again, that *events* make true or false—verify or confute—our predictions; and the event might be somebody's action. Since occurrence of an event is one kind of fact, the meaning of 'making true' is the same in both sorts of statements; but it is in the case of 'verification of a prediction by an event' that it seems most plausible to say that verification means making true in the sense of causing to become true. I shall therefore limit myself here to analysis of the meaning of 'making true' in a case of prediction. The analysis will apply automatically to the other sort of statement.

---

[1] I do not understand Nagel's objection (*Journal of Symbolic Logic,* vol. VI, p. 160) that 'since it is not stated under what conditions a proposition is true if the [testing] procedure were *not* applied, the definition [of truth] is incomplete'. For this seems like saying that a definition of, for instance, the 'fusibility' of gold is incomplete unless it states under what conditions gold is fusible if it is *not* subjected to the conditions of fusion. Fusibility is a *capacity* irrespective of time, for behaviour of a certain kind in the presence of certain conditions. Similarly, the definition of truth in view defines truth as the *capacity* of some propositions, irrespective of time, to cause a certain sort of effect (perhaps, for instance, to compel belief) under certain conditions. A property or capacity is a law of the behaviour of the entity which has the property; and a law is a respect of invariance through time, and has no date.

[2] This contention, like that just discussed, has a variant which would define truth as verifiability 'in principle' instead of as actual verifiability, and would define 'in principle' in the manner already described. What would have to be said concerning this variant may be gathered from what was said concerning the other, together with what is now about to be said.

It must be recalled to begin with that ordinary language does not systematically distinguish between propositions, propositional functions, sentences, opinions, judgements; and that it accordingly applies to all of these the adjectives 'true' and 'false' without realizing that they mean very different things as applied to each. We are concerned here, however, with their meaning as applied to propositions. How, then, is a prediction related to a proposition?

The statement: 'Jim will sing tomorrow from 3 to 4 p.m.' formulates a prediction because the time at which it is uttered is earlier than the time it mentions. But the proposition itself, which is content of the opinion formulated by that statement, is not a prediction. Futureness, pastness, or presentness are in no way constituents of *it*. This is shown by the fact that the time which is a constituent of the proposition could be specified simply by naming it; for example, as 'Aug. 31, 1943, from 3 to 4 p.m.', instead of by means of its relation to the time of utterance of the statement.

Let us suppose that the proposition as to Jim's singing on August 31, 1943, from 3 to 4 p.m. is true. Then, a statement that it is true would have a slightly different form according to the time of its utterance:

If uttered on August 30 it would be: That Jim *will sing* on August 31 1943, from 3 to 4 *is* true (*not* will be true). The statement *then* is a prediction.

If uttered between 3 and 4 on August 31, it would be: That Jim *is singing* from 3 to 4 on August 31, 1943, *is* true.

If uttered on September 1, it would be: That Jim *was singing* from 3 to 4 on August 31, 1943, *is* true (*not*, was true). The statement is then a 'postdiction'.

Thus, the proposition as to Jim's singing on August 31 from 3 to 4 does not become false, or neither true nor false, after 4 p.m., for *it* has nothing to do with any time after 4. Nor for a similar reason, was that proposition false, or neither true nor false, before 3. Truth and falsity have no dates at all, because they are not events. What is an event, and occurs from 3 to 4 if the proposition is true, is singing, not truth; and it is also singing, not truth, which Jim's decision to sing makes happen.

Discovery by us that the proposition is true occurs at that same time if we happen to be present; but might happen only later, through testimony, if we were not there at the time. For three dates are to be carefully distinguished: (a) the date which is a constituent of the proposition; (b) the date on which we assert the proposition; and (c) the date on which we verify, i.e., discover the truth-value of, the proposition. The date of assertion and that of verification may, but need not be the same; and also may, but need not be the same as the date which is a constituent of the proposition.

What then is it that 'makes true' a prediction, and in what sense of 'making true'?

As we have seen, a prediction is not itself a proposition but is the *asserting* (or denying) of a proposition. A prediction, then, is an *opinion*; and 'true' and 'false', if applied to an opinion, mean 'sound' and 'erroneous'. Whether an opinion is sound or erroneous, however, is a matter of whether the asserting or denying which is a constituent of it—the believing or disbelieving—*accords with* the truth-value of the proposition which is content of the opinion: if the proposition is true *and is believed*, or false *and disbelieved,* the opinion is sound. Otherwise, erroneous. Hence, what makes an opinion 'true', i.e., sound, or 'false', i.e., erroneous is *that accord or disaccord.* And 'makes' therefore means here, not, 'causes' soundness or erroneousness of the opinion, but *constitutes* soundness or erroneousness of it.[1]

11. *The correspondence theory of truth*

What the correspondence theory is depends on what specifically it is, which is supposed to correspond to what. If what is in question is correspondence of a declaratory sentence to the opinion it is intended to formulate, then correspondence and non-correspondence mean, not truth and falsity of propositions, but semantical and syntactical correctness and incorrectness of wording. If what

---

[1] It is true that a given proposition can be now believed, and later disbelieved. This change of epistemic attitude *causes* replacement of an erroneous opinion by a sound one; or vice versa. But if one describes this by saying '*becomes* sound', instead of 'is replaced by a sound opinion', then what one is speaking about is an *opinional function,* not an opinion. And similarly, if one speaks of a *change* of truth-value, it is a propositional function, not a proposition, one is speaking of; i.e., changing the value assigned to the variable in a propositional function yields a different proposition, not a change in the truth-value of the same proposition.

is in question is the accord or disaccord of one's belief or disbelief with the truth-value of a given proposition, then correspondence means, again not truth and falsity of propositions, but soundness and erroneousness of opinions.

When it has been 'ideas', in the sense of entities mental or subjective, that have been supposed to correspond, or not, to 'reality' or to 'facts' in the sense of entities nonmental or objective, then correspondence has usually been held to mean *likeness* of the former to the latter. Likeness or unlikeness, however, is something knowable only by comparing the two entities concerned; and the question remains, how, under the initial assumption, this can be possible. Moreover, if we are in position to observe both of the terms to be compared—the 'reality' itself, as well as the 'idea'—then no function seems to remain for the idea. Hence, when we speak of comparing our idea with 'the fact', 'the fact' is likely to be only the opinion that resulted or will result from some more elementary, and, we hope, less precarious, cognitive attempt—such perhaps as a perceptual instead of a speculative one.[1]

If correspondence or non-correspondence, however, are to mean truth or falsity of a proposition, then they can only be correspondence or non-correspondence between the *quid* constituent and the *ubi* constituent of the proposition itself. That is, the correspondence or absence of it must be internal to the proposition, and not as between the proposition and something external to it. Even then, however, the question remains, as to just what relation it is, which constitutes 'correspondence' between the *ubi* and the *quid*, and how we can know whether, in any given case, it obtains or does not. Calling it correspondence is no more of a theory as to this than is calling it truth.

12. *The self-evidence theory of truth*

As regards the self-evidence theory, which is perhaps most justly associated with the name of Descartes, I shall at this point only mention briefly some objections to which it is manifestly open. They are essentially, (a) that some things which are not self-evident are nevertheless known to be true; (b) that some things which are or have been claimed self-evident are nevertheless false; and,

---

[1] cf. A. C. Ewing, op. cit., p. 198.

therefore, that (c) to determine whether something is really or only seemingly self-evident, we need a criterion of self-evidence, which criterion, then, rather than self-evidence itself, is the ultimate criterion of truth. Lastly, there is the difficulty that (d) the term self-evidence is itself ambiguous: We need not only a method for identifying in practice the *cases* of 'self-evidence', but also, and first, to know what *kind* of thing is meant by the word—how, for example, it is related to *complete* evidence, and to *direct* or *immediate* *evidence*.

Since, in earlier sections of this part of the paper, I have endorsed, at least by implication, the 'self-evidence' theory of truth, I mention these objections to make clear the nature of the task which confronts any proponent of a theory so labelled. How adequately I may have succeeded in performing that task in the remaining part of the paper will have to be judged by the reader.

5

13. *Attainment of knowledge of the truth-value of any proposition is a* *conscious event*

That we know *some* propositions to be true seems to me wholly certain. Were any one to question it, his questioning it would constitute complete proof that the proposition that it can be questioned is true. But if the truth of *this* proposition is completely proved, this proposition is then known to be true. Therefore, *some* propositions—at least this one—are known to be true.

But, as was pointed out in earlier comments on the coherence and the pragmatic theories, whatever proposition P it be, which we know or may come to know to be true; and whatever may be the process by which we come to know it to be true; the process itself, or if not, then at least the consummating step of it—that last step upon which, but not until which, knowledge of the truth of P is actually attained—must consist of a change of some kind in our own immediate consciousness. To come to know, for instance, that it is true that the temperature of a given liquid is 180°, we may proceed by immersing a thermometer into the liquid and looking at the graduation on a level with which the top of the mercury comes to rest. But even then we cannot know that it is true the temperature is 180° unless our looking, together with various

172

things we already know, causes a certain specific change in our state of consciousness.

Again, the alteration in one's external relations which constitutes becoming an uncle is one event; but knowing that it is true one has become an uncle is another event, which cannot occur unless there occurs in our immediate consciousness a change of a certain specific sort, brought about more or less indirectly by the birth of the child.

Thus, the truth or falsity of any proposition we may come to know to be true or to be false must ultimately be the two values of which is capable the independent variable of some causal function (however direct or indirect) whose dependent variable has for *its* two possible values one or the other of a certain two kinds of states of consciousness. Only some state of consciousness can be the ultimate criterion of the truth or falsity of any proposition we may come to know to be true or to be false, since otherwise the process of discovery of truth or falsity, however far it had gone, would stop just short of consummation.

This same crucial point may be put otherwise by saying that, on any occasion on which we obtain knowledge that proposition P is true, either the knowledge is being obtained *through* (as final step) a clear immediate experience of some sort, which is then the ultimate sign or criterion of the truth of P; or else the proposition P itself is *that* we are having a certain clear immediate experience; in which case knowing that P is true *consists in* occurrence of that very experience.

14. *Truth and its ultimate criterion*

I now submit that the immediate experience which is the ultimate criterion of truth is the experience called *belief*; and of falsity, disbelief; and that the truth itself of a proposition consists in *ultimate* undisbelievability of the proposition; and falsity, in *ultimate* unbelievability of it.

This contention, if not misunderstood, should give neither comfort to fideists nor offence to scientists; but since much is packed into the qualifying adjective, 'ultimate' and also into the word 'proposition', misunderstanding will be unavoidable unless the cautions and explanations that follow are given their full weight.

15. *Two possibilities of confusion*

For one thing, it is necessary to guard against the possibilities of confusion arising from the fact that, when we are attempting to ascertain whether a given proposition is true or is false, there are two other tasks one or the other of which we often have to perform at nearly the same time, and which, therefore, we may easily mistake for the former or for a part of it.

One of these two other tasks is that of *deciphering* the verbal expression which formulates the proposition we are concerned with. For most of the propositions the truth or falsity of which we judge in the course of a discussion or as we read become objects of our attention as a result of our deciphering the sentences we hear spoken or see on the page. But our deciphering of a sentence may be correct or incorrect in the sense that the proposition which it brings to our attention may be either the same or not the same as the one the utterer of the sentence intended it to formulate. And the point I wish to emphasize is that the question as to the correctness or incorrectness of our deciphering must not be confused with the question as to the truth or falsity of the proposition the utterer intended his sentence to formulate. If our deciphering happens to be incorrect, then our Yes or our No does not really represent agreement or disagreement by us as to the truth-value claimed for the proposition by the utterer of the sentence; it represents only misapprehension on our part as to what proposition he asserted.

The other task, which also must not be confused with that of discovering the truth-value of a proposition, is that of ourselves *formulating* the proposition concerned. This task is not always required, for sometimes we are able to judge the proposition without first formulating it. For example, if in looking through a house I think of renting I perceive a door in one of the rooms, I may wonder whether or not it opens into a closet; but for this I do not need at all to put the topic of my wonder, i.e. the proposition as to the truth-value of which I am curious, into uttered words or even word-images. And I may also not formulate the discovery I make when I open the door. If I do formulate it, however, the question arises whether my formulation of it is correct or incorrect according to the syntactical and semantical rules of the language I mean to use. But this question too is not to be confused with the question as to whether the proposition itself, which I attempted to formulate, is true or is false.

16. *Ultimate versus initial undisbelievability*

Again, my contention as to the nature of truth must not be taken as implying denial of the plain fact that many persons believe some false propositions and disbelieve some true propositions. For what I contend is not that the propositions concerned in these cases are *initially* unbelievable or undisbelievable, but only that they are so *ultimately*, i.e. at whatever time decisive evidence as to their truth-value may be in and have been grasped.

Obviously, so long as only part of what would be decisive evidence is in, all we can be *certain* of, i.e. can know to be true, is that, on this partial evidence, the *probability* that the given proposition is true is, as the case may be, greater or less than, or the same as, on the still more limited evidence we had earlier; or perhaps, how the probability of it on that evidence compares with the probabilities of truth of certain other propositions on specified bodies of evidence.

That most of the propositions of which we know the truth-value are propositions only as to the comparative probabilities of certain other propositions is doubtless regrettable. Yet to know even this is much better than to know nothing at all; for probability, which has been called the guide of life, is a useful even if not an infallible guide. At all events, the important point to notice here is that, unless our 'quest for certainty' were *completely* successful as to *some* things, we would not have even probabilities as to any other things.

There is no space here, however, to consider the nature of probability or its relation to truth. My remaining task is only to make clear what 'self-evidence' means in the case of the propositions whose truth-value must, (as was pointed out in part 4), be 'self-evident' if coherence, or success of a plan, or fulfilment of a prediction, or correspondence, etc., is to be even an intermediary criterion of truth; and to show that the claim to 'self-evidence', for *these* propositions, is not invalidated by the objections which do invalidate it in other cases.

As a last remark before passing to this, however, attention may be called to the fact that truth and falsity, defined as ultimate un-disbelievability and ultimate unbelievability, are *properties* of pro-positions in the sense of 'property' mentioned earlier. A property in that sense is, let it be stated once more, a *power or capacity* of the thing that has it—sometimes exercised and sometimes latent—for some form of behaviour, or of action on something else. Ultimate undisbelievability or unbelievability—whether at a given moment manifest or latent—are thus properties of propositions just as cor-rosiveness, i.e., capacity to corrode certain things, is a property of some acids; poisonousness, a property of some substances; in-visibility, sapidity, etc., properties of some others.

17. *Evidence*

The adjective, self-evident, is often used in the sense of *perfectly* evident. I propose, however to use it only in the strict sense which contrasts 'being self-evident' with 'being made evident by some-thing else'. Within the latter category, it is important further to distinguish between the cases where the evidenced is *directly* evi-denced by a given evidential item, and the cases where it is so *indirectly*, i.e., through an intermediary evidential chain, whether long or short. We have, then the three categories, being indirectly made evident by. . .; being directly made evident by. . . .; and being self-evident. In the last, the evidenced item is strictly identi-cal with the evidencing item. For these three categories I shall use the terms *indirectly evident, directly evident, and self-evident* (or *in-herently evident*).

Moreover, I shall concern myself here only with the cases in which 'evident' means *perfectly* evident; for, as pointed out earlier, unless *some* things were perfectly evident, nothing could be evi-dent even in degrees short of perfection. Furthermore, so far as I can see, there is no reason to suppose that only what is self-evident can be perfectly evident. It seems quite possible that something should be perfectly evident directly, or even indirectly.

Examples of propositions the truth-value of which is perfectly evident *directly*, would be all propositions as to the apparent occur-rence, or the apparent nature, or the apparent interrelations, of appearances as such, i.e., of appearances considered independently of whether or not they are appearances *of*—signs of—something other than themselves. No mistake by the person concerned is possible as to the truth-value of such propositions, for where appearances as such alone are concerned, appearances constitute reality and reality consists in appearance.

For example, the truth of the proposition that the colour I intuit as I look at the letters on this page, and the colour I intuit as I look at the spaces between the letters, appear to me different is *perfectly* evident to me; that is, it is known by me beyond all possibility of error.

If the question is now asked, *how* the truth of that proposition is known to me, i.e., what is the evidence or criterion of its truth, the answer is that when I try to disbelieve that proposition, even then I still believe it completely. That I so believe it is, in this and every other such proposition, the sole and sufficient evidence of its truth, and it is *direct* evidence of it.

Another proposition of this type would be that, as I look at these two dashes:— —, the direction of the line I intuit as I look at the first appears to me exactly the same as that of the line I intuit as I look at the second. This example is specially interesting because it illustrates the sort of judgement ultimately involved in all the pointer-readings of the physical sciences.

Other propositions of the class under consideration would be those each of us would ordinarily formulate in such sentences as 'I wonder', 'I am afraid', 'I feel pain', 'I feel nausea', 'I itch', 'I taste bitter', etc. Other propositions, not of the same class, but, I submit the truth of which is likewise perfectly evident, and likewise evidenced directly by the fact that they are believed, notwithstanding any effort to disbelieve them, by everyone who apprehends their constituents, would be those we would normally be intending to formulate by such sentences as the following: 'If all men are mortal and Socrates is a man, Socrates is mortal'; 'If a man is both tall and handsome, he is tall'; 'If none of the beans in a bag of beans is a lima bean, it is impossible that a bean drawn at random from them should be a lima bean'; 'If there is one lima bean among them, it is then possible'; 'If there are ten, the probability of it is greater than if there is only one'; etc.

That propositions such as those which these statements are intended to formulate are known to be true is what makes even imperfect *indirect* evidence possible. The question whether, or how far, such propositions as just illustrated are verbal rather than 'real' is of course legitimate, but is irrelevant to the question whether, even if they are verbal, the evidence we have for their truth is perfect, and of what nature it is.

Let us, however, now return to the first example considered. The evidence which guarantees to me the truth of the proposition that the colour I see as I look at the letters, and the one I see as I look at the spaces between, appear different to me is, it was pointed out, simply that I believe the colours look different to me. But, we may now finally ask, what evidence have I *that I believe* that the colours look to me different? The answer to this is that *occurrence of belief is its own evidence*. Like light, which reveals not only other things but also itself, belief certifies not only the proposition here believed (as to the colours), but also the proposition as to its own occurrence at the time. This, moreover, is the only case where truth *consists in* belief and belief *constitutes* truth (not, is direct or indirect evidence of truth). That is, this is the only case of *self-evidence* strictly so called. For even in the case of disbelief, that it is true I disbelieve a given proposition is itself finally established solely by the fact that I *believe* that I disbelieve the given proposition. Of course, it is possible to be in doubt as to whether one believes something; but what is then certain is that one is in doubt about it, and this is certified by one's *belief* that one is in doubt.

12.

PROPOSITIONS, OPINIONS, SENTENCES, AND FACTS*

There is perhaps no question more basic for the theory of knowledge than that of the nature of propositions and their relations to
judgements, sentences, facts, and inferences. Yet even the philosophers who give it explicit consideration seldom heed consistently in practice the implications of their own answers to it. In
this paper I attempt to formulate with some precision at least the
main points of what seems to me the right answer to that question,
and to exhibit a number of interesting and important consequences
of it.

1. The 'epistemic attitudes'

Stebbing states that 'A proposition is anything that is believed,
disbelieved, doubted, or supposed'[1]. But since, as Stebbing herself
would probably grant, there are countless propositions never yet
considered and therefore never yet believed, disbelieved,
doubted, or supposed by anybody, her statement should be
amended to read that a proposition is anything *susceptible* of being
believed, disbelieved, or doubted. Let us first consider belief, disbelief, and doubt.

These, as W. E. Johnson has emphasized, are no part of any
propositions but are *attitudes* that some persons have towards some
propositions.[2] I propose to say that belief and disbelief are respectively the extremes of a unique kind of attitude, which has degrees.

* *The Journal of Philosophy*, vol. XXXVII, No. 26, 1940.
[1] *A Modern Introduction to Logic,* p. 33.
[2] Cases in which belief, disbelief, or doubt is present but is not towards
any proposition are relevant not to epistemology but to psychopathology.

If we call this kind of attitude 'inclination to believe',[1] then belief will be defined as its maximum (100%) degree and disbelief as its minimum (0%) degree; or if we prefer to call the attitude 'inclination to disbelieve', belief is then its minimum and disbelief its maximum. Any degree of 'inclination to believe' (e.g., 25%) is thus one and the same thing with the *supplementary* degree (here, 75%) of 'inclination to disbelieve'. The various degrees of this sort of attitude I shall call the various *epistemic attitudes*.[2]

Cases where inclination to believe is *greater* than inclination to disbelieve will be called cases of *positive inclination to believe* (or negative inclination to disbelieve); and cases where it is *smaller* will be called cases of *negative inclination to believe* (or positive inclination to disbelieve).

Cases where inclination to believe is *positive* or is *negative* are cases of *opinion*; and any epistemic attitude consisting of some degree of positive or of negative inclination to believe is an *opinative* attitude.[3]

The degree of inclination to believe which is *neither* positive nor negative will be called *dubitancy* rather than doubt, for 'doubt' in ordinary usage has several senses. In phrases such as 'I am in doubt as to whether or not . . . ,' or 'The point in doubt is whether or not . . . ,' 'doubt' has approximately the meaning for which I have just proposed 'dubitancy'. But in the more frequent cases where 'doubt' is followed by 'that' or 'what', e.g., 'I doubt that he will come', 'I doubt what he asserts', 'to doubt' rather means to have positive but not maximal inclination *to disbelieve*. Nevertheless, we should ordinarily also be said to have 'some doubt' even in the opposite cases, viz., those where we have positive but not maximal inclination *to believe*. To avoid ambiguity, then, let us

---

[1] I am using these words not as a description of the attitude, but as *a name* for it.

[2] No claim is intended that the degrees of inclination to believe can be accurately quantified. Such figures as 25%, 75%, are used here only as expository devices.

[3] The term 'inclination to believe' as used here is formally analogous to the term 'probability'. That is, just as in non-technical usage 'probable' is opposed to 'improbable', but in technical usage covers the whole range from 'certainty' (or better, necessity) to impossibility, so the term 'inclination to believe' would in non-technical usage mean what has been called above *positive* inclination to believe, but in the technical usage proposed it covers the whole range from belief to disbelief, both inclusive.

gree that 'doubt', as a technical term, will be the name for any degree of inclination to believe *other* than the maximal and minimal. Dubitancy will thus be the exactly middle degree of doubt.

The diagram (below) represents the various degrees of inclination to believe by the various positions above the horizontal of a

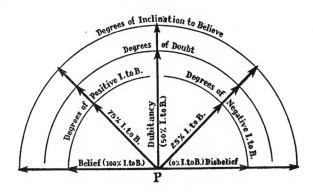

pointer revolving about the point *P*. The various arcs drawn are labelled in accordance with the definitions given. Where an arc is drawn, terminating just short of the horizontal or vertical, this means that only the degree represented by the horizontal or vertical is excluded from the degrees represented by the arc.

2. *Propositions, opinions, and judgements*

A belief, or *a* disbelief, is a proposition *together with,* respectively, the attitude of belief or of disbelief towards it. More generally, *an* opinion is a proposition together with some degree of positive or of negative inclination to believe it. To refer to a proposition together with the dubitancy attitude towards it, the terms 'a dubitancy' or 'a dubitation' would be awkward, and the term 'a doubt' would be ambiguous. The best term I can think of is 'a question', if used with the proviso that the interrogative sentence which formulates a question shall not also itself be called 'a question' (as often it is in non-technical usage).

As regards *judgement*, to judge is to decide between alternatives and the term '*a* judgement' is therefore best reserved for *an opinion reached through choice between alternatives.* Since many opinions are reached without consciousness of their alternatives, simply by imitation or suggestion, 'opinion' is a wider term than 'judgement'. All judgements are opinions but not all opinions are judgements. Lastly, for a proposition together with *any* one of the epistemic attitudes towards it, I shall use the term '*a predication*'.

3. *Sentences*

The formulation, i.e., the discursive symbol, of a predication is a *sentence*. The discursive symbol of an opinion is a *declarative* sentence; of a question, an *interrogative* sentence. A sentence is normally, but not invariably, a sign that the person who utters it has, towards the proposition it formulates, the particular epistemic attitude the sentence *also* formulates. A case where it is not a sign of this would be an interrogative sentence in a paper setting an examination, or any case where one formulates an opinion not held by oneself—the uttering of the sentence then constituting either quoting or lying.

It is important to realize that an opinion, e.g., a belief, may exist without formulation. When, for instance, a clerk unrolls paper with which to wrap a parcel, there comes a moment when he *believes*—indeed, believes through judgement—that the length of paper unrolled is sufficient to go around the parcel. But for this belief to exist in him formulation of it is not in the least required. That is, the words 'This length is enough' need not at all be uttered or imagined by the clerk and in fact seldom are.

4. *Symbols of epistemic attitudes and of propositions*

Perhaps no precaution avoids so many epistemological pitfalls as that of distinguishing in a sentence between the constituents of it which symbolize the proposition concerned (I shall call it the '*content*' of the predication the sentence formulates), and the constituents which symbolize the epistemic attitude towards that proposition. The latter constituents are such words as 'is' or 'is not' or more generally, the *affirmative* or *negative* form of the verb whether or not modalized (e.g., by 'may', 'must', 'cannot', 'probably', etc.).[1]

---

[1] This parenthesis is not to be taken as claiming that 'It is probable that . . .', or the adverb 'probably', always means simply that the person who

If we eliminate these constituents from the sentence, then what we have left of it symbolizes *only* the proposition. For example, in the sentence 'Napoleon was short', 'was' formulates the attitude of belief,[1] and 'Napoleon, short' formulates the proposition believed. In the sentence 'Napoleon was not short', the proposition is the same, viz., 'Napoleon, short' but the words 'was not' symbolize disbelief.[2] Again, if from the relational sentence 'John loves Mary' we eliminate the symbol of the epistemic attitude, viz., here the affirmative form of the verb, we have left 'John loving Mary' as symbol of the proposition believed. The sentence 'John does not love Mary' formulates the *same* proposition, but disbelief instead of belief towards it.

The question of negative terms naturally suggests itself here, but I think need not be gone into at any length for the purposes of this paper. I shall only say that I would accept 'not short' as a negative term only if it is taken as synonymous with 'either tall or medium-sized'; but not if it is taken as synonymous with 'either tall, or medium, or dark-eyed, or soluble in alcohol, or divisible by 3, or . . . (every adjective *other* than 'short' and other than any implying 'short')'. I do not think anybody who declares 'Napoleon was not short' ever intends to express thereby belief that Napoleon was 'not short' in the *latter* sense. Rather, what he intends to express is belief that Napoleon was either medium or tall; or else disbelief that Napoleon was short.

The fact that a sentence symbolizes not only a proposition but also an epistemic attitude towards it—the two together being

---

utters the words has positive inclination to believe the proposition concerned. The claim is only that often, in ordinary discourse, a person who so speaks is actually expressing thereby only the presence in him of positive inclination to believe; and not also perception by him of a certain relation between the opinion he voices and certain items of evidence.

[1] Also, of course, the fact that the time of utterance of the sentence is later than the time of Napoleon.

[2] W. E. Johnson says that 'is' symbolizes two things at once—the assertive attitude and the 'characterizing tie', *Logic,* vol. I, p. 13. The latter, however, as he himself notes, is symbolized automatically by the mere juxtaposition of a substantive and an adjective. Therefore no separate, additional symbol for it is needed nor, I believe, occurs in ordinary language. That is, the declarative forms of the verb 'to be', as occurring between a substantive and an adjective, symbolize (in addition to the time and other relations symbolized by the various 'modes' of any verb) *only* the epistemic attitude present in the particular case.

what an opinion is—has the epistemologically important consequence that the examples of 'propositions' given in textbooks are in fact in almost all classes examples of *opinions*, and that opinions —not propositions simply—are then what is actually discussed there, usually unawares. And when the difference between propositions and opinions is kept in mind, it becomes obvious that, contrary to the usual teaching, *propositions are neither affirmative nor negative*. The distinction between affirmative and negative applies only to opinions and to the sentences which formulate them.

It also becomes obvious that the constituents of syllogisms or, more generally, of inferences are not propositions simply but opinions; and this in turn suggests that, as I shall try to show on some other occasion, not only frequencies, but also the degrees of inclination to believe these frequencies, are intrinsic to the concept of probability.

The distinctions pointed out in this and the preceding sections have other interesting consequences, some of which may now be pointed out.

5. *A sentence formulates a given opinion correctly or incorrectly*

A sentence considered as attempted formulation in a given language of an opinion, has one or the other of the two 'values', *correctness* and *incorrectness*. A sentence is a correct formulation of a given opinion in a given language if it presents to other users of that language exactly the same opinion the utterer of the sentence intended to present. If the sentence presents to them a different opinion, it is incorrect. Correctness or incorrectness of a sentence thus has nothing to do with the merits of the opinion the sentence attempts to formulate.

If a declaratory sentence, uttered without quotation marks or their equivalent, is intended by the utterer to symbolize an opinion he does not himself hold, then his utterance is *mendacious*. In the opposite case, it is *veracious*.

6. *An opinion is sound or erroneous*

'Truth' is often contrasted with 'error', but it is of the greatest importance to notice that since error is one thing and falsity another, *'truth' as opposite of 'error' is a different concept from 'truth' as opposite f 'falsity'*. Error is positive inclination to believe a proposition which is false, or negative inclination to believe a proposition which is true; and the opposite of error, which, to avoid ambiguity, I shall call *'soundness'* rather than 'truth', is what we have when we positively incline to believe a proposition which is true, or negatively incline to believe a proposition which is false. Thus, erroneousness and soundness are 'values' that only opinions, not propositions simply, can have.

Perception of this makes clear the inadvisability of speaking of a *sentence* as 'true' or 'false' unless we then specify whether by a 'true sentence' we mean one formulating a given opinion *correctly*; or one formulating a *sound opinion*; or one formulating an opinion the content of which is a *true proposition* (and analogously with 'a false sentence'). For the proposition which is the content of a sound opinion is not necessarily a true proposition: if I disbelieve a proposition which is false, my opinion is sound although its content is a false proposition. And if I disbelieve a proposition which is true, my opinion is erroneous although its content is a true proposition.

7. *A proposition is true or false*

When the question is raised what a proposition is, it often is answered by saying that a proposition is the sort of thing (and the only sort of thing) susceptible of being true or false. This answer, which so far as it goes I accept, means, more specifically, that every proposition has one of these two 'truth-values' and that no proposition has both; but that if one knows about something only that it is a proposition, then one does not know whether its truth-value is 'truth' or is 'falsity'.

The statement is occasionally met with today, however, that propositions are susceptible of other truth-values besides 'true' and 'false', e.g., 'probably true', 'necessarily true', etc. The opinion this statement is intended to formulate would be sound if it were *only* that a many-valued symbolic system is as possible as a two-valued one, and that the many values may, for formal purposes, be given any *names* one pleases, e.g., 'necessarily true', 'possibly false', 'not known to be true'; or indeed, 'anna', 'cora', 'dora', etc.[1]

---

[1] cf. C. A. Baylis, 'Are Some Propositions Neither True Nor False?' *Philosophy of Science,* vol. 3 (1936), pp. 156–66.

Otherwise it is unsound and rests on confusions between truth-value (of propositions), soundness-value (of opinions), and probability-value (of inferences); and between implication (which is a relation between propositions simply) and inference (which is an operation performed by some mind and having as its constituents not propositions simply but opinions).[1]

8. *Unlike truth and falsity, soundness and erroneousness have degrees*

The only epistemic attitude which would be *completely* appropriate theoretically towards a true proposition would be belief; and towards a false proposition, disbelief. But every proposition has one and only one of the two truth-values, 'true', 'false'. Therefore, even without knowing whether a given proposition P is true or is false, we know that any degree of inclination to believe it, other than either the maximal or the minimal, is theoretically inappropriate in some degree. This means that *there are degrees of soundness and erroneousness* although there are no degrees of truth or of falsity: If the proposition which is content of an opinion is true, and the inclination to believe that proposition is positive, the opinion is sound; but if the positive inclination to believe the proposition is *great*, the opinion is *sounder* than if the positive inclination is small. Again, if the content-proposition is true, and the inclination to believe it is negative, the opinion is erroneous; but if the negative inclination to believe is great, the opinion is *more erroneous* than if the negative inclination is small.

It should be noted, however, that 'error' is often used in another sense than the one already defined. In the latter, 'erroneousness' has 'soundness' as opposite. In this sense, two opinions, of which one is more erroneous than the other, both have as content *the*

---

[1] For a particularly glaring example of a *non sequitur* resulting from neglect of these distinctions, see P. W. Bridgman, *The Nature of Physical Theory*, p. 41. Bridgman there considers the statement that somewhere in the decimal expansion of π there occurs the sequence 0 1 2 3 4 5 6 7 8 9. He then argues that because today this statement cannot be either proved true or proved false, it is neither true nor false; whereas obviously the conclusion warranted is only that *today no one knows* whether it is true or false. In saying this, I am not objecting by implication to the defining of 'truth' in terms of verifiability, for I would myself so define it. But to define it *tenably* in such terms, it is indispensable to distinguish sharply between 'verifiability' as property of certain propositions, and 'verifiability' as ability of a given human being at a given time to verify certain propositions.

same proposition; and their difference in degree of erroneousness is a matter solely of their difference in degree of inclination to believe.

In the other sense, however, 'error' is used to refer also to the various degrees of *approximateness*, and its opposite is then '*exactness*'. When an opinion is said in this sense to be more erroneous than another, the two have as contents *two propositions in part different*. For example, if the fact is that a given shot did hit the bull's eye, then the opinion consisting in belief of the proposition 'This shot, having hit *far* from the bull's eye' is more erroneous (contains a greater error) than the opinion consisting in belief of the proposition 'This shot, having hit *near* the bull's eye'. It is in this sense that we speak of 'errors of measurement', the 'probable error' of a set of observations, etc. Both senses, however, have in common the element that the inclination to believe is negative where it should be positive, or positive where it should be negative.

9. *Subject and predicate*

It has often been asserted in recent years that some propositions, and in particular relational propositions, do not have a subject and predicate. The truth, I believe, is that *no* propositions, but all *judgements*, have subject and predicate; and this because the distinction between subject and predicate is neither formal nor objective, but solely epistemic. That is, it can be defined only in terms of the constituents of epistemic attempts.

An epistemic attempt is an attempt to resolve some question—some cognitional problem. And in every such attempt there is both a *datum* and a *dubitatum*. There is something the problem *is about* and something the problem *is as to*—something about which the question is (but not itself in question), and something in question about it. For example, the question stated by the interrogative sentence 'Was Napoleon short?' would ordinarily be *about* Napoleon (whose existence is then not in question but given), and *as to* stature or, more specifically, shortness of stature. And in the opinion reached *by deciding this question*, that is, in the judgement that, let us say, Napoleon was short, or in *any* judgement, the distinction between what was given and what has been found about it— the distinction between *datum* and *repertum*—is the distinction between the *subject* of the judgement and its *predicate*. A relational judgement, e.g., John loves Mary, then obviously has subject and predicate like any other. But its subject or predicate cannot be identified by examination either of the sentence which formulates it or of the proposition which is its content, but only by examination of the question the judgement actually attempts to resolve. For example, if the question was 'whom does John love?' then 'Mary' is the predicate; if the question was 'What emotional relation does John have to Mary?' then 'loves' is the predicate; if the question was 'Does the relation "loves" exist anywhere?' then 'From John to Mary' is the predicate, etc.

It is important, however, to notice that the distinction between subject and predicate, as defined above, is not the same as that between substance and attribute, or object and character, or particular and universal, or substantive and adjective.[1] In the first example used above, indeed, the subject of the judgement was a substance and the predicate was a character. But if the question had been not what sort of stature Napoleon had, but whether any cases of shortness of stature have existed, then, in formulating the resolving judgement, we should either have had to stress the word 'Napoleon', writing: '*Napoleon* was short' (instead of 'Napoleon was *short*'); or to rephrase the sentence to read: 'Shortness of stature existed in Napoleon'; for our question would then have been *about* shortness of stature, not about Napoleon, and *as to* existence of it. That is, shortness of stature would have been the *datum* or subject of our judgement and Napoleon its *repertum* or predicate. Thus, in descriptive (or, as I should prefer to say, quiddative) judgements the subject is an existent and the predicate a character; but in existential judgements the subject is a character and the predicate an existent.

The very same *proposition,* however, viz., 'Napoleon, short', was the content alike of the descriptive and of the existential judgements used as examples. Each of its constituents, therefore, was susceptible of functioning as subject (of a certain judgement) or as predicate (of a certain other); and the distinction between subject and predicate therefore cannot be made within the proposition itself. What can be said of a proposition is only that, since any proposition is the potential content of at least one pair of judgements (one existential and one quiddative), a proposition

---

[1] The last three pairs of terms are here used in Johnson's sense. See his *Logic,* vol. I, 5.

must always be analysable (in one or in several ways) into two constituents —one capable of functioning as *datum* of an existential or as *repertum* of a quiddative judgement, and the other as *repertum* of an existential judgement or as *datum* of a quiddative. In this paper, however, there is no room to indicate more explicitly than above what sort of intrinsic nature it is, which fits the constituents of the proposition to function in the ways just mentioned.

10. *Propositions and facts*

Some authors assert that the word 'fact' has a variety of senses. Cohen and Nagel, for instance, attempt to describe and illustrate four:[1] (1) 'Certain discriminated elements in sense perception', e.g., that which is denoted by the expression 'This band of colour lies between those two bands'. (2) 'The propositions which *interpret* what is given to us in sense experience', e.g., 'This is a mirror'. (3) 'Propositions which truly assert an invariable sequence or conjunction of characters', e.g., 'All gold is malleable'. (4) 'Those things existing in space or time, together with the relations between them, in virtue of which a proposition is true. Facts in this sense are neither true nor false, they simply *are*'.

Examination of these descriptions and illustrations of the alleged several senses of the word 'fact' reveals first that although these writers earlier[2] warned their readers against confusing propositions either with sentences or with the mental acts required to think of propositions, they themselves here lose sight of the distinction. Otherwise they could not speak of *propositions* as *interpreting* what is given us in sense experience; for interpreting is a mental act performed by us, whereas a proposition neither is a mental act nor performs any. The interpreting by us of 'what is given us in sense experience' consists in our *thinking of and affirming* a certain proposition. Again, these authors speak in the third statement quoted of propositions *as asserting*. But a propositions does not assert or deny anything: *we* assert or deny it.

I contend that '*a fact*' and '*a true proposition*' *mean identically the same thing*. The evidence is that the expression 'It is true that . . .' can always be substituted for 'It is a fact that . . .' and vice versa;

---

[1] *An Introduction to Logic and Scientific Method,* pp. 217–18.
[2] Loc. cit., p. 28.

and that nothing can be deduced from what either expression formulates, which cannot be deduced from what the other formulates. Furthermore, examination of Cohen's and Nagel's illustrations of the alleged four senses of 'fact' reveals that in each case the illustrating fact consists of *a proposition which is true,* and that what these authors distinguish are not four *senses* of the word 'fact' but four *kinds* of facts; and this—as perfectly proper in the context where they make the distinction—chiefly on the basis of the kind of evidence which makes known to us the truth of the propositions concerned.

Additional comments, however, are called for by their statement that 'facts' in the sense of things in space or time, together with the relations between them, simply *are*.[1] It may be noted first that, of *true* propositions, we can similarly say that they 'simply are', and cannot say (except redundantly) that they are true, nor (without a contradiction) that they are false. On the other hand, the expression 'true facts', which actually is not uncommon,[2] is improper only in that it contains a redundancy, and 'false facts' in that it contains a contradiction. Thus there is still an exact parallelism between what we can and cannot say of 'facts', and of 'true propositions'. And further, if we ask what exactly can be meant by the assertion that facts 'simply *are*', the answer would seem to be that if it is not the mere tautology that 'facts are facts', it must be that 'facts exist', i.e., that 'there are facts'. But then, similarly, one can say that 'true propositions exist', i.e., that 'there are true propositions'.

The truth of the matter would seem to be that the fourth of the alleged senses of the word 'fact' is, like each of the other three, only a fourth *class* of facts, viz., those loosely said to consist of 'things' and 'events' (as when we say that a tree, or an explosion, is a fact); but strictly consisting of *the existence* of a kind of thing or *the occurrence of* a kind of event, at some specific place in space or time or both. And 'existence of a tree here now', or 'occurrence of an explosion there then', are statements of *propositions*; and of *true* propositions if of facts at all.

If, by 'proposition', we mean the sort of thing alone susceptible

---

[1] cf. Stebbing, op. cit. 'Facts simply *are*; they are neither true nor false.'
[2] See, for instance, Whewell, *Nov. Org. Renov.* Table of Contents. There (p. xiv) art. 1 of chapter III is entitled 'Facts must be true.' See also p. 51.

of being believed, disbelieved, or doubted, then 'a fact' and 'a true proposition' mean identically the same thing. But of course, if by 'a proposition' we mean a *sentence*, or a certain sort of *thought* (not what is *thought of* by it), then indeed a 'true proposition' in either of these two senses is not the same thing as a 'fact'. Rather it then 'represents' or 'corresponds to' a fact. But I ask, what sort of thing is then the 'fact' corresponded to by the sentence or the thought? I submit that it is nothing other than *a true proposition,* in the sense of 'proposition' defined as the sort of thing alone susceptible of being believed, disbelieved, or doubted. That is, one cannot consistently *both* accept this sense, and deny that 'a fact' and 'a true proposition' are the same thing.

If the truth of a proposition cannot be said to consist in 'correspondence' of the proposition to a fact, what then can it consist in? I believe it can still be described as 'correspondence', but *as between the constituents themselves of the proposition.* What 'correspondence' means there, however, is too long a story for the present occasion.

13.

MOORE'S 'THE REFUTATION
OF IDEALISM'*

Professor Moore's 'The Refutation of Idealism', published in
1903, is still one of the most famous articles written in philosophy
since the turn of the century. Its acute and searching criticism of
the proposition that *esse* is *percipi* has been widely held to have
finally proved its falsity and thus to have robbed of their basis the
idealistic philosophies which in one way or another had been
built upon it. It is true that in the preface to his *Philosophical Studies*
—in which the article was reprinted in 1922—Moore writes that
'this paper now appears to me to be very confused, as well as to
embody a good many downright mistakes'. These, however, are
not specified, and, since he does not repudiate the article as a whole
it may be presumed that he still adheres at least to its essential contention. In any case, because of the influence the wide acceptance
of its argument has had on the course of subsequent philosophical
thought, the article as published is now a classic and commensur-
ate in importance with the celebrated proposition it attacks. This
is enough to justify a critical examination of it on the present
occasion.

As against Moore, I believe there is a certain class of cases concerning which it is true that *esse* is *percipi*. This class, moreover, is
the very one in terms of an instance of which his discussion is
worded. I think it can be definitely proved that, so far as this class
is concerned, Moore's argument does not prove, as it claims to do
—or even render more probable than not—that *esse* is *percipi* is
false. I shall, however, try to show not only this but also that, for
this class of cases, *esse* is *percipi* is true. The latter will be more

* From *The Philosophy of G. E. Moore*: vol. IV, *The Library of Living
Philosophers*.

difficult to demonstrate conclusively, but I believe I shall be able to show at least that the burden of proof definitely rests on those who would deny that even in these cases *esse* is *percipi*.

The considerations I shall set forth, however, will not constitute an argument for idealism, for I believe that there is also another class of cases concerning which it is false that *esse* is *percipi*. Accordingly, even if my argument is successful, its effect will not be to open the way for idealism; but only, on the one hand, to rob of its basis the kind of realism Moore's article has been used to support, and on the other and chiefly, to make clear that certain facts do belong to Mind, which that realism rejects from Mind.

1. *Moore's argument*

In what I shall say, familiarity on the reader's part with the text of Moore's article will be assumed, but I may state here briefly what I understand to be the essence of its argument. Using the sensation of blue as example, Moore points out that the sensation of blue admittedly differs from the sensation of green, but that both are nevertheless sensations. Therefore they have (1) something in common, which he proposes to call 'consciousness', and (2) something else, in respect of which one differs from the other; and he proposes to call this the 'object' of each sensation. We have then, he says, 'in every sensation two distinct elements'; and therefore assertion that one of them exists, assertion that the other exists, and assertion that both exist, are three different assertions. From this it follows that 'if anyone tells us that to say "Blue exists" is the *same* thing as to say that "Both blue and consciousness exist", he makes a mistake and a self-contradictory mistake.'[1] Just because the *esse* of blue is something distinct from the *esse* of the *percipi* of blue, there is no logical difficulty in supposing blue to exist without consciousness of blue.

The point on which turns the validity or invalidity of this argument is of course what sort of distinctness is to be granted between the sensation or consciousness and the blue; for existential independence is not a corollary of every sort of distinctness. Existential independence is entailed by distinctness of the sort we admit when we say that for instance cat and dog or green and sweet

---

[1] *Philosophical Studies,* Harcourt Brace & Co. (1922), 17–18.

are distinct, but not by the sort of distinctness we admit when we say that cat and spinal cord or blue and colour are distinct.

Moore believes that blue and the *percipi* of blue are 'as distinct as "green" and "sweet" '[1]; and if existential independence is to follow from this, 'as distinct' must be taken to mean here that the distinctness is of the same logical sort as that of green from sweet. To show that it is of the same sort Moore advances both destructive and constructive considerations. The destructive consist of his criticism (which I do not pause here to summarize) of the hypothesis that blue is 'content' of the sensation of blue; the constructive, of the positive account he himself offers of the relation of sensation to blue or, more generally, of awareness or experience to its 'objects'. This account is substantially as follows. A sensation is a case of 'knowing' or 'experiencing' or 'being aware of' something; and this awareness is not merely

> something distinct and unique, utterly different from blue: it also has a perfectly distinct and unique relation to blue. . . . This relation is just that which we mean in every case by 'knowing'[2] . . . the relation of a sensation to its object is certainly the same as that of any other instance of experience to its object[3] . . . the awareness is and must be in all cases of such a nature that its object, when we are aware of it, is precisely what it would be, if we were not aware.[4]

As against these contentions, I shall argue that if 'knowing' is taken as the name of a unique relation, then this relation is a generic one and two species of it have to be distinguished; that one of these allows the object known to exist independently of the knowing of it, but the other forbids it; that in the case of the latter relation the known is 'content' of the knowing in a sense not disposed of by Moore's criticism of that term and that in this very sense blue is 'content' of the sensation of blue and therefore cannot exist independently of it.

2. *Cognate vs. objective accusative*

I shall lay the basis for my argument by calling attention to a certain distinction mentioned and used by S. Alexander. It is the dis-

---

[1] ibid., 16.   [2] ibid., 26–7.   [3] ibid., 28.   [4] ibid., 29.

tinction between what is expressed in language by, respectively, the cognate accusative and the objective accusative—between, for instance, striking a stroke and striking a man, or waving a farewell and waving a flag.[1]

There is not, I believe, any word in the language to denote *that in general* (or perhaps *that ambiguously*) which has, to the activity a verb names, the same relation that *a noun in the accusative in general*—i.e., in the accusative no matter whether cognate or objective—has to the verb. I shall, however, need a word for this and will therefore borrow for the purpose from grammar the word 'accusative' itself—as W. E. Johnson, similarly, borrows from grammar the word 'adjective' to refer to the sort of entity which any word grammar calls an adjective stands for.[2] Thus, for example, I would speak of a stroke struck as cognate accusative, but of a man struck as objective accusative, of the sort of activity called 'striking'. But, for reasons of euphony which will appear later, I shall, instead of 'cognate', use the synonymous form 'connate'. Also, since the relation of 'objects' of awareness to the awareness thereof is what we shall ultimately be concerned with, and we must not allow our terminology to prejudge for us surreptitiously the nature of that relation, I shall use the term 'alien accusative' for what would otherwise be called 'objective accusative'. That is, I shall say that an accusative of an activity may be connate with or alien to—homogeneous with or heterogeneous to—the activity. For example, in what is expressed by the phrase 'jumping a jump', the jump is *connate accusative* of the activity called 'jumping', whereas in what is expressed by 'jumping a ditch', the ditch is *alien accusative* of the jumping.

3. *Accusatives co-ordinate or subordinate in generality to a given activity*

Let us next notice that the relations 'connate with' and 'alien to' (as they concern an activity and an accusative of it) may each be either symmetrical or unsymmetrical. Each is symmetrical when its terms are of strictly *co-ordinate* generality as for instance 'jumping' and 'jump' (connate accusative), or 'jumping' and 'obstacle' (alien accusative). An activity and an accusative of it, which, like these, are co-ordinate in generality I shall call respectively *connately*

---

[1] *Space, Time, and Deity*, vol. 1, 12.
[2] *Logic*, vol. 1, 9.

co-ordinate (or co-ordinately connate), and *alienly co-ordinate* (or co-ordinately alien).

On the other hand, the relations 'connate with' and 'alien to' are unsymmetrical when the accusative of the activity concerned is *subordinate* in generality to the activity. Accordingly I shall say that an accusative—for instance a leap—which is subordinate in generality to an activity which—like jumping—is connate with it, is *connately subordinate to* (or subordinately connate with) that activity. And similarly I shall say that an accusative—for instance a fence—which is subordinate in generality to an activity which—like jumping—is alien to it, is *alienly subordinate* (or subordinately alien) to that activity.

4. *An accusative connate with a given activity exists only in occurrence of that activity*

Close attention must now be given to the implications as to existence which go, or do not go, with connate and alien co-ordinateness and subordinateness. There will be four cases. I list and illustrate all four but the last two will be the ones of special interest for the purposes of my argument.

(1) When an accusative, e.g., an obstacle, is *alienly co-ordinate* with an activity, e.g., jumping, then obviously this accusative may exist independently of existence, i.e., of occurrence, of the activity: obstacles exist which are not being jumped, have not been jumped, and will not be jumped. On the other hand, in so far as the activity is of the kind represented by a transitive verb, it cannot occur independently of existence of an accusative alienly co-ordinate with it: jumping, in so far as transitive, obviously cannot occur without existence of some obstacle—some distance or thing—being jumped. Similarly striking, in so far as transitive, cannot occur without existence of some object—be it only empty air—being struck.

(2) When an accusative, e.g., a fence, is *alienly subordinate* to an activity, e.g., jumping, then again this accusative may exist independently of occurrence of the activity: a fence, for instance, which is a species of obstacle, may exist which is not jumped at any time. But here the activity, even when it is of a transitive kind, can occur independently of existence of a *given* accusative alienly subordinate to it: transitive jumping could occur even if for instance no fences existed but ditches did.

We now come to the two cases of special interest for the purposes of this paper—the two where the accusative is connate with the activity.

(3) When an accusative, e.g., a jump, is *connately co-ordinate* with an activity, viz., jumping, then this accusative cannot exist independently of existence, i.e., of occurrence, of the activity: a jump exists only in the jumping, a stroke in the striking, a dance in the dancing, etc.—the *esse* of a *saltus* is its *saltari*. But, although this obviously is true, it may be well nevertheless to pause here a moment to point out why it is true.

To do so, we must ask what exactly is the logical relation between jump and jumping, between the dance and dancing, etc., i.e., between the connately co-ordinate accusative of an activity and the occurrences of that activity. The answer is that the *nouns* 'jump', 'dance', 'stroke', name each a *kind*, viz., a kind of activity, considered independently of occurrence of cases of it; whereas the *verbs* 'jumping', 'dancing', 'striking', are the linguistic entities which not only likewise name the kind but in addition allude to *existence*, i.e., *occurrence, of a case* of the kind of activity they name. The various tenses of which the verb admits express the various possible time-relations between the time *of discourse about* a particular occurrence of an event of the given kind, and the time ascribed *by discourse* to that particular occurrence: the time of that occurrence may be earlier or later than, or the same as, the time of our discourse about it. The noun-form, on the other hand, wholly ignores these temporal relations because it denotes a *kind* of event— not a *case*, i.e., not an occurrence, of that kind—and kinds as such have no dates. Yet the kinds we are here considering are kinds *of events*, i.e., they are kinds the existence of a case of which consists in an *occurrence*—a particular event—at a particular time. Attention to these considerations enables us to answer our question: The reason why no jump, for instance, can exist except in the jumping, and why jumping, at whatever time, is always and necessarily the jumping of a jump, is that *jump stands to jumping as kind stands to existence of a case thereof.*

(4) Let us now finally consider an accusative, e.g., a leap, *connately subordinate* to an activity, e.g., jumping. It is obvious that the activity can exist, i.e., can occur, at dates when *the given* accusative does not: jumping may be of a jump of some species other than a leap; dancing may be of a dance of some species

other than the waltz; striking, of a sort other than a jab; etc.

On the other hand, *an accusative connately subordinate to a given activity cannot exist independently of that activity*: a leap exists only in the jumping thereof, a waltz only in the dancing, a jab only in the striking. That this is true is again evident even without explicit mention of the reason why it is true; but in any event the reason is that leap, waltz, jab, etc., respectively, stand to jump, dance, stroke etc., each as species to genus; that a case of the species cannot exist unless a case of the genus exists; and that, as pointed out above, existence of a case of the genera, jump, dance, stroke, etc., consists in, respectively, jumping, dancing, striking, etc., at some time.

5. A cognitum connate with the cognizing thereof exists only in the cognizing

So much being now clear, it may next be emphasized that although the activities so far used as examples were activities both motor and voluntary, the distinctions pointed out—between connate and alien accusatives and between accusatives co-ordinate and subordinate in generality to a given activity—in no way depend on the activities being motor and voluntary ones; and therefore that the implications as to existence which we found rooted in these distinctions do not depend upon these characters either. Rather, the distinctions and their existential implications are perfectly general: any sort of activity whatever has a connate accusative, and any sort of activity which is transitive has in addition an alien accusative; and further, *whatever the nature of the activity, an accusative connate with it (whether co-ordinately or subordinately) exists only in the occurrences of the activity.* Because this is true universally, it is true, in particular, of the sort of activity which is of special interest to us in these pages—viz., the one called 'cognizing' or 'experiencing'—notwithstanding that it is not, like jumping, a motor activity and notwithstanding that some species of it, e.g., sensing, are involuntary instead of, like jumping, voluntary. If we now agree to call any accusative of the cognitive activity a *cognitum,* then, in the light of the considerations that precede, it will, I believe, be admitted as evident that *any cognitum connate with a cognitive activity exists only in the occurrences of that activity.*

6. *Nature of the hypothesis I shall oppose to Moore's*

The question we now face, however, is whether such cognita as blue or bitter or sweet are connate with the species of experiencing called 'sensing', or on the contrary are alien to it; for on the answer to this depends, as we have now seen, the answer to the question whether the *esse* of blue or bitter or sweet is their *percipi*. Moore believes they are what I have called alien cognita of the experiencing. My contention will be on the contrary that they are cognita connate with the experiencing. At this point, however, I shall not attempt to prove this contention but only, first, to explain more fully what it means, and second, to dispose of two *prima facie* plausible objections to it. This will make evident that there does exist a genuine alternative to Moore's contention regarding the relation of blue to the sensing of blue; and will enable me to show that it is an alternative he neither disposes of nor considers. To show this, however, will only be to show that his argument does not prove what it claims to prove, i.e., does not prove that the blue can exist independently of the sensing of blue. Only after this has been done shall I give the positive evidence I have to offer in support of my own contention that the blue cannot exist independently of the sensing of blue.

The hypothesis, then, which I present as alternative to Moore's is that 'blue', 'bitter', 'sweet', etc., are names not of objects of experience nor of species of objects of experience but of *species of experience itself*. What this means is perhaps made clearest by saying that to sense blue is then to sense *bluely,* just as to dance the waltz is to dance 'waltzily' (i.e., in the manner called 'to waltz') to jump a leap is to jump 'leapily' (i.e., in the manner called 'to leap') etc. Sensing blue, that is to say, is I hold a species of sensing—a specific variety of the sort of activity generically called 'sensing' which, however (unlike dancing or jumping), is an involuntary and nonmotor kind of activity. In this as in all cases where the known is connate with the knowing, what is known by the knowing activity is then *its own determinate nature on the given occasion.*

With regard to the relation between blue and sensing blue, I further contend that the same remarks apply that were made above concerning the relation of jump and leap to jumping: the noun 'blue' is the word we use to mention merely a certain *kind* of activity (just as are the nouns 'waltz', 'leap', etc.); whereas the verb 'to sense blue' is the linguistic form we use when we wish not only to mention that same kind of activity but also at the same time to mention some *case*, i.e., some *occurrence*, of that kind of activity—the various tenses of the verb expressing the various possible temporal relations between the *time at which we mention* some case of that kind of activity and the time we mention as *time of that case itself*.

7. *The objection that what is sensed is not 'blue' but a case of 'blue'*

It might be urged, however—perhaps under the belief that it constitutes a difficulty precluding acceptance of my hypothesis—that what we sense is never blue or bitter in general, i.e., a *kind*, but always *a* blue or *a* bitter, i.e., (it would then be alleged) some *case* of blue or bitter.

To this I reply that 'blue' and 'bitter' are the names of certain *determinable* kinds, and that '*a* blue' or '*a* bitter' are expressions by which we refer *not to cases but to determinates,* i.e., to *infimae species,* of that determinable kind.[1] That a determinate shade of blue is logically not a case but a species, viz., an infima species, of blue is shown by the fact that even a perfectly determinate shade of blue is susceptible of existing many times, or no times, or only once, etc. That is, *qualitative determinateness neither constitutes existence nor entails existence.* Existence of qualitatively determinate blue, bitter, etc., is a matter of presence of them *at some determinate place in time.*

On the basis of these considerations, my reply to the objection mentioned above is then that we do not *sense a case* of blue, but that our sensing blue of a determinate species, i.e., our sensing bluely-in-some-completely-specific-manner, *constitutes occurrence of a case* of blue. That is, it constitutes *presence at a determinate time* of blue of that determinate shade, and therefore of course, of blue; just as our waltzing—which if we do it at all we do in some com-

---

[1] W. E. Johnson, in his chapter on 'The Determinable' (*Logic*, vol. I, ch. XI) misleadingly uses the names of the various colours as illustrations of names of determinates; whereas the fact obviously is that blue, for instance, is a determinable having as sub-determinables cerulaean blue, prussian blue, etc.; and that no names exist in the language for the truly determinate colours —for instance for cerulaean blue completely determinate as to hue and as to degree of brightness and of saturation. But we could, if we wished, assign names to the various *infimae* species of cerulaean blue—calling a certain one, perhaps, Anna cerulaean, another, Bertha cerulaean, etc.

pletely determinate manner—constitutes presence at a determinate time (and place) of that determinate species of waltz, and therefore automatically also of its genus, the waltz.

8. *The objection that one may be aware without being aware that one is aware*

If in any case of awareness of blue what one is aware of is, as I contend, the determinate nature of one's awareness on that occasion, then, it may be objected, it would follow that being aware of blue would be one and the same thing with being aware that one is aware of blue; whereas obviously they are not the same thing. To meet this objection, I shall first analyse the nature of the difference which is felt and which I acknowledge exists; and then I shall point out why this difference leaves untouched the essence of my contention.

If on an occasion when one has asserted 'I am aware of blue' one is asked or asks oneself whether this is really so, one then makes an additional judgement which (if affirmative) one formulates by saying 'I am aware that I am aware of blue'. I submit, however, that *this* judgement concerns the *appropriateness* of the concept, 'being aware' to the fact one is attempting to describe by saying 'I am aware of blue'. Or similarly, if I have asserted 'I know that Mary is eight years old' and I am asked or ask myself whether I 'really know' it and conclude 'I know that I know that Mary is eight years old', the question this answers is whether the concept labelled 'knowing' fits the status conferred upon my belief that Mary is eight years old by the grounds I have for the belief. I compare the particular sort of relation between grounds and belief, called 'knowing', with the actually existing relation between my grounds and my belief in the case of Mary's age, and ask myself whether this actually existing relation is a case of that sort of relation. This comparison—and not the examining of additional evidence as to Mary's age—is the ground of my assertion that I know that I know that Mary is eight years old. Just this sort of difference, I submit, is the difference between knowing and knowing that one knows, or being aware and being aware that one is aware.

But the statement 'I am aware that I am aware', which is a correct formulation of the sort of fact just illustrated, would not be a correct formulation of the fact—of a quite different nature—that whenever I am aware at all I am 'aware of an awareness' *in the same sense of the accusative* in which it is true that whenever I strike at all I strike a stroke, or that whenever I know at all I know a knowledge, or that whenever I dance at all I dance a dance. To express this sort of accusative of a given verb no *verb form* can correctly be used but only a *noun*; that is, for this sort of accusative of 'being aware' we cannot, except misleadingly, use the verb forms 'that I am aware' or 'of being aware', but must use 'of an awareness'. In this sense of the accusative, moreover, it is true not only that whenever I dance at all I dance a dance, but also that I dance in some specific manner, e.g., 'waltzily'. Similarly in this sense of the accusative, it is true not only that whenever I am aware at all I am aware (intuitively, not discursively) of an awareness, but also that I am aware in some specific manner, e.g., bluely.

Having now made clear the nature of my hypothesis as to the relation of blue to sensing blue, and defended that hypothesis from two *prima facie* plausible objections to it, I may add that the relation the hypothesis describes is the one I shall mean whenever I say that blue is *content* of sensing blue. That is, when I so use this term I shall mean that blue stands to sensing blue (or more generally, that any given species of experience or awareness stands to experiencing or being aware) as kind stands to occurrence of a case thereof. With this understood, let us now turn to Moore's criticism of what he calls the 'content' hypothesis.

9. *Professor Moore's criticism of the hypothesis that blue is 'content' of the sensing of blue*

The only place at which Moore's criticism of the contention that blue is content of the sensing or awareness of blue could be considered relevant to the meaning of 'content' I have stated to be mine is the place where he raises the question 'whether or not, when I have the sensation of blue, my consciousness or awareness is ... blue'.[1] He acknowledges that offence may be taken at the expression 'a blue awareness', but asserts that it nevertheless 'expresses just what should be and is meant by saying that blue is, in this case, a *content* of consciousness or experience'.

As to this, I can only reply that what I mean (as defined above) when I say that blue is the content of my awareness of blue is not

---

[1] Moore, op. cit., 26.

properly expressible by saying that my awareness is then blue *unless blue be taken as the name, instead of as an adjective*, of my awareness at the moment. That is, what I mean when I refer to blue as content of my awareness of blue is that my awareness is at the moment of the determinate sort *called 'blue'*, and not that it has, like *lapis lazuli*, the property of being blue; for when I assert, *of lapis lazuli*, that it is blue, what I mean is that it is such that, whenever I turn my eyes upon it in daylight, it causes me to experience something called 'blue'; whereas I mean nothing like this when I say, *of my awareness*, that at a given moment it is of the particular sort called 'blue'.

To speak of a blue awareness, I would insist, is improper in the same way it would be improper to speak of an iron metal. We can properly speak of a species of metal called 'iron', but if we wish to use 'iron' as an *adjective*, we have to apply it to something—for instance a kettle or a door—which stands to iron *not*, like 'metal', *as genus to species*, but *as substance to property*.

I conclude here, then, that Moore's criticism of the contention that blue is content of the awareness of blue is not a criticism of the contention that blue is a species of awareness—which is what I mean when I assert that blue is content of the awareness of blue. His criticism does not consider *this* contention at all and therefore does not refute it.

10. *Does existential independence follow from the fact that the awareness is* OF *blue?*

It is only because Moore does not in his paper consider as a possible meaning of 'blue awareness' the hypothesis that blue is a species of awareness rather than a property of it, that he is able to dismiss the possibility that 'awareness is blue' as unimportant even if true—saying that, in any case, the awareness is *of* blue, and 'has to blue the simple and unique relation the existence of which alone justifies us in distinguishing knowledge of a thing from the thing known'.[1] For he believes this relation entails in all cases that the known may exist independently of the knowing of it. But we have seen that this is so only in some cases. We do indeed speak of the tasting *of* a taste—e.g., of the taste called 'bitter'—and also of the tasting *of* quinine; but although 'tasting' in each case denotes a

---

[1] ibid., 26.

species of knowing, it obviously does not denote the same species
in both cases: the relation of tasting to taste (or to bitter) is not
the same as the relation of tasting to quinine or to cheese, etc.
Similarly, when we speak of the smelling *of* a smell and of the
smelling *of* a rose, of the hearing *of* a tone and of the hearing *of* a
bell, or—as Moore himself points out elsewhere[1]—of the seeing
of a colour, e.g., brown, and of the seeing *of* a coin, we are obviously using 'smelling', 'hearing', 'seeing', each in *two* senses notwithstanding that in each sense it is a species of knowing, and
notwithstanding that in each sense the knowing is *of* something.
Were any proof needed that the senses are two, it would be provided by the following consideration.

The two sentences 'I see red' and 'I see a rose' each represent an
attempt to describe in English a judgement made by the utterer—
something he believes. Now it is possible that 'red' or 'a rose' are
not the right words to describe in English what he believes he sees;
that is, either sentence may be an *incorrect wording* of his belief. But
in the case of the sentence 'I see red' the belief itself, which he uses
that sentence to describe, cannot possibly be a mistaken belief. It
cannot be erroneous because that which he believes is not anything more at all than is actually and literally seen by him at the
moment. In the case of the sentence 'I see a rose', on the other
hand, not only as before may the sentence be an incorrect wording
of his belief, but now in addition *his belief itself may be mistaken*:
that, which he believes he sees, may not be what he believes it to
be. It may be something else which *looks* the same as what he believes to be there, but the other characters of which are very different; for these other characters, e.g., tactual, olfactory, gustatory
ones, etc., of course cannot literally be *seen*. Odour, taste, hardness,
can be 'seen' only in the elliptical sense that the colours literally
seen *predict* to us a certain odour, taste, etc. But whenever what
we believe is something the nature of which is predicted or signified even in part instead of literally and totally observed at the
moment, error is possible.

The relation between seeing and seen or more generally between knowing and known is thus not as Moore's paper asserts 'a
simple and unique relation' (unless considered generically only)
but is of at least the two kinds just illustrated. Moreover if, as I

---

[1] *Philosophical Studies*, 187.

contend, the first of these two relations between knowing and known is the very relation between cognizing and a cognitum *connate* therewith, then in *no* case of that first relation is the known existentially independent of the knowing thereof. Therefore, from the fact that in *all* cases of knowing the knowing is *of* something, *nothing general* follows as to the existential independence or dependence of the known upon the knowing.

To prove such independence in a given case it would be necessary to show that when we speak of, e.g., the tasting of bitter or the seeing of blue, the tasting is existentially related to the bitter or the seeing to the blue not (as I contend) as cognizing is to cognitum (subordinately) connate therewith, but on the contrary, as, for instance, green is existentially related to sweet. But this is not shown by anything in Moore's paper. As just pointed out, the fact that the sensing or seeing is *of* blue does nothing to show it and, as I shall now make clear, neither does a certain additional fact to which Moore appeals.

11. *Does existential independence follow from the introspective distinguishability of the awareness from the blue?*

Moore asserts that in any case of awareness of blue it is possible (even if not easy) to distinguish by careful introspective observation the awareness from the blue. This I readily grant, but I deny that it constitutes any evidence at all of the existential independence it is adduced to prove, for the fact that the awareness is observationally distinguishable from the blue leaves wholly open the question which is crucial here. This question is whether the awareness is distinguishable from the blue as for instance green is from sweet—i.e., as a case of one species from a case of a logically independent species—or on the contrary (as I contend) as a case of a genus is distinguishable (by abstractive observation) within a case of any one of its species—for instance, as a case of the generic activity, 'to dance', is by abstractive observation distinguishable within any case of the species of that genus called 'to waltz'. That is, we can observe that a person is moving with the specific rhythm and steps called 'waltzing'; and then we can abstract our attention from the specific nature of the rhythm and steps and notice only the fact (common to the waltz, polka, one-step, fox trot, etc.) that he takes steps in a rhythmical manner, i.e., that he is 'dancing'. Indeed, observation *merely* that the genus 'dance' is the one to which belongs a case of activity concretely before us is what would normally occur if—perhaps through the rapid opening and shutting of a door—we had only a brief glimpse of the dancing going on in a room.

To prove that blue and awareness are distinct in the manner which entails existential independence, we should have to have the same sort of evidence on which is based our knowledge that green and sweet are existentially independent: we have observed, for instance, that some apples are green and not sweet, and that some are sweet and not green. That is, we should have to observe —i.e., to be aware—that at a certain time blue exists but awareness does not, and that at a certain other time awareness exists but blue does not. Of the latter we have a case whenever what we are aware of is something other than blue, for instance, sweet or green, etc.; but of the *former* it is impossible that we should ever have a case, for to be aware that one is not at the time aware is a contradiction.

This situation, it is true, does not prove that blue is existentially *dependent* on awareness of blue; yet just that sort of situation is what would confront us if blue *were* existentially dependent on awareness of blue; therefore that the situation we do confront *is* of that sort is circumstantial evidence, so far as it goes, of such dependence.

12. *Comment on some relevant remarks of C. D. Broad's*

It might be claimed, however, that the introspective observation by which, in awareness of blue, we distinguish the awareness from the blue is not of the abstractive kind I have described, but on the contrary of the same 'total' kind for the awareness as for the blue. This is perhaps what Moore means to assert when he says that 'to be aware of the sensation of blue is . . . to be aware of an awareness of blue; awareness being used, in both cases, in exactly the same sense.'[1]

Some light will perhaps be thrown on the issue by examination of certain remarks made by Broad. He observes that a sensation of red (the case would of course be the same with blue) seems obviously to involve an act of sensing and a red 'object'. But it is of particular interest to note his further remark that it does not seem

---

[1] Ibid., 25.

similarly obvious 'that a sensation of headache involves an act of sensing and a "headachy" object.'[1]

To me also it is evident that there is a difference between the two cases; and the important point is that, on Moore's view, there ought not to be any. *Both* cases ought to be introspectively analysable alike into an awareness—a sensing—and an 'object', viz., respectively, red and headache. The explanation of the difference is, I submit, as follows.

The eye, which is the sense organ with which the sensation of red is connected, is an organ susceptible of being oriented and focused. That is, the eye is capable of *looking*; and it does look in this sense whenever any colour is seen or even imaged, for the eye always has *some* orientation and *some* accommodation. But with any orientation and accommodation of the eye there goes a certain sort of kinaesthetic sensa (the sort connected with the muscles of the eyeball and of the lens). And these *kinaesthetic sensa*, I submit, are what Broad finds present in the sensation of red but absent in that of headache; for the latter is not, like the former, connected with an organ susceptible of orientation and accommodation and is therefore not, like the former, accompanied by characteristic kinaesthetic sensa. The difference Broad notices is really present, but it is not rightly described as presence in the one case of an 'act of sensing' absent in the other. What he calls an 'act of sensing' (or we can say more specifically, of 'seeing') is in fact only the kinaesthetic sensa which accompany the physical act of *looking*. Similarly one must distinguish between acts of *hearing, smelling,* etc., and the kinaesthetic sensa which always accompany the physical acts of *listening, sniffing,* etc.

The red, indeed, is existentially independent of the accompanying ocular kinaesthetic sensa for, on the one hand, a completely blind person (who of course does not see even black) has them and, on the other hand, if the eye muscles of a normal person were anaesthetized he could undoubtedly nevertheless sense red. But kinaesthetic sensa are not an 'act of sensing' the red. The genuine act of sensing, on the contrary, is distinguishable in the sensation of headache as well as in that of red; but it is not distinguishable from the red as the headache *as* red is from kinaesthetic sensa or from sweet, but, I now urge again in the light provided by

---

[1] *Scientific Thought,* 254.

removal of the confusion just discussed, *as* a case of the dance is distinguishable within any case of the waltz.

The point is now reached where I believe that the first part of the task I undertook has been accomplished. I submit, namely, that the preceding pages have shown that Moore's argument to prove that blue can exist independently of the sensing or the being aware of blue neither proves this nor proves it to be more probable than not. I now therefore turn to the second part of my task, which is to show that blue, bitter, or any other 'sensa' cannot exist independently of the experiencing thereof. This will be proved if I prove that blue, bitter, etc., are, as I have claimed, species, not objects, of experiencing.

13. *The hypothesis that bitter, blue, etc. are 'directly present' to the mind*

For this positive attempt I shall take as starting point a fact already mentioned. It is that if, in answer to the question 'What do you taste?' we answer at one time 'I taste bitter' and at another time 'I taste quinine', the relation of the tasting to bitter is *different* from that of the tasting to quinine. Or, to take another example, if, having been asked 'What do you see?' we answer at one time 'I see blue' and at another 'I see some *lapis lazuli*', it is obvious that the relation of the blue to the seeing of it is not the same as that of the *lapis lazuli* to the seeing of it. Or again, if to the question 'What do you hear?' we answer 'I hear middle C', and at another time 'I hear a bell', it is evident that the relation of middle C to the hearing of it is different from that of a bell to the hearing of it.

That it is different is obvious, but if it needed any proof it would be found in the fact that the judgement expressed by 'I hear a bell' is the judgement that the cause of my hearing the tone I hear at the moment is a thing of the kind called a bell; or that the judgement 'I see *lapis lazuli*' is the judgement that the cause of my seeing the blue I see is a substance of the kind called *lapis lazuli*; or that the judgement 'I taste quinine' is the judgement that the substance, presence of which on my tongue is causing me to taste the bitter taste I am tasting, is a substance of the kind called quinine. That is, in these examples, to taste or see or hear an 'object' is to take a taste or colour or tone one is experiencing as *sign* that the cause of the experiencing of it is, respectively, something of the kind called quinine, *lapis lazuli*, a bell. To have *this* relation to one's experiencing of a taste, colour, or tone is, in these examples, what being 'object' tasted, seen, or heard consists of.

Therefore if bitter, blue, and middle C are also to be spoken of as 'objects' respectively tasted, seen, and heard, it can be only in some *other* sense, not yet considered, of the word 'object'; for obviously it could not be maintained that 'I taste bitter' means (as in the case of quinine) that the cause of my tasting the bitter I taste is presence on my tongue of a substance called bitter taste, for 'bitter' is not the name of any kind of substance but of a kind of taste.

Our situation is then this. We have considered so far two sorts of relation a cognitum may have to the cognizing of it: one, the relation I have called 'content of', and the other, the relation ordinarily called 'object of', illustrated by the example of quinine as cognitum of tasting. *This* sense of 'object of' I shall label *sense A*, for convenience of reference. Now our problem was: is bitter (or) blue, etc.) *content of*, or *object of*, the tasting (or the seeing, etc., thereof? Admittedly, it is not 'object of' the tasting *in sense A*. But this does not force us to conclude that bitter is (as I maintain) content of the tasting if there happens to be some *third* sort of relation, which a cognitum could have to the cognizing of it, and which is also called 'object of' but constitutes what we shall now label *sense B* of 'object of'. The question therefore now is whether there is such a third sort of possible relation, and if so what exactly it is. The epistemologists who believe there is, usually describe it as 'direct presence' of the blue or bitter to, or 'immediate apprehension' of these by, the mind or consciousness. As against them I maintain that either these phrases are only other names for what I have called 'content of', or else they are figures of speech for which no literal meaning that is not absurd is available. I shall now attempt to make the latter evident.

The facts which, without our noticing it, suggest to us the employment of the words 'direct' or 'immediate' in the phrases mentioned consist of examples of directness or immediacy such as the direct contact of quinine with the tongue, or the immediate presence of a piece of *lapis lazuli* before the eyes. The presence is in these cases 'direct' or 'immediate' in the sense that *there is nothing discernible between* the object and the sense organ—no medium or instrument discernible at the time between them. And when these same words—'direct' or 'immediate' presence—are used to describe also the relation between bitter or blue and the mind, the only *literal* meaning they can have there is that the latter relation *resembles* that of the *lapis* to the eye or the quinine to the tongue in the respect that, in both relations, *there is nothing discernible between* the terms they relate.

But if (as of course we must where blue or bitter and the mind are the terms) we divest the word 'between' of the only sense, viz., the *spatial*, which it had when quinine and the tongue or *lapis* and the eye were the terms, then, I submit, the words 'nothing between' describe *no hypothesis at all* as to the nature of the relation of the blue or bitter to the mind. This means that when one of the terms of a certain relation is the mind, then—since the mind is not, like the head or sense organs, an entity having a place in space— nothing whatever is being said as to the nature of that relation by employing the words 'direct presence' to describe it unless some definite meaning *other than the spatial one* is explicitly provided for those words. But everybody seems either to have assumed their meaning to be obvious and not incongruous to the cases concerned, or else to have defined the words ostensively only, as meaning the sort of relation there is between blue or bitter, etc., and consciousness of these. But of course to define 'direct presence' thus only ostensively is not in the least to *analyse* the sort of relation the words apply to. In particular, it is not to offer the least evidence that analysis would not reveal it to be the very relation I have called 'content of'.

Aside from this, however, even if one supposes that bitter tastes are entities which would exist even if no minds existed, and one should be willing to accept the absurdity that not only minds but also bitter tastes (and likewise, of course, nauseas, dizzinesses, fears, etc.) have like tongues and quinine places in space and can move about or be moved about independently of each other so that a bitter taste or a nausea could become 'present' to a mind in the sense of travelling to its spatial neighbourhood until nothing remained spatially between them—even then, I submit, one would have to accept the further absurdity that this mere spatial juxtaposition *without that mind's being in any way affected by it*, i.e., *without any change being caused in that mind by it*, would constitute cognition of bitter by that mind. For if one were to say that the juxtaposition does cause in the mind a specific change, viz., one to be called not 'smelling' or 'hearing' etc., but 'tasting', this would amount to erecting bitter taste into as strictly a physical substance as quinine, and therefore to saying that tasting bitter taste and tasting quinine are both 'tasting' in essentially the same (causal) sense. Yet it was obvious and admitted from the start that 'tasting' does not have the same sense in both cases.

But further still, even if 'presence of bitter taste in the spatial neighbourhood of a mind' were not an absurdity, and even if such 'presence' did cause in that mind a change called 'tasting', even then there would still remain to give an account of that mind's *intuitive cognition of its own tasting at the time it occurs*, i.e., of the event *in that mind itself* caused to occur by the advent of the bitter taste in the spatial neighbourhood of that mind. And this would face us then anyway with the need for my hypothesis that 'tasting bitter taste' is the name of a specific variety of the activity called 'tasting', viz., the variety called 'tasting *bitterly*' (in the literal not the figurative sense of this adverb), and that what the activity cognizes on every such occasion is its own specific nature on the occasion.

But everything for the doing of which we need a relation of a kind other than that of quinine to tasting is, I submit, adequately done for us by the relation just described, which I maintain is the one of bitter to tasting; and this relation does not entail the absurdities required to give a literal *sense B* (distinct from both 'content of' and *sense A* of 'object of') to the 'direct presence' hypothesis. Moreover, because the two relations 'content of' and 'object of' in *sense A* adequately account for every case, Occam's razor enables us to dismiss the still other nominal supposition—which might be resorted to *in extremis*, that bitter is 'object of' tasting in some unique and indefinable other *sense C* of the words.

14. *Taste is a species, not an object, of experience*

If the discussion in the preceding section has succeeded in what it attempted, it has shown that the phrase 'direct presence to a mind' either is but another name for the relation between cognitive activity and the cognita connate therewith, or else is only a figure of speech for which no literal meaning not ultimately involving absurdities is forthcoming. If this has been shown, then the allegedly third hypothesis, which *prima facie* seemed meaningful and was the only one seeming to offer an acceptable alternative to mine, has been disposed of. I shall not rest my case here, however, but will now attempt to show that when the issues are sharply presented my assertion that blue, bitter, etc., are not objects of experience, nor species of objects of experience, but species *of experience itself*, is the very assertion common sense then finds itself ready to make. What is needed for this is only to put the question in a manner making it impossible for our judgement to be confused by the ambiguity which may still cling to the phrase 'object of' in spite of what was said in the preceding section. To make the meaning of the question unmistakably clear, I then ask first what would be indubitable examples of the four possible kinds of accusatives (viz., of cognita), of 'experiencing'. I submit the following:

The *alienly co-ordinate* cognitum of 'experiencing' is 'object' or 'objective event'.

The *connately co-ordinate* cognitum of 'experiencing' is 'experience'.

An *alienly subordinate* cognitum of 'experiencing' is 'quinine', or 'a rose', etc.

A *connately subordinate* cognitum of 'experiencing' is 'taste', or 'smell', etc.

I believe the first three examples will be readily accepted as correct; but the fourth might be disputed, for if it is accepted my case is won.

'Taste', 'smell', etc., I may be told, are not, as the above would imply, *species* of experience but *'objects'* of experience. If this is said, however, I ask what then would be right examples of *connately* subordinate cognita of experiencing; or—which is equivalent since experience is the connately co-ordinate cognitum of experiencing—what then would be right examples of *species* of experience? I believe it would not be disputed that tasting, smelling, etc., are species of experiencing; and I submit it is equally natural and proper and indeed unavoidable to say that taste and smell are species of experience, or that there is a species of experience called 'taste'. For the only alternative to this is to say that taste is an 'object' of experience in the same sense that quinine is an object of experience; and this is plainly false.

Moreover, one who would deny that taste is a species of experience is called upon to say what then would be the cognitum co-ordinately connate with the species of experienc*ing* called 'tasting'. If it is not taste, what then might it be? I for one can no more think of an answer than if I were asked what would be the co-ordinately connate accusative of striking if it were not stroke.

15. *Bitter is a species, not an object, of taste*

To emphasize the point of the considerations just advanced, they will now be reiterated, but at the more determinate level where the relation of bitter to tasting is in question instead of that of taste to experiencing. Again I ask, what would be indubitable examples of the four possible sorts of cognita of tasting, and I submit the following:

The *alienly co-ordinate* cognitum of 'tasting' is 'physical substance'.
The *connately co-ordinate* cognitum of 'tasting' is 'taste'.
An *alienly subordinate* cognitum of 'tasting' is 'quinine'.
A *connately subordinate* cognitum of 'tasting' is 'bitter'.

Here again, to say that bitter is not a species but an 'object' of taste is to say that bitter is related to tasting in essentially the same manner as quinine is to tasting; and this is patently false. Moreover, one who would deny that when bitter is tasted what is tasted is a species of taste is called upon to say what then would be a cognitum *connately* subordinate to tasting. If bitter is not such a cognitum, what then might be one? Again here, I can no more think of an answer than I could to the question what might be a subordinately connate accusative of striking if jab were not one.

16. *Linguistic inertia is responsible for the error that taste is object of experience*

It is easy to see how one is led into the error that taste is an object of experience or bitter an object of taste. What leads one into it is the tendency—which we may call linguistic inertia or linguistic optimism—to believe that when a word is the same it means the same, and that when it is not the same it does not mean the same. The sameness in this case is that of the word 'of', which occurs equally and in grammatically similar positions when we speak of the experiencing *of* taste and of the experiencing *of* quinine; or of the tasting *of* bitter and of the tasting *of* quinine. The temptation to believe that 'of' means the same in both halves of each pair is likely to vanish only when we realize that we likewise speak of the striking *of* a jab and of the striking *of* a man—in which case it is quite obvious that the two 'of's do not mean the same relation.

On the other hand, because the two words 'experiencing' and

'taste', or 'tasting' and 'bitter', are not *linguistically* connate, linguistic inertia tempts us to believe that the cognitive activity and the cognitum in each case, for which those words stand, are not connate either. And this temptation again is likely to vanish only when we realize that 'dancing' and 'waltz', or 'striking' and 'jab', or 'jumping' and 'leap', etc., are not *linguistically* connate either, but that in each case the accusative nevertheless is obviously connate (subordinately) with the activity.

17. *'Bitter' as name of a species of taste vs. of a property of some substances*

The adjective 'bitter' can be applied both to tastes and to substances: we speak both of a bitter taste and of a bitter substance. Owing to linguistic inertia, this tempts us to believe that the relation between what the adjective and the noun stand for in the one and in the other case is the same relation. But that the relation is on the contrary very different in the two cases becomes obvious if we note that the expression 'bitter taste' expands into 'taste of the species called "bitter"', whereas the expression 'bitter substance' cannot similarly be expanded into 'substance of the species called "bitter"' (since 'bitter' is not the name of any species of substance), but only into 'substance having the *property* "being bitter"'. In the case of 'bitter taste' the relation of bitter to taste is that of *species to genus*; whereas in the case of 'bitter substance' the relation of bitter to substance is that of *property to substance*. The various properties of a substance are mutually conjunct; the various (coordinate) species of a genus on the contrary mutually disjunct. A property, moreover, is essentially of the nature of a law: to say that a substance has the property 'being bitter' is to say the substance is such that, if placed on the tongue, then the sort of taste called 'bitter taste' occurs. But when one speaks of 'bitter taste', the adjective 'bitter' is not here similarly the name of a certain law but the name of a certain quality.

18. *Special sources of confusion when visual sensa are taken as examples*

My argument has been formulated at most places in terms of gustatory sensa, but if it is valid for them it obviously is equally so for sensa of any other kinds. The reason for having presented the argument in terms of an example from the realm of taste rather than from the favourite one of sight was that the question at issue being a very difficult one, its exact nature could be exhibited more clearly by a simple example than by one where—as in the case of sight—special risks of confusion are present. The chief of these arises from the fact that the organ of sight, viz., the eye, yields to us not only colour intuitions but also place and shape intuitions. This fact means that when our eye is focused upon, for instance, an apple, we see not only a colour (say, green) but also 'see' a *place* at which the colour is. But simultaneously (because our own nose as well as the apple is in front of our eye) we see, although inattentively, also another colour (say, pink) and a place at which it is, different from the place of the green. And the fact that the place at which the green is seen and that at which the pink is seen are *literally*, i.e., spatially, *external* to each other seems to provide for some philosophers an irresistible temptation to believe that the green attended to (and the pink too if attention is called to it) are 'external' also in the *metaphorical* sense the word has when we speak of externality *to the mind*, i.e., are existentially independent of their being experienced. Obviously, however, spatial externality to each other of the places at which two colours are seen, or of the places of two physical things such as our own eye and an apple, is something totally irrelevant to the question whether the colours (or, for that matter, the physical things), are 'external to the mind' in the sense of existing independently of their being experienced.

19. *Summary and conclusion*

The essential steps of the argument of this paper may now in conclusion briefly be reviewed. First, attention was called to the distinction between accusatives connate with and alien to a given activity, and to the fact that an accusative of either sort may in point of generality, be either co-ordinate with or subordinate to the corresponding activity. It was then pointed out that any accusative connate with a given activity exists only in the performances of that activity and therefore in particular that any cognitum connate with a given cognitive activity exists only in the performances of it. That is, the *esse* of any cognitum connate with the cognizing is its *cognosci*. The question as to whether a sensum, e.g., blue or bitter, can or cannot exist independently of the *percipi* of it then reduces to the question whether the blue or bitter is a cognitum (subordinately) connate with or on the contrary alien to the cognizing thereof. My contention, I then stated, is that the sensum is a cognitum (subordinately) connate with the cognizing of it, i.e., that what is cognized (intuitively not discursively) in cognition of it is the specific nature the sensing activity has on the given occasion; and that, in just this sense, blue or bitter are 'contents' of sensing and not 'objects', i.e., not alien cognita, of sensing. It was next pointed out that Moore's criticism of the 'content' hypothesis concerns a hypothesis *other* than the one just described, which therefore remains a possible alternative to his own hypothesis that blue or bitter are 'objects' of sensing. But since Moore's paper does not disprove or even consider that alternative hypothesis, and that hypothesis entails that the blue or bitter would exist only in the sensing thereof, his paper does not prove what it seeks to prove, viz., that there is no cognitum of which it is true that its *esse* is its *percipi*. I then passed to the attempt to show that blue, bitter, etc., *are* cognita connate with the sensing thereof, and therefore that their *esse* is their *percipi*. To do so, I first pointed to the fact— stated by Moore himself in another paper—that seeing brown and seeing a coin, hearing middle C and hearing a bell, tasting bitter and tasting quinine, are not 'seeing', 'hearing' and 'tasting' in the same sense in both cases; and therefore that if the coin, the bell, and the quinine have to the seeing, hearing, and tasting the relation 'object of', then brown, middle C and bitter either are not 'objects of' these activities at all, or else are 'objects of' them in some *other* sense of the term. The allegation that 'direct presence to the mind' describes such another sense was then examined and shown to be false; and this left as the only answer in sight concerning the relation of sensa to the sensing of them, the one I had advanced. I then further attempted to show that it is the very answer common sense renders when the question is thoroughly freed of its ordinary ambiguity. Finally, some explanations were added to show how the error that sensa are 'objects' of cognition arises. The upshot of the argument is that the distinction between sensing and sensum, to which appeal is commonly made nowadays and for which Moore's paper is generally regarded as the warrant, is an *invalid* distinction, if it is taken as the one from which would follow the possibility of existential independence of the sensum from the sensing. On the other hand, there *is* a valid distinction between sensum and sensing but it is the one I have described, and from it what follows is that the existence of the sensum consists in the sensing thereof.

Whether my argument, of which this is but a brief summary, succeeds in the two tasks it undertook to perform is something that must now be left to the decision of the reader.

14.

PHILOSOPHY AND NATURAL SCIENCE*

There is a philosophical problem which is perhaps the most fundamental of all but to which philosophical books, when they mention it at all, give for the most part only a few pages in an introductory chapter. This problem is, what specifically distinguishes philosophy from other human enterprises and what sort of method is appropriate to its tasks. The need to deal with this question much more thoroughly than is customary is forced on our attention today by the glaring contrast between the states of affairs prevailing respectively in philosophy and in the sciences. For in the latter, we find a steady progress which has resulted in the accumulation of a vast body of positive knowledge; whereas in philosophy what we find is, to quote Hoernlé, 'that all new theories do but add to the babel and confusion, that there is no cumulative co-operative advance from generation to generation, no funded stock of philosophical truths which can be taught as its established rudiments to beginners, and which are taken for granted by all experts as the basis of further enquiry. The same problems are ever examined afresh ... the old problems remain persistently open.'[1]

This situation in philosophy would I believe rapidly improve if philosophers knew more clearly than I think they usually do just what it is that distinguishes philosophy from the sciences. The layman often asks us what exactly is philosophy, and I venture there is no question we find harder to answer to his satisfaction, or, I suspect, really to our own. Because of its basic importance for

---

* *The Philosophical Review*, vol. XLIX, No. 2, 1940.
[1] *Studies in Contemporary Metaphysics,* 48.

the future progress of philosophy, and because none of the answers currently given to it seem to me really defensible, I propose on this occasion to outline the one which a careful examination of the facts appears to me to dictate.

1. *Some current hypotheses as to the nature of philosophy*

It is only proper, however, that I should first indicate the grounds for my belief that none of the usual answers is acceptable. Unfortunately, limitations of time will not now permit more than a very few words for this—too few, I am afraid, to pass as adequately presenting the opinions criticized or as effectively disposing of them.

Of these opinions, the one probably most often met with is that the problems of philosophy differ from those of science in being more general. According to Herbert Spencer, for instance, philosophy carries the process of generalization one stage higher than do the sciences, so that the truths of philosophy 'bear the same relation to the highest scientific truths that each of these bears to lower scientific truths'.[1] Unfortunately for this view, however, it is in vain that we seek in the writings of philosophers for any truths from which, to take one of Spencer's own examples, one could deduce the laws at once of dynamics, of thermotics, and of economics, as one can deduce, for instance, the laws of the dynamics of fluids from those of general dynamics. Moreover, that the propositions of philosophy are not more general than such laws, but are about something else, is indicated by the fact that, unlike these laws, they lay no claim to the power of predicting events in Nature. It is sometimes said, of course, that each science represents a species of knowledge, whereas what philosophy, or more specifically epistemology, studies is knowledge in general; and that the subject-matter of epistemology therefore differs from that of any of the sciences in being more general. But this is only to confuse knowledge in the sense of *facts known* with knowledge in the sense of *knowing*. The various sciences are not various species of knowing, but are the knowing of various species of facts. And what epistemology studies is not these same facts at a more general level but the relation, called knowing, which the scientist seeks to establish between his mind and those facts.

---

[1] *First Principles*, § 3.

Again, some metaphysicians have conceived the task of philosophy to be the construction of a picture of the universe such that man, as a seeker of values, should feel at home in it or at least find life in it acceptable. But if construction of such world-views is philosophy, then philosophy is essentially wishful thinking, and the world-views it formulates represent, not knowledge, but each only a more or less self-consistent content for a comforting possible faith. I submit, however, that philosophy is neither poetry nor the inventing of possible articles of faith, but definitely a knowledge-seeking enterprise.

The task of philosophy, again, has been described by some writers as consisting in the analysis of concepts. But the sciences too analyse some concepts; and if one should then say with C. D. Broad that the concepts philosophy analyses are 'fundamental' ones, this only raises the question what marks a concept as fundamental. Broad does not answer it, but only mentions some of the concepts he would so label. Yet the answer to it is what we must have if we are to know exactly what then differentiates philosophy from the sciences.

Yet another view of philosophy is that urged by Carnap and certain other writers. He believes that if, from the variety of questions philosophers have discussed, we reject the many which represent only pseudo-problems, all that then remain are questions concerning the logic of science. These, he contends, appear to be questions about objects, but all really are questions concerning the syntax of the language of science. And he therefore concludes that philosophy, in so far as its problems are not spurious, is the study of the syntax of the language of science.

It may be observed first, however, that the language of science is not the only language there is. We have also the language of art, the language of religion, the language of law, of morals, and so on; for man is not exclusively a cognitive, science-building animal. And these other languages too have their respective syntaxes. If problems of syntax are philosophical problems at all, then I submit that they are such no matter whether the syntax concerned is that of the language of science or of religion, of morals or of art, or of any other basic human interest; and therefore that philosophy has a much broader field than the view under consideration assigns to it.

But the opinion that philosophical problems are syntactical

problems at all seems to me definitely erroneous. Carnap bases it on the contention that there exist two 'modes of speech', which he calls respectively the material and the formal modes; and that assertions in the material mode of speech can be translated into the formal mode. The assertions of philosophy, he observes, present themselves mostly in the material mode of speech. Like all assertions in this mode they appear to be about objects, but really are about words; and this becomes obvious when they are translated into the formal mode of speech.

Let us, however, examine the alleged translating. In some of Carnap's examples, it consists only in restating unambiguously something that was stated vaguely or incorrectly. This, of course, is strictly not translating but construing; and has anyway no particular bearing on the contention that philosophy is logical syntax. The examples that are crucial for this contention are of a different kind. Their kind may be illustrated by the sentence 'This book treats of Africa', which is said to be in the material mode of speech, and is said to be translated into the formal mode by the sentence 'This book contains the word Africa' (or an expression synonymous with it). I submit, however, that to call this *translation* is obviously to misuse the term, for translation consists in saying the same thing in different words; whereas these two sentences do not say the same thing at all, but different things. If this should need any proof, it would be furnished by the fact that the truth-value of each sentence is independent of the truth-value of the other; for there *can* be a book which treats of Africa but does not contain the word 'Africa' or any expression synonymous with it; and there *can* be a book containing the word 'Africa' but not treating of Africa, for instance a rhyming dictionary.

In this and similar examples, the so-called two modes of speech thus are not two sets of words for saying one and the same thing, but two sets of words for saying each a different thing. The continent, called 'Africa', is one topic and the word, 'Africa', is another; and no statement to the effect that the word, 'Africa', has certain relations to certain other words is a translation, properly so called, of any statement about the continent, called 'Africa'. It may be possible, of course, to give a rule for matching certain statements about the continent called 'Africa', each with a statement about the word 'Africa' having the same truth-value. The two sets of statements would then be *parallel as to truth-value*. But even then they would be each about a different thing, the ones about a piece of land and the others about a word. And therefore to describe the ones as *translations* of the others would be to misconceive their relation.

But just this misconception appears to be the whole basis for the contention that philosophy is the study of logical syntax, for this contention is rested squarely on the assumption that a statement *about a word* and giving its relation to certain other words can be truly a translation of, that is, be strictly synonymous with, a statement *about something other than a word*. This assumption, however, is obviously false, and its falsity implies that such statements in the material mode of speech as we are now considering cannot, strictly speaking, be translated into the formal mode of speech. And from this it follows that although the study of logical syntax may well be exceedingly useful for philosophical purposes, and is perhaps even a part of philosophy, it nevertheless is the study of a subject at least narrower than that of philosophy.

Another current conception of philosophy still remains to be mentioned, the one, namely, according to which philosophy is essentially 'vision, imagination, reflection', employed to guide to a prosperous issue actions dealing with social and moral problems. This is the view represented by Dewey's famous statement that philosophy 'recovers itself when it ceases to be a device for dealing with the problems of philosophers and becomes a method, cultivated by philosophers, for dealing with the problems of men'.[1] In America today, action practical in ways both obvious and direct is an object of well-nigh universal worship, and a view of philosophy which assigns to it a function practical in this glamorous sense therefore commends itself to the spirit of the age. But reflection forces on us the fact that to contrast the problems of philosophers with the problems of men is to forget that philosophers too are men, and therefore that the problems of philosophers are some of the problems of men just as truly as are the problems of astronomers and mathematicians, of poets and musicians, of social and moral reformers, or of the persons for whose benefit the reforms are proposed. For man does not live by economic, political, social or other practical conditions alone. In him, thought is capable of being a *mode of life* even in cases where its usual function as an

---

[1] *Creative Intelligence,* 65.

instrument for life is indiscernible or totally absent. And I submit that man's capacity to be impractical and to starve in a garret for the sake of thought or of art or of religion indicates more truly what man distinctively is than does the capacity he shares with the animals to use the intelligence he has to minister to his more obvious needs. For after all, when man erects even an Empire State building or a Hoover dam, the end to which he is then devoting his superior intelligence is of exactly the same sort as that which an animal such as the beaver is striving to achieve.

2. *Philosophy seeks knowledge and its method must therefore be scientific*

The hypothesis as to the nature of philosophy for which I shall now argue takes it for granted at the outset that the enterprise of philosophy is distinct both from that of religion and of poetry, and distinct also from that of the natural sciences. But it takes for granted that philosophy, like these sciences, seeks knowledge. The knowledge it seeks, moreover, is not knowledge in a different or less rigorous sense but in the very same sense, that, namely, in which knowledge is contrasted with guesses, articles of faith, snap-judgements, vague or unsupported opinions, prejudices, or wish-born beliefs. But if philosophy seeks knowledge in this same sense, then its method must necessarily be likewise scientific, for 'scientific' means nothing more and nothing less than *knowledge-yielding*. This, however, does not imply that scientific method will take in philosophy the same specific forms it has in physics or in biology, or even in mathematics. For such specific forms are dictated by specific subject-matter and differ even as between one and another of the sciences.

3. *Philosophy has a subject-matter distinct from that of the natural or the formal sciences*

Thus what essentially differentiates philosophy from the other sciences can be only a subject-matter distinct from theirs. Of course, we hear it said today that, beside the subject-matter of the natural sciences and that of the formal sciences, none remains for philosophy to claim as its own. But I shall try to show that this is not the case.

To avoid misunderstandings, however, let us agree to begin

with that by the 'formal' sciences will be meant pure logic and pure mathematics, and by the 'natural' sciences all the sciences that study what has commonly been called Nature or the material world. These sciences will thus include, for instance, physics and chemistry, astronomy, geology, biology, and both physiological and behaviouristic psychology: also the social sciences if these are taken only as studies of human behaviour. But in the social sciences I would class on the contrary as applied philosophy, whatever there may be other than study of behaviour. As regards history, the term usually designates particularly the study of human societies or human activities in their time-dimension; but there is of course also such a thing as the history of the solar system, or of the earth, or of a given tree, etc. More generally, then, we may say that history is the study, in the time-dimension, of any sort of facts that exist in time.

4. *Primitive and derivative subject-matter*

Turning now to the question of the subject-matter distinctive of philosophy, it will be useful as a first step to see what form an answer to the corresponding question would take in the easier case of the natural sciences.

To say, as we did a moment ago, that their subject-matter is Nature or the world of material events only raises the question what exactly we mean by these terms. And it is not easy to find for them a definition that will apply equally to things as diverse as light and heat, the causes of earthquakes, the differences in basal metabolism for different races, the mechanisms of heredity, the varieties of sub-atomic particles, the marriage customs of the Dyaks, the determinants of the properties of alloys, etc., all of which belong to this Nature that the natural sciences investigate. A solution of the difficulty becomes discernible only when it occurs to us to make a certain most important distinction, that, namely, between what we may call the *primitive* facts of a science, and its *derivative* facts.

The primitive facts of a science are those which, for the given science, are beyond question. They comprise, on the one hand, the facts about which are the very first, most elementary questions that the science asks, and on the other the facts to which the science ultimately appeals in testing the validity of its hypotheses. The primitive facts of a science are thus the sort of facts which originate or terminate its inquiries. An example of a primitive fact which originates inquiry in physics would be the rising and falling of the tide. *That* the tide does rise and fall is obvious at many places and is then not questioned; but it is something *about which* many questions occur to the physicist. Other facts primitive for a physicist would be, on certain occasions, that a given string is stretched; that he plucks it; that a sound occurs; that a certain string is longer than a certain other; that certain metal filings are clinging to a certain metal bar; that a certain body is moving, etc. About these facts many questions would arise, but in many cases the facts themselves would be regarded as established beyond question by ordinary perceptual observation. On the other hand, examples of primitive facts functioning in certain cases as terminative rather than as originative of physical inquiries would be that a certain pointer is at a certain place on a graduated scale; that on a certain occasion no sound occurs when a given bell is struck; that on a certain occasion two falling bodies do not reach the ground at the same time, etc.

The derivative facts of a given science, on the other hand, are those eventually discovered as a result of the attempt to analyse or synthesize its primitive facts. A derivative fact, after it has been discovered, may itself become the subject of new questions, or may serve to answer certain other questions. Examples of terms, again from physics, which name derivative facts and which enter into the formulation of the derivative facts we call laws and explanations would be magnetic field, atom, proton, electric charge, electric potential, velocity, mass, acceleration, energy, etc.

In the light of the distinction between primitive and derivative facts, we may now say that *the subject-matter distinctive of a science consists of the sort of facts that are primitive for it, plus any facts implicit in the primitives and about which problems may arise in turn.* The illustrations given make obvious something very important to notice, namely, that in physics or any other science at all advanced, the overwhelming majority of the statements made by the science are explicitly and directly not about its primitive but about its derivative facts. And, because of this, the latter may easily seem to be what the science is really about. But since they are known at all only derivatively from the primitive and more vulgar ones, and indeed have claim to belong to the given science only because they are implicit in the primitives of specifically that science, those primitives, although seldom explicitly mentioned in the assertions reached by the science, are nevertheless what all its assertions are *ultimately* about. And this means that the subject-matter distinctive of a given science is ultimately defined by the very ones among its facts which it least often explicitly mentions in the statements of its results. This, as we shall see, is true likewise of philosophy.

5. *The subject-matter of the natural sciences*

In the light of these remarks, what can we now say is the subject-matter distinctive of the natural sciences as a group? I submit that their primitive facts are *any facts ascertainable by ordinary external perception*; that is, facts that are *perceptually public* in the sense that common perceptual observation is what establishes them as beyond question for all the practitioners of those sciences. It is true that we may doubt the factuality of what perception exhibits in a given case; but, if we were to doubt it in *every* case, there would then be nothing left at all of the problems the natural sciences investigate. For there is no such thing as a problem without data, and the primitive data of the natural sciences are perceived data. This being clear, we may now say that *Nature*, which is the subject-matter distinctive of the natural sciences, consists *of such facts as are susceptible of being perceptually public, plus such facts as are analytically or synthetically implicit in these.*

6. *The subject-matter of the formal sciences*

A word more briefly now as to the subject-matter of the formal sciences. Their primitive facts, I submit, consist of certain entities created by us through stipulations. These stipulations are of the kinds we call postulates, definitions, and rules of formation and of transformation. The entities created by such stipulations are created exclusively out of the sort of material which we may call discursive or verbal material, that is, *utterable* material, it being theoretically indifferent whether the utterances of it be in a given case graphic, oral, or other.

The derivative facts of the formal sciences, on the other hand, which we may call their *theorems*, consist of the sentences which may be derived from the primitive verbal facts just described, by means of the rules that are a part of the latter. The knowledge given us by the formal sciences is thus *a priori* knowledge, for the differentia of *a priori* knowledge is, I submit, that the truth-value of its propositions is *determined by choices of our own*. But although so determined in all cases, their truth-value may be known to us either *directly* in the making of the choices, as when we lay down postulates, definitions, and rules, or only *indirectly* by deduction from these, as in the case of theorems.

7. *Is Mind the subject-matter distinctive of philosophy?*

The outcome of our inquiry as to the subject-matter distinctive of the natural sciences now makes evident that there does exist a range of facts not investigated by them, nor, except perhaps in one of its parts, by the formal sciences. It consists of *the facts ascertainable by introspection, and of those implicit in them*. But if I were to claim at this point that these facts constitute the subject-matter distinctive of philosophy, and that philosophy is therefore the science of Mind, several apparently insuperable objections would immediately suggest themselves. One would be that facts of introspection are not verifiable, and therefore that a science of them is not genuinely possible. A second would be that even if a science of them were possible, its right name would be not philosophy but introspective psychology. A third objection would be that although philosophy has some concern with Mind, it is concerned also with the relation between Nature and Mind, and with Reality in general. And a fourth objection, of course, would be that contemporary naturalism has shown Mind to be a part of Nature, and therefore that to assume Mind to be distinct from Nature is a fundamental error. I believe, however, and will now attempt to show, that these seemingly formidable objections are based not on superior insights but much rather mostly on confusions of thought.

8. *Is Mind a part of Nature?*

Let us examine them; and first let us consider the contention of contemporary naturalism that Mind is a part of Nature. It is easy, of course, so to define the word Mind that Mind shall then be a part of Nature, just as, by defining black as a species of white, it is easy to prove that negroes are a part of the white race. But such high-handed verbal procedures are obviously futile. What they do is only to construct an arbitrary language which, by using familiar words in novel senses, makes it seem that one is talking about the things these words familiarly denote when in fact one is talking about something very different. For example, what naturalism chooses to call Mind is something which in ordinary English would be called *the behaviour of bodies that have minds*. Study of the behaviour of such bodies is perfectly legitimate and very important, but it is not study of the same thing that the word Mind denotes in ordinary English, namely, *the realm of facts accessible only through introspection*. Only confusion results from using the same word for both of these very different subjects of study; for to do so leads to the belief that naturalism has made important discoveries about that which in ordinary English is denoted by the word Mind, whereas the truth is that a consistent naturalism is not interested at all in that, but in something which remains quite different from that even when arbitrarily called by the same name.

It thus turns out that the claim of naturalism that Mind is a part of Nature represents only its own initial resolution to make every term it uses, and in particular the term Mind, denote at any cost something *in Nature,* that is, something *in the perceptually accessible world.* But, let it be well noted, this resolution is not forced on those who make it by any facts. It represents only the initial and perfectly free espousal, by certain thinkers, of the ontological position which defines both the scope and the limits of all natural science. This seldom stated and seldom conscious ontological commitment is this: *To be real is to be either something susceptible of being perceptually public, or something implicit therein.* To commit oneself to such a position is of course to commit oneself to ignore the world of introspectively accessible facts, that is, the world of Mind; but to have thus decided to ignore it is not in the least to have invalidated the contrast traditionally expressed by the words Mind and Nature or Mind and Matter. This contrast is based on the existence of two modes of observation namely, introspection and objective perception, which common sense regards, and I believe rightly, as irreducibly distinct. On the present occasion there is unfortunately no time for me to argue their distinctness. I can only state that I take it to be a fact; and, to avoid misunderstandings, add that—in agreement I believe with most introspective psychologists—I regard attention to our own sensations as a case of introspective observation. My statement of this may on the present occasion be taken only as clarifying what I propose to mean by introspection, for there is not time to go into the merits of the question. I can at most mention in connection with it that, although I do admit a distinction between *sensing* and *sensum*, I take it to be not as usually assumed one between sensing and *object* of sensing, but between sensing and *species* of sensing. That is, when we speak for instance of tasting quinine, quinine is the name of an *object* of taste; but when we speak of tasting bitter, bitter is the name of a *species* of taste. Thus tasting a substance and tasting a taste are tasting in two radically different senses of the word. In the first, tasting is a case of objective perception, but in the second tasting is a case of introspection.

9. *Are assertions about introspectable facts verifiable?*

I turn now to the contention that the facts of introspection, because of their private character, are not amenable to scientific study. Let us suppose that someone asserts, as generalizations from his own introspective experience, that jealousy is a more unpleasant feeling than anxiety, or that hearing the word 'triangle' regularly causes to arise the image of a three-sided closed figure. These generalizations are statements of alleged properties of some human minds. Another person cannot directly verify whether they are indeed possessed by the mind of the person who has stated them; but he can decide by introspection whether his own mind possesses them. And, by obtaining the testimony of other persons, he can decide what percentage more or less of human minds possess them.

A statistical inquiry concerning the properties of human minds differs from statistical inquiries concerning the properties of objects in Nature only in that in the former, but not in the latter, the taking of testimony is an indispensable part of the process of verification and the assumption has to be made that those who give the testimony are not lying. But this same assumption is often also made and considered legitimate in the case of statistical inquiries concerning Nature which, although theoretically they could be pursued without recourse to testimony, actually in many cases are carried on by means of it.

Testimony, however, presupposes that the terms used by the witness and by the inquirer have the same meaning for both of them. How do we make sure they do? In the case of terms referring to Nature, community of meaning is established, in ultimate analysis, through the process of publicly pointing at perceptually public facts of the kind to which a given term is intended to refer. In the case of terms referring to Mind, this cannot be done. Community of meaning in their case is established in a less direct way, namely, in ultimate analysis, by attaching them to the sorts of states introspectively observable by any normal persons who are in given sorts of perceptually public physical conditions. The kind of psychical event called pain, for instance, is identified as the one introspection reveals to any normal person at times when, for example, his body is being cut, or burned, or bruised, etc.; and whether a person is normal or abnormal is itself a matter of whether the relations, such as likeness, or unlikeness, or causation, which he discovers introspectively among the psychical states identified in the manner just stated, and which he reports, are the same relations that most other persons introspectively find among them. This is the way in which for instance the abnormality called colour-blindness is discovered.

Terms enabling us to talk to one another about events of psychical kinds thus are possible only through correlation between certain psychical events and certain perceptually public physical events. But from this it does not at all follow that the terms so established denote these physical events themselves. For to denote the latter we have certain *other* terms. For example, whereas the term 'anger' denotes a psychical event, the *other* terms, 'anger-behaviour' and 'anger-provoking-situation', denote physical events. The upshot of these remarks is then that we do possess the language needed for taking testimony concerning the properties of other minds, and can therefore verify assertions as to the similarity of several minds in respect to a given property.

10. *Introspective psychologists have cultivated only a small part of the science of Mind*

This, however, brings us to the objection that the science of Mind is not philosophy but introspective psychology. My answer to it in brief will be that philosophy includes what introspective psychologists have had to say, but that what they have had to say represents only a small part of the comprehensive science of Mind, which philosophy is. To regard introspective psychology as a part of philosophy is of course anything but a novel proposal, since it is on the contrary the traditional view. What is not a part of philosophy is the study of animal and human behaviour and of its physiological mechanisms, which in recent years has arbitrarily called itself by a name, psychology, that hitherto had always designated something else. I may add in this connection that when some months ago I mentioned this to a group of behaviouristic psychologists, their retort was that if I wished to claim introspective psychology as a part of philosophy, I was welcome to it, for *they* did not want it! I propose to accept the gift, but to point out now what a comprehensive science of Mind includes in addition to what introspective psychologists have discovered. To see what they have discovered, let us look into one of their textbooks. The one by the late E. B. Titchener may be taken as representative. The larger number of its pages, we find, deal with the physical conditions under which certain kinds of introspectable facts, chiefly sensations, occur; and this, of course, is not strictly introspective psychology but is a hybrid science which may be called psycho-physics or psycho-physiology. The proportion of pages devoted to introspective psychology proper, that is, to study of the relations of introspectable facts *to one another*, is relatively small, and the content of a science of Mind as represented in those relatively few pages would be rather meagre. For about all it would include would be an inventory of the kinds of sensations and other mental states; an account of certain of the elements and dimensions of some complex mental states; and an account of the general laws according to which mental elements become discriminated or submerged, dissociated or associated. As Titchener himself suggests, a science of Mind that was limited to this 'would stand to scientific psychology very much as the old-fashioned natural histories stand to modern textbooks of biology'.[1] A scientific psychology, he says, must not only describe but also explain.

But then he strangely assumes that no mental process can cause another mental process; and since he also assumes, without argument, that no process in the nervous system can cause any mental

[1] Op. cit., 38.

process, he concludes that the explanation of mental processes consists in tracing correspondences between them and nervous processes. The latter, he says, explain the former in the sense in which a map can be said to explain the country of which it is a map. But I submit, first, that, if this is explanation at all, it is certainly not explanation in the sense in which the term is used in the other sciences, where it means either the tracing of effects to their causes, or the deduction of known empirical laws from theoretical constructs. And, second, the search for correlations between psychical and physiological processes is anyhow not introspective psychology proper but, as already pointed out, psycho-physiology.

But further, as regards Titchener's assumption that no mental process can cause another nor therefore explain another, I submit that on the contrary such causation is just what we do have in any case of association of ideas; and therefore in all the numberless mental connections constituted by cases of the relation of symbol to symbolized, or of sign to signified. Investigation of these very relations is what investigation of a given mind chiefly consists in; and establishment or alteration of such relations is what constitutes education of a mind. For symbols and signs, even the artificial ones of which a language consists, are not as it were a species of trained seals, which their trainer can endow with modes of behaviour *of their own* by the process of laying down rules of combination and transformation. Such rules, obviously, are nothing whatever but *habits* either already possessed or to be adopted, and habits not of the words or symbols themselves, but of a particular mind or minds. These rules, in short, are simply some of the laws or properties that certain minds have or acquire, and the study of them is thus a part but only a part of the science of Mind, that is, of philosophy.

Another artificial limitation, which introspective psychologists have gratuitously imposed on the science of Mind, arises from the assumption that there can be no facts in Mind other than those susceptible of being introspectively observed. But to see how unscientific this assumption is, we need only consider what would be the parallel assumption in the case of Nature. It would be that there can be no facts in Nature other than those susceptible of being perceptually observed. As already pointed out, however, the vast majority of the facts revealed by the natural sciences are not directly perceptible at all. They are accepted as facts, and as

facts *in Nature*, only because postulation of them enables us to deduce facts in Nature already perceived or laws of Nature already
discovered inductively, and additional ones that turn out to be
verified by further observations of Nature. And I submit that in
the science of Mind we have exactly as good a right, and the very
same sort of right, to postulate and to call mental certain entities
which introspection does not exhibit at all, but which similarly
enable us to deduce facts that introspection has already revealed
and additional ones that introspection eventually verifies. Examples of such entities would be the countless opinions, beliefs,
and mental associations which all of us have, but of the having
which we are totally unconscious at most times. They are properties of our minds, and our minds possess them even at times when
they are not introspectively manifest, just as the property called
combustibility is possessed by this sheet of paper even at times,
such as the present, when it is not perceptually manifest. The realm
of Mind, like that of Nature, thus includes vastly more than is ever
directly revealed by observation of it.

11. *Psychological vs. e.g., epistemological questions*

But there are certain questions, for example, those of the theory of
knowledge or of ethics, which it is customary to contrast, as philosophical in a narrower sense, with certain others referred to as
'purely psychological'. If, as I claim, *both* these sorts of questions
belong to the science of Mind, there is need to point out exactly
where and how, within that science, we pass from the ones called
purely psychological to the ones called epistemological, ethical,
etc.

To do this, I must return to the matter of causation among
psychical events, mentioned a moment ago, and call attention to
what I should like to call *the interpretive activities*. By an interpretive
activity, I mean a kind of psychical process consisting in this, that
*occurrence of a psychical event of a given kind, in a psychical context of a
given kind, regularly causes in us occurrence of a psychical event of a certain
other kind.* This definition it should be noted, stipulates nothing as
to the character of the psychical events concerned, and therefore
equally covers the cases where these events have the peculiar
character called objective reference, and the cases where they do

not have it. As so defined, a mode of interpretive activity is simply a psychical habit or a psychical disposition, and is the same thing as a property or law, whether acquired or native, of the particular mind concerned.

But now, among interpretive activities, there are certain ones called *appraisals*. How exactly they differ from others is an important question, but one into which we neither can nor need to inquire on the present occasion. For the contention I now wish to put forward is only that the cases of interpretive activity that *are* appraisals constitute the primitive subject-matter which distinguishes the so-called normative sciences, such as ethics or the theory of knowledge, from the part of the science of Mind whose problems are called 'merely psychological'. The whole of the theory of knowledge, for example, develops out of a persistent attempt to discover and describe exhaustively the differences between, and the presuppositions of, the sorts of appraisals expressed by such words as *erroneous* and *sound, mendacious* and *veracious, fallacious* and *valid*, etc. But since appraisal is a species of interpretive activity, the normative sciences, although they do go beyond the study of interpretive activities in general, are not independent of this study nor therefore of the study of mental events in general.

But the example of the theory of knowledge, just mentioned, may serve to call attention to the important fact that the sciences called normative are not, as sometimes thought, normative in the sense that they prescribe norms, but only in the sense that they discover and describe them. For a norm must not be confused with a desideratum or an aim. A norm is simply an appropriate form, the sort of form, namely, that an entity of a given sort has when it does satisfy a given sort of desire, or that an activity of a given sort has when it does cause the sort of effects that were aimed at. For example, the *aim* of the sort of activity called research is to attain knowledge, but the *norm* for this activity is *the manner of performing it* that regularly results in attainment of knowledge. What this norm is cannot be prescribed but has to be humbly discovered. A norm becomes itself an aim only in cases where, after we have discovered it, we then seek to impose it upon something for which it is the norm but which does not conform to it, for instance, to impose it upon some activity of our own which has been unsuccessful because its form has been defective.

12. *Metaphysics and the science of Mind*

To my contention that philosophy is the science of Mind, there still remains the objection that the branch of philosophy called metaphysics deals not only with Mind but also with Nature and with Reality in general. To deal with this objection I shall submit three remarks.

In the first place, I submit that in a large part of what has gone by the name of metaphysics the meaning of the terms employed is so vague and the transitions of thought so loose that the conclusions drawn have no title to the name of knowledge, even of probabilities. Such so-called metaphysics therefore seems to me to be just what Broad calls it, namely, moonshine. It is not really philosophy but only the manifestation of a methodological disease from which philosophy is gradually freeing itself. But the need to purge of this disease the philosophical problems it has most infected, namely those of the nature of Reality and of the relation of Nature to Mind, does not imply that these problems are spurious. I believe on the contrary that both are genuine and that both belong to the science of Mind, but I believe also that the true nature of each has been widely misconceived and therefore that each has to be re-stated before it can admit of solution.

To deal first with the problem of the nature of Reality, I believe that the adjectives, 'real' and 'unreal', describe no character that things have independently of human interest in them, but are on the contrary adjectives of human appraisal. But the sort of appraisal they describe is different from the appraisals mentioned already, in that the latter concerned the form of things or activities that were considered *as means to the satisfaction of some interest,* whereas the adjective 'real' voices appraisal of something as being *of a species which is itself an object of interest* at the time to the person who is calling it 'real'; and the adjective 'unreal', on the contrary, appraisal of something as belonging to a species of no interest to him at the time and therefore as to be ignored by him. This implies that a general statement as to the nature of Reality, that is, a statement of the form 'To be real is to be such and such', does not formulate a hypothesis and is therefore not susceptible of being proved, disproved, or assigned a probability; but rather formulates simply the *criterion of interestingness* which we use or propose to use at a given time in appraising any given thing as interesting or uninteresting to us. To be using, or to choose, such a criterion is to be occupying, or to take, an ontological position. And since an ontological position is thus not a hypothesis but a ruling interest, an ontological position is not the sort of thing susceptible of being either erroneous or the opposite. An ontological position may be queer and unusual, or on the contrary widespread; or it may be perhaps foolish or wise in the long run; or it may be taken or given up or not taken; but it may not be either refuted, demonstrated, or shown to be more or less probable than another. That adoption of an ontological position consists in choice of a criterion of interestingness was evident already in the statement given a while ago of the ontological position which determines both the scope and the limits of natural science, the position, namely, that, for the natural scientist, to be real—that is, to be of interest—is to be either perceptually public, or implicit in what is so.

From these considerations it follows that ontology is the part of the science of Mind which inquires first, as we have just done, what exactly is represented by any statement of the form 'To be real is to be such and such', and further inquires what principal varieties of such ontological choices there may be, how they are mutually related, what consistency with each implicitly demands, and so on.

I come now to my last remark, which concerns the objection that, if philosophy inquires into the relation of Nature to Mind, it then is occupying itself not only with Mind but also with Nature. To deal with this objection, I must first mention briefly two sorts of problems concerning Nature that do not belong to philosophy. One is the problem of the relations of the parts of Nature *to one another,* which is the task of the natural sciences exclusively; and the other is that of discovering such correlations as there may be between specific kinds of mental events and specific kinds of nervous processes. This is the task of the hybrid science already referred to as psycho-physiology, which from the start takes mental events on the one hand, and nervous processes on the other, as somehow both known, and, without inquiring how each is known, occupies itself with the discovery of particular correlations between them.

But philosophy cannot take mental events on the one hand, and nervous processes or other parts of Nature on the other, as *independently* known. For in the absence of the mental events called sensations, we should not perceive or even be able to conceive such things as brains, nerves, sense-organs, or other parts of Nature. Nature is thus in ultimate analysis known to us at all only somehow *through* our sensations, in the cases, namely, when these are not themselves the centre of our interest but, to borrow a phrase from Broad, are being *used by us to perceive with.* That is, there are times when the sensations we are having are making known to us not merely or even chiefly themselves, but somehow also something other than themselves as existing independently of them. The independently existing something somehow then made known to us by them is what we call a part of 'Nature' or an 'object of perception'; and, for philosophy, the problem of the relation between Mind and Nature is that of describing *without circularity*, that is, *otherwise than in terms of objects of perception,* what exactly the introspectable process called 'perceiving an object' consists in. That *this* problem genuinely belongs to the science of Mind is, I submit, evident from the mere formulation of it, irrespective of what in particular the solution of it may be.

I believe that although it is not one of the easier problems of philosophy, it is nevertheless perfectly soluble; but even a bare outline of what seems to me the solution of it would now be too long a story, for the time has come to rest my case. I have based it first on the distinction between the primitive and the derivative facts of a science; and further on the contention that the primitive facts distinctive of the natural sciences consist exclusively of facts susceptible of being perceptually public, whereas the primitive facts distinctive of philosophy consist exclusively of facts introspectively observable. If this contention is sound, it directly entails that the only reason why a naturalistic theory of so-called 'Mind' is not bad philosophy is that it is not philosophy at all but natural science, and indeed good natural science. To my thesis that philosophy is the science of Mind, certain apparently formidable objections immediately suggested themselves. I have considered them and have attempted to show that, on careful scrutiny, each of them turns out to be without force. That, in the brief time at my disposal, I have succeeded in making this fully evident is hardly probable; and the most I can hope to have shown is therefore that the case for the contention that philosophy is the science of Mind is far stronger than appears at first sight, strong enough, perhaps, to merit much more searching examination of it than was possible in this address.

15.

THE METHOD OF KNOWLEDGE
IN PHILOSOPHY*

Even among philosophers, the part of philosophy called meta-physics enjoys today no great popularity, but rather is the subject of many strictures. Some of its critics allege that its problems are too remote from those of plain men to have any practical import-ance. Hence they urge philosophers to forget them and to occupy themselves instead with the problems of social and political philo-sophy. Others claim that the age-long failure of metaphysicians to settle their differences is enough to show that any answers pro-posed to the questions they discuss cannot represent knowledge, but only personal opinions or temperamental preferences. And others yet contend that the problems of metaphysicians are not genuine problems at all and hence cannot be solved, but that they can be eliminated by bringing to light the false assumptions on which they rest.

Since our being assembled here must be reckoned as a long-range effect of the late Professor Howison's distinguished lectures on metaphysics, I shall assume that most of those present share my own belief that these criticisms of metaphysics are at most but partially justified. I shall therefore not reply to them at any length, but simply indicate at this point in a general way how the matter seems to me really to stand.

I believe, then, that although some of the problems metaphysi-cians have discussed are indeed pseudo problems, and that some others, although genuine, do not belong to philosophy at all, nevertheless certain others of them are, or contain, genuine prob-

* The Howison Lecture for 1944. From *University of California Publications in Philosophy,* vol. 16, No. 7, 1945.

lems, which are philosophical and are perfectly capable of solution.

I believe, moreover, that these genuine problems of metaphysics are connected with certain of the plain man's difficulties as intimately and in much the same manner as are, for instance, the problems of theoretical physics with certain others of his difficulties. For the plain man every day passes judgements of approval or disapproval on sundry concrete issues in the fields of morals, of art, of social policy, of religion, of reasoning, and so on; and when the validity of these judgements is challenged and the clash of appraisals does not arise from misinformation as to the concrete facts judged, the plain man finds that he can defend his appraisal of those facts only by appeal to a philosophy of the subject they concern.

The philosophy of it which he improvises at such times may seem to him independent of the more technical problems philosophers discuss. But it is bound to be ambiguous, fragmentary, and inconsistent; and if he were to try to purge it of these defects, he would find that the more careful and thoroughgoing reflections necessary for this would face him sooner or later with the very problems studied in the abstract and theoretical parts of philosophy.

The problems of theoretical physics, it would be granted, have remote but practical implications for the task of putting into the hands of the plain man means to attain the physical ends he chooses to pursue. And the problems of theoretical philosophy have likewise remote yet also practical bearing on something still more important, namely, on the discernment of wisdom from folly in the choices man makes of ends to pursue and of means to reach them. Hence, as G. P. Adams remarked on a certain occasion not long ago, philosophy need not *try* to be practical; it is practical inherently. But it takes already some wisdom to perceive how this is true.

Finally, a word concerning the allegation that one's metaphysics is a matter of one's temperament rather than of truths one has discovered. The fact seems to me to be, as I shall try to show later, that certain metaphysical questions call, and quite properly, for an answer expressing not a hypothesis but a basic choice or ruling interest. On the other hand, the answers called for by certain other metaphysical questions are genuinely hypotheses; and if these are but clear and specific enough, they are as capable of being tested and either confirmed or disproved as are hypotheses in any other field.

I believe, thus, that metaphysics, or, more generally, theoretical inquiry in philosophy, can reach results having title to the name of knowledge. But I also believe that, for this, the modes of investigation used must be purged of the defects which have too often made philosophical inquiry heuristically barren and thus tended to bring it into disrepute. These defects have been such as looseness of inference, ambiguity of terms, confusion of issues, inadequate testing of hypotheses; and they seem to me traceable in the main to two sources.

One of these sources is the assumption, widespread even among philosophers that in philosophy it is possible to reach knowledge through reasonings carried on in the vague terms of ordinary language without bothering to use a technical apparatus of thought. But the truth is that as soon as inquiry, whether in philosophy or elsewhere, comes to questions more difficult than those which everyday experience or casual reflection is able to answer, a technical terminology becomes a *sine qua non* of fruitful thinking. For a technical term is simply a term whose meaning is known exactly; and hence, not to bother to use technical terms is not to bother to think with precision. One can easily imagine how far chemistry or geometry, for instance, would have progressed if chemists had not bothered to use more exact conceptions of alcohol, of acid, or of ether; or mathematicians, of points, planes, or circles; than the vague conceptions those words stand for in ordinary language. The situation of philosophy is no different. Unpopular as a plea for technical language in philosophy is sure to be today, the fact must be faced that at the point where one ceases to be superficial, there, technical language, far from making for unintelligibility, is on the contrary the only means of being intelligible and of making dependable inferences. This is true in the sciences and equally so in philosophy.

Technical terms, however, must not be confused with jargon terms. A jargon term is not necessarily precise. It is merely one which is not understood by most persons because it designates things with which only a comparatively few persons occupy themselves. Thus, every trade, art, and craft, as well as every science, has its own jargon. But the jargon terms of the sciences—unlike most of those of the trades or the crafts—get defined exactly; and therefore, in addition to being esoteric like the latter, they become technical.

On the other hand, even terms in common use—such as alcohol, acid, and circle; or, in philosophy, property, truth, substance, proposition, and so on—become technical terms as soon as their meaning is stated exactly.

Philosophers, it is true, have sometimes defined their terms, and sometimes, although more rarely, defined them with some precision. This brings me to the second of the two sources of defective method in philosophy to which I alluded a moment ago. It is that to specify exactly the meaning of a term is not enough to insure that it will be an effective implement for the winning of knowledge. For this, what is needed besides is that its meaning shall not be assigned to it arbitrarily, but shall represent characters which there is reason to believe are possessed by the things the term is used to think about.

Unfortunately, the definitions offered by philosophers have often failed to satisfy this capital requirement, and have then represented mere speculations. Of course, speculation, which is but the making of hypotheses, is just as legitimate and indeed necessary in philosophy as in the natural sciences; but before any conclusions can be based on a speculation, adequate testing of it is as indispensable in philosophy as elsewhere.

Why then have philosophers so often failed to test adequately, or at all, the hypotheses that constituted the definitions they gave of their terms? The chief reason, I believe, has been that they have not realized clearly enough the nature of the facts by which these hypotheses could be tested empirically. Because of this, the testing has too much been limited to a checking of the mutual consistency of the various hypotheses entering into a system—the system as a whole, however, being then left more or less hanging in the air for lack of empirical verification of its hypotheses.

But every genuine problem has data, that is, facts not themselves questioned, about which the problem is and by reference to which any proposed solution of it can be empirically tested. And since in philosophy what these facts are is often not very obvious, one of the basic maxims of knowledge-yielding method in philosophy should be that, when a question is to be investigated, one should not only ask oneself just which facts it is about, but also state them explicitly. Actually, however, they are too often merely alluded to, as if oneself and everybody else already understood quite well what they are.

The procedure I suggest will not only make clear the way to test empirically any hypothesis made about those facts, but will also greatly facilitate compliance with a second, equally important methodological maxim. It is that one should again not be content merely to name or allude to the question which is to be answered about the facts one has listed, but that the question too should be stated as explicitly and unambiguously as possible. Observance of these two maxims will automatically lead one to distinguish, and to treat separately, each of the several questions one's initial vague statement of a problem may unawares have been propounding all at once. This will not only clear away such difficulties as confusions breed, but will also be of positive help in solving the questions one isolates, for a sharply formulated question is one of the most fertile sources of ideas.

These two maxims, however, are not so easy to comply with in philosophy that they need for this only to be accepted. The concrete nature of the method they define, as well as the power this method may possess to solve the problems to which it is applied, can be made fully clear only by an example. In the remainder of my remarks I shall therefore illustrate its use by applying it to the central and most ancient of the problems of metaphysics.

This problem is commonly referred to merely as that of the nature of reality, but it is sometimes formulated more explicitly. A. E. Taylor, for instance, describes metaphysics as 'a systematic and impartial inquiry as to what we really mean by the familiar distinction between "seems" and "is", that is to say, a scientific inquiry into the general characteristic by which reality or real being is distinguished from mere appearance, not in one special sphere of study, but universally.'[1]

But even this formulation fails to specify the data of the problem. Moreover, it tends to suggest that the data of the problem as to the nature of reality are of the same logical type as would be, for instance, those of a problem as to the nature of chalk, or of rubber; and therefore that to solve it we must compare concrete samples of real being with concrete samples of merely apparent or

---

[1] *Elements of Metaphysics*, p. 4.

unreal being, and observe what characteristics differentiate the former from the latter. But that the problem is not of this logical type is perhaps sufficiently shown by the fact that since some philosophers are idealists, some materialists, and others adherents of still other doctrines, samples of real being could not be picked without begging in the very act what the contending philosophers would regard as the question at issue.

To avoid this, the data to which we look as starting point must be of quite a different kind. I submit that they can consist only of concrete examples of the manner or manners in which the word 'real' or its cognates, 'really' and 'reality', are used predicatively. That is, our data will have to consist of *statements* such as that a certain substance, which seems to be paper, is really asbestos; or that mermaids do not really exist; or that trees far away appear blue but in reality are green; and so on. Such concrete instances of the predicative use of the word 'real' or its cognates constitute the factual data which a hypothesis as to the meaning of those words must fit and by reference to which its tenability can be empirically tested; for the problem then is as to what those words mean *as applied in the given examples*.

Of course, I take it that what we are interested to analyse is examples which, like those given, illustrate commonly accepted usage; but it is worth noting that if examples of some freak usage of those same words were given instead, then, if it interested us to do so, we could analyse equally well the meaning those words had there. The essential point is that either *no* applications of those words are given us, and then we can make them mean anything we please; or else concrete examples of *some* applicative usage of them are furnished, and then we have data by which to test empirically the soundness of any proposed definition of what they mean in that particular sort of context. A definition of them so reached will be a so-called real or objective definition, as distinguished from an arbitrary, merely verbal definition.

Our second maxim of method, it will be recalled, enjoins us to state explicitly what we are seeking to discover about the data the first maxim requires us to list. In the present case, then, what we wish to discover is the meaning the word 'real' or its cognates have in the sample statements we take as data. Any hypothesis as to this will therefore have the form of a definition of the word concerned; and since a definition is good if and only if it is exactly equivalent to the term defined, the test of the adequacy of any definition that occurs to us will consist in the possibility of replacing the term defined by the definition proposed, in any of the sample statements taken as data.

But what will be the test of that possibility itself? It will be, I submit, that this replacement shall not result in making false any of the statements that were true, nor in making true any that were false, nor in altering the truth or the falsity of any other statement implying or implied by the given ones. For this test will be met automatically if a definition expresses a genuine equivalence, and will not be met unless it does.

The nature of the method I propose having now been described in general, let us next apply it in particular to the problem of the nature of reality, and see what it will do for us.

As soon as, in compliance with it, we begin listing statements in which the word 'real' or one of its cognates is used predicatively, the suspicion forces itself upon us that the word may mean one thing in some of them, and something else in certain others. We are therefore led to divide our sample statements into several groups and to scrutinize each group separately.

The first may well consist of examples in which the adjective 'real' is evidently used in some special, purely technical sense. In law, for instance, real property is contrasted with personal or portable property, and 'real' therefore means nonpersonal or immovable. In mathematics, certain numbers are called real numbers and contrasted with imaginary numbers, although both kinds are real enough, in an ordinary sense of the term, to be accurately described and fruitfully employed by mathematicians. Again, in logic real definitions are contrasted with verbal or nominal definitions, although words are just as real, in an ordinary sense, as are things other than words. It is clear that no problem involving the distinction between reality and appearances arises in connection with these or possible other equally technical uses of the word 'real'. We may therefore dismiss them from consideration.

The group we come to next is much more significant. It consists of statements such as that a certain dog looks or seems or appears ferocious, but is not so really or in reality; or that a certain seemingly valid argument is really fallacious; or that the stone in a certain ring, although it appears to be glass, is a real diamond; or that a certain substance seems to be paper but is in reality asbestos; and so on. All these, let it be noted, are descriptive statements. That is, in each some entity, for example a substance, is given, and the hypothesis is offered that it is of a certain kind, for example, of the kind called paper. For the sake of generality, let us call E the entity given in any of them, and call K the kind to which it is claimed to belong; and let us note that, whatever the kind K may be, there is always some set of characters, a, b, c, d, such that, if and only if a given entity possesses *all* of them, it is of kind K. This simple analysis puts us in position to describe exactly the occasions which give rise to the question as to whether a given entity E really is, or only appears to be, of a kind K.

They are occasions on which *only some* of the characters of E are manifest to observation, and on which these manifest characters— which constitute the *appearance* of E at the time—happen to be the same characters as would be manifest in the existing circumstances if E should happen to be of kind K.

For example, under present circumstances, the colour, shape, texture, and flexibility of the sheet I hold are manifest to observation; they are its present appearance; whereas the combustibility of it, if it be combustible, is not now manifest. But further, the colour, flexibility, and other now manifest characters of the sheet, are the *same* characters as would be manifest under present circumstances if the sheet *were* of the kind called paper.

Now, if the things which in our past experience manifested this same colour, flexibility, and so on, did later turn out in most cases to possess *also* combustibility and the remaining characters of paper, then what we naturally say in the present case is that this sheet *seems* or *appears* to be paper; that is, its present appearance is the same as that of paper.

Furthermore, if, on applying the proper tests, we find that this sheet does have *also* those remaining characters of paper, then we express this by saying that it not only appears to be paper, but *really* is paper; whereas, if it turns out to lack some of them, what we say is that, although it appears to be paper, it is *not really* so, or is not real paper.

Thus, in terms of an entity E, and of a set of characters a, b, c, d, *all* of which must be possessed by it if it is to be of kind K, but *only some* of which are at the time manifest in it, we have defined exactly the types of situations which govern the use of the notions of appearance and reality in cases where the nature of the thing a descriptive statement describes consists of a complex of characters. When on the contrary a single character is concerned, as when we say that the trees on a distant hillside appear blue but really are green, the analysis of 'really' is very different. We shall consider it farther on at the appropriate place.

What now can we conclude is the qualification introduced by the words 'real' or 'really' in statements of the kind we have been examining? A moment's reflection makes evident that in our example what is qualified as 'real' is not in fact the paper itself at all, for paper does not have two species—one called real paper and the other unreal or seeming paper. What is not really paper is not paper at all. Rather, what is qualified is the descriptive proposition 'This is paper', and the effect of inserting the word 'really' into it is simply to assert that *that proposition is true*: to say 'this is really paper' is exactly the same as to say, 'truly, this is paper', or 'that this is paper, is true'.

Accordingly, the occasions on which we say 'this is *really* paper', instead of simply 'this is paper', are occasions on which we wish to assert that, notwithstanding some item of evidence to the contrary, it is *true* that this is paper. On the other hand, the occasions on which we say simply 'this is paper' are those on which we are answering the question 'What is this?' without anything having suggested that it is not paper.

These remarks complete the analysis of the notion of reality as it enters in statements of the type we have been examining. I turn now to examples of a different kind. They consist of existential assertions, that is, of assertions which, instead of answering as before the question 'What is this?' answer the question 'Are there any so and so's?'

Instances of existential assertions in which the notion of reality enters would be that, in reality, no mermaids exist; that the man called Hamlet by Shakespeare did not really exist; that Utopia is an imaginary country but that Spain is real; that there is really such a psychological state as hypnosis; or that black swans really exist but green swans do not.

In some of these statements, it looks as if 'is real' means simply 'exists', but in others the notion of reality clearly is additional to that of existence. The examples which are of the latter sort may be dealt with first and briefly, since in them the import of the word 'really' or of either of its cognates is essentially the same as in the descriptive statements we have considered. That is, in existential statements too, its import is to assert that the statement in which the word enters is *true* notwithstanding some doubt or item of evidence to the contrary.

For example, the sort of occasion on which one would naturally say 'mermaids do not really exist', or 'mermaids are not real', instead of simply 'no mermaids exist', would be one on which, perhaps, a child had been reading a story about mermaids or had seen a moving picture representing some. For the simplest explanation of such a story or picture would naturally be that there are mermaids, and the story or picture therefore constitutes an item of circumstantial evidence that mermaids exist. The import of the statement that mermaids do not *really* exist would thus be that that evidence is misleading—that, in spite of it, the truth is that mermaids do not exist.

In such examples, realness is thus not a character differentiating one species of existence from another and inferior species called unreal or seeming existence; any more than, in our earlier example, realness differentiated one species of paper from an inferior one called seeming or unreal paper. In both groups of examples alike, what the word 'really' or either of its cognates qualifies is the statement itself in which it occurs, and its force is the same as that of the adverbs 'truly' or 'certainly'.

Let us now return to the sort of assertions in which 'is real' is used simply as synonymous with 'exists'. Our task here is then to analyse the meaning of 'to exist'. This will not only make explicit the meaning of these assertions, but also clarify by contrast that of assertions—such as those just discussed and certain others yet to be considered—in which the notion of reality is added to that of existence.

The question as to what exactly it means, to say that something of a given kind K exists, is best approached by limiting attention at first to cases where what is in view is specifically physical existence, as distinguished from, for example, mathematical or psychological existence.

In all such cases, the assertion that there exists something of a kind *K* is, I submit, exactly synonymous with the assertion that something of that kind *is somewhere*; that is, occupies some place in space at some time. It is important to notice, however, that an assertion of existence may be more or less determinate.

For example, least determinately, one might assert that there are black swans, or, which is the same thing, that black swans exist; that is, are at *some* place, not specified.

But, somewhat more determinately, the assertion made might be instead that there are black swans *somewhere within a specified region*—for instance, in Australia.

Or thirdly and now quite determinately, the assertion made might be that there is a black swan *here now*; that is, at the specific place to which one is pointing at the time.

These examples make evident that, in the phrases 'there is' or 'there are', one is using the word 'there' not in some idiomatic sense but literally, that is, as indicative of spatial location whether completely indeterminate or partially or wholly determinate. In these phrases, moreover, temporal location also is indicated, likewise more or less determinately, at least by the past, present, or future tense of the verb, and often through specification by date of some period or particular moment also.

Physical existence, thus, is essentially spatio-temporal ubiety; and that which has or lacks ubiety, that is, is or is not present at some place in space at some time, is always some *what* or *kind*—which may be a kind of substance, or of property, or of relation, or of activity, or of change, or of state, and so on.

When existence other than physical is in view—for instance, mathematical existence—the meaning of existence is closely analogous. The difference is only that the place concerned is a place in some order other than the space-time order.

Thus, for example, the assertion that a square root of 9 exists, but no square root of 3, means that the character 'being square root of 9' characterizes a certain place in the order of the whole numbers, namely, the determinate place called 3; whereas the character 'being square root of 3' characterizes none of the places in the series of whole numbers.

In any assertion of existence, thus, no matter whether it be more particularly one of physical existence, or of mathematical, or psychological, or mythological, or other existence, two components always are essentially involved, namely, a *what* and a *where*. And generically a *where* or place is the sort of thing specifiable in terms of *ordinal* relations; that is, of relations such as between, next to, beyond, among, outside of, and so on.

This analysis, it should be noted, incidentally results in making explicit also the meaning possessed by the word 'reality' when it is used not as an abstract term synonymous with 'realness', but as a concrete, *denotative* term; as, for example, in such statements as that reality is exclusively material, or exclusively mental, or of both these kinds, or of the nature of will, and so on. When the word 'reality' is so used, it means 'everything that exists'. It is obvious that reality in this sense is not the opposite of appearance, but of non-existence, or nothing.

At this point, it may be remarked in passing that when the word 'reality' is used thus denotatively, then that, *if anything*, which it denotes, is known to us, that is, known to us *to exist*, only if our existential judgements or other existential apprehensions are *true*. Hence, if their truth (or erroneousness) is to be something ascertainable at all, it cannot possibly be defined as correspondence (or non-correspondence) to reality, that is, to something known at all to exist only if those very apprehensions or judgements of existence happen to be true.

We shall now examine next a use of the word 'really' or its cognates radically different from any we have so far considered. An example of it would be the statement that the wood of the table is really a cloud of minute particles at relatively vast distances from one another; and another example, that water is really a compound of oxygen and hydrogen.

When this is asserted about water, the word 'really' cannot have the same meaning as when we say that the liquid in a given glass is really water. For the statement that water is really H_2O evidently does not mean that water only seems to be water but in truth is something else; nor does it mean that it only seems to have the familiar properties of liquidity, tastelessness, capacity to quench thirst and fire, and so on, but has *instead* of these the property of being analysable into oxygen and hydrogen; nor does it mean simply that it is true that the composition of water is H_2O.

What it means, I submit, is that, *for certain purposes*, such as some of those of chemists, the property of being analysable into and synthesizable out of hydrogen and oxygen is *the important or relevant* property; whereas for such purposes the other, more familiar properties of water are irrelevant.

In statements of this type, then, the definition of realness which, at the time they are made, tacitly governs the use in them of the word 'really' is that *to be real is to be relevant to the purposes or interests which rule at the time.* In such cases, the opposite of 'to be real' is thus not, as before, to be a deceptive appearance, nor to be non-existent, but to be irrelevant, unimportant, insignificant, negligible, of no interest or value for the purposes ruling at the time.

Additional examples belonging to this group would be such statements as that the real way to talk to a mob is such and such; that you really must do this or that; that such and such a proposal is not realistic; that nothing is more real than an idea; that such and such a consideration is very real; and so on. The example mentioned earlier, in which we say that the trees on the distant hillside seem blue but really are green, analyses in a manner slightly different from that in which we say that water is really H_2O; but in it, too, realness consists in relevance to interests or purposes postulated as for the time ruling. For, evidently, that the trees display the colour blue when they are observed from far away is exactly as true as that they display the colour green when they are observed from a distance of a few feet. The two properties are perfectly compatible and the trees truly possess both. Which colour we say the trees 'really' have is therefore a matter only of whether only the near point of observation is relevant to the purposes which rule us at the time (as when they are the ordinary practical or scientific purposes), or of whether on the contrary any point of observation we have chosen is relevant to our then ruling purposes (as when we are landscape painters).

We have studied so far four main types of statements in which the word 'really' or one of its cognates figured. The four types differed markedly in certain respects, but they were nevertheless alike in a respect to which attention must now be called, namely, all of them were statements of something or other that had the status of *hypothesis.* That is, what they formulated was in each case something that was either true or false, and was therefore susceptible of being more or less fully verified or confuted.

But now we must notice yet another group of statements in which the notion of reality enters, but which express not hypotheses at all, but something else altogether, to which the categories of truth, falsity, probability, confirmation, proof, or disproof do not apply at all. What they express I shall call *ontological positions*.

Just what an ontological position is, as distinguished from a hypothesis in which the notion of reality figures, will become clear if we return to the tacit major premise which, as we saw, was assumed by the assertion that water really is H_2O. That tacit premise, it will be recalled, was that to be real is to be relevant to certain of the purposes of chemists. Now, to adopt this or any similar major premise for one's activities through a given time is to *take a position* as to what, for the time, one will mean by 'being real'. And to be governed, even if unawares, by such a major premise at a given time is to be then *occupying a position* as to what it is to be real. That is, the statement of such a major premise is the statement of an ontological position. It is always of the form 'to be real is to have such and such a character'.

An ontological position, thus, is essentially of the nature of an exclusive or basic interest in the things which have a certain character; it is a rule one adopts as to what things one will regard as alone of interest, or will rank as basic or primary. For example, the ontological position that to be real is to have a certain character C would consist in interest exclusively or basically in things having this character; it would be the rule of admitting to consideration only the things having character C, or at least of positing them as fundamental and absolutely prior in interest or importance.

Now, an ontological position may be consciously embraced, or it may be occupied unawares. It may be occupied by many persons, or by few. It may be congenial to one person, and repugnant to another. It may be occupied at a certain moment, and relinquished the next in favour of a different one. But just because an ontological position is not a contention at all but essentially an interest at the time ruling, an ontological position cannot be true or be false; nor therefore can it be shown more or less probably true than another, or be refuted, or be proved. These possibilities exist only in the case of hypotheses.

The ontological position, for example, which natural scientists, while functioning as such, occupy, is that to be real is to be perceptually public or implicit in what is so. But it is evident that these words do not formulate a hypothesis as to properties empirically discoverable in some concretely given entity called reality; for no empirical facts one might adduce could prove or disprove what those words expressed, or render it probable, doubtful, or improbable. Plainly, they describe no hypothesis at all, but simply the criterion by which the things in which the natural sciences interest themselves are distinguished from the things these sciences ignore.

Truth, falsity, and probability are thus categories logically incongruous to ontological positions—as inapplicable to them as would be the predicates thirsty or bitter to logarithms or to algebraic equations. Ontological positions may only be occupied or not occupied, be embraced or abandoned. This analysis of their nature and logical status, I may say, seems to me in essential agreement with conclusions reached by J. Loewenberg in a penetrating article entitled 'The Question of Priority' which he published some years ago;[1] and I therefore look to him hopefully for moral support in a conception of the nature of ontological positions which, I realize, is likely to shock many philosophers.

Additional instances of ontological positions that have been held or might be held would be that to be real is to be introspectively observable or implicit in what is so; that to be real is to be individual; that to be real is to be unique and changeless; that to be real is to be free from contradictions; that to be real is to be a coherent whole; and so on.

There is one ontological position, however, worth special mention here. It is the one occupied by *any* ontologist—and therefore by ourselves here now—at the time he is engaged in an inquiry as to the nature of reality. This position is that to be real is to be relevant to the problem of the nature of reality, appearance, and unreality. Evidently, it is a position different from the idealistic, or materialistic, or other conclusion as to the nature of reality, which an ontologist may believe his reflections on the subject eventually dictate.

But this very remark now leads us to ask whether our inventory of the variety of statements in which the notion of reality figures has been complete. Is there any problem as to the nature of reality which is a genuine, not a pseudo problem, but which we have not yet considered? It might be contended that such metaphysical

---

[1] *University of California Publications in Philosophy*, vol. 13, pp. 37–69.

doctrines as idealism, materialism, voluntarism, and so on, purport to be answers to a question about reality distinct from all those we have examined. An adequate scrutiny of this contention would require more time than I can now dispose of, but I can indicate briefly why I believe it to be mistaken.

The statement, for example, that reality is exclusively mental may be construed in either one of two ways. First, it may be taken as but another way of saying that to be real is to be either a mind or a mind's idea. If so, it is evidently the statement of what we have called an ontological position, not of a hypothesis; and, as pointed out, it is then not the sort of thing which either is true or false. It only declares the primacy, for the idealist, of minds and their ideas, and his intent to construe everything in terms of them.

But the statement that reality is exclusively mental may be interpreted otherwise. In it, the word 'reality' may be taken denotatively, that is, taken to mean 'everything that exists'. The statement that reality is mental then means that only minds and their ideas exist.

In ordinary usage, however, the words 'mental things' denote only such things as feelings, thoughts, volitions, hopes, memory images, and so on, or the minds comprising them; whereas such things as the wood of the table, which beyond question, also exists, are normally denoted by the words 'material things'. I submit, therefore, that the statement that reality is exclusively mental, as meaning that everything which exists is minds and ideas—or similarly, that reality is exclusively material—cannot possibly be true unless some meaning at variance with the customary is forced, ad hoc, by means of the qualification 'really', either on the verb 'to exist', or else on the adjective 'mental', or 'material'.

A materialist, for example, might say that what he contends is that nothing which is not material has real existence. But then this would be but saying that the realm of material existence is the only one he chooses to acknowledge—the only one of interest to him. Thus, because he would be restricting his assertion to a particular realm of existence, which he elects to rank as alone or supremely interesting to him, he would in fact again not be stating a hypothesis as to the nature of everything that exists, but again only declaring the ontological position he chooses to take.

But instead of using the word 'really' to limit arbitrarily the scope of 'to exist', one might use it instead to stretch, equally arbitrarily, the denotation of the terms 'mental' or 'material'.

An idealist, for example, might say that what he maintains is that everything which exists is *really* mental, that is, *really* consists of minds and their ideas. But then, since, beyond question, the wood of this table can be sawed, scraped, sandpapered, soaked in oil, and so on, it would automatically follow that minds, or their ideas, can in some cases be sandpapered, soaked in oil, used as a table, and so on. But these are the very kind of operations we mean when we speak of material operations.

I submit, therefore, that to assert that the wood on which such operations can be performed is mental would not be to reveal a hitherto unsuspected but verifiable property of the wood. It would only be to reveal that one has arbitrarily elected to employ the word 'mental' to denote not only the things it is customarily used to denote, but also those customarily denoted by the word 'material'. To do this, however, would be exactly the same logically, and just as futile, as proposing to say henceforth that white men are really negroes, or that negroes are really white men. This would not be revealing any hitherto hidden fact as to the colour of their skins, but only tampering wantonly with language.

But the idealist who asserts that reality is mental, or the materialist who asserts it to be material, usually believes himself to be revealing some generally unrecognized fact about such things as wood, or about such things as thoughts, and thus to be solving a genuine problem. Yet, as I have briefly tried to show, he is in truth doing no such thing, but either stating the ontological position he chooses to take, or else dealing with only a pseudo problem, which evaporates when one distinguishes and analyses as we have done the different meanings the word 'reality' or its cognates have in the several sorts of contexts in which they function in the language.

There is, however, a genuine problem as to mind and matter. But it is not as to whether everything is mental and nothing material, or everything material and nothing mental. For there is no doubt at all that some existing things have and others do not have the properties, such as those I have mentioned, which we mean when we speak of material properties; nor that some existing things have and others do not have the properties we mean to refer to when we speak of mental properties. The datum of the genuine problem as to mind and matter is that certain things, such as wood, in fact are *called* material and not mental, and others, such as thoughts, in fact are *called* mental and not material. And the problem itself is as to what exactly the words 'material' and 'mental' mean *as* so applied and so denied.

Then, when this has been discovered, the further problem arises as to what, in the light of the discovery, may be the relation between mind and matter. But the remarks which have preceded show that the relation cannot possibly be that of identity.

In concluding, let me say that the analyses I have offered of the several meanings of the word 'reality' or its cognates may well have contained mistakes. But the method of inquiry we have used, which has required that the several kinds of contexts in which these words occur be not just alluded to but be unambiguously specified by concrete examples, has thereby furnished the very facts by reference to which the correctness of those analyses can be empirically tested, and the analyses rectified if need be.

I hope, however, that the results we have obtained by that method in our discussion of the ancient problem as to the nature of reality may be judged sufficiently sound and substantial to recommend the use of the same method in dealing with other philosophical problems.

International Library of Philosophy & Scientific Method

Editor: Ted Honderich
Advisory Editor: Bernard Williams

List of titles, page two

International Library of Psychology Philosophy & Scientific Method

Editor: C K Ogden

List of titles, page six

ROUTLEDGE AND KEGAN PAUL LTD
68 Carter Lane London EC4

International Library of Philosophy and Scientific Method
(Demy 8vo)

Allen, R. E. (Ed.)
Studies in Plato's Metaphysics
Contributors: J. L. Ackrill, R. E. Allen, R. S. Bluck, H. F. Cherniss, F. M.
Cornford, R. C. Cross, P. T. Geach, R. Hackforth, W. F. Hicken, A. C. Lloyd,
G. R. Morrow, G. E. L. Owen, G. Ryle, W. G. Runciman, G. Vlastos
464 pp. 1965. (2nd Impression 1967.) 70s.

Armstrong, D. M.
Perception and the Physical World
208 pp. 1961. (3rd Impression 1966.) 25s.

A Materialist Theory of the Mind
376 pp. 1967. about 45s.

Bambrough, Renford (Ed.)
New Essays on Plato and Aristotle
Contributors: J. L. Ackrill, G. E. M. Anscombe, Renford Bambrough,
R. M. Hare, D. M. MacKinnon, G. E. L. Owen, G. Ryle, G. Vlastos
184 pp. 1965. (2nd Impression 1967.) 28s.

Barry, Brian
Political Argument
382 pp. 1965. 50s.

Bird, Graham
Kant's Theory of Knowledge:
An Outline of One Central Argument in the *Critique of Pure Reason*
220 pp. 1962. (2nd Impression 1965.) 28s.

Brentano, Franz
The True and the Evident
Edited and narrated by Professor R. Chisholm
218 pp. 1965. 40s.

Broad, C. D.
Lectures on Psychical Research
Incorporating the Perrott Lectures given in Cambridge University in 1959
and 1960
461 pp. 1962. (2nd Impression 1966.) 56s.

Crombie, I. M.
An Examination of Plato's Doctrine
I. Plato on Man and Society
408 pp. 1962. (2nd Impression 1966.) 42s.
II. Plato on Knowledge and Reality
583 pp. 1963. (2nd Impression 1967.) 63s.

Day, John Patrick
Inductive Probability
352 pp. 1961. 40s.

International Library of Philosophy and Scientific Method
(Demy 8vo)

Edel, Abraham
Method in Ethical Theory
379 pp. 1963. 32s.

Flew, Anthony
Hume's Philosophy of Belief
A Study of his First "Inquiry"
296 pp. 1961. (2nd Impression 1966.) 30s.

Fogelin, Robert J.
Evidence and Meaning
Studies in Analytical Philosophy
200 pp. 1967. 25s.

Gale, Richard
The Language of Time
256 pp. 1967. about 30s.

Goldman, Lucien
The Hidden God
A Study of Tragic Vision in the *Pensées* of Pascal and the Tragedies of
Racine. Translated from the French by Philip Thody
424 pp. 1964. 70s.

Hamlyn, D. W.
Sensation and Perception
A History of the Philosophy of Perception
222 pp. 1961. (3rd Impression 1967.) 25s.

Kemp, J.
Reason, Action and Morality
216 pp. 1964. 30s.

Körner, Stephan
Experience and Theory
An Essay in the Philosophy of Science
272 pp. 1966. 45s.

Lazerowitz, Morris
Studies in Metaphilosophy
276 pp. 1964. 35s.

Linsky, Leonard
Referring
152 pp. 1967. about 28s.

Merleau-Ponty, M.
Phenomenology of Perception
Translated from the French by Colin Smith
487 pp. 1962. (4th Impression 1967.) 56s.

International Library of Philosophy and Scientific Method

(Demy 8vo)

Perelman, Chaim
The Idea of Justice and the Problem of Argument
Introduction by H. L. A. Hart. Translated from the French by John Petrie
224 pp. 1963. 28s.

Ross, Alf
Directives, Norms and their Logic
192 pp. 1967. about 25s.

Schlesinger, G.
Method in the Physical Sciences
148 pp. 1963. 21s.

Sellars, W. F.
Science, Perception and Reality
374 pp. 1963. (2nd Impression 1966.) 50s.

Shwayder, D. S.
The Stratification of Behaviour
A System of Definitions Propounded and Defended
428 pp. 1965. 56s.

Skolimowski, Henryk
Polish Analytical Philosophy
288 pp. 1967. 40s.

Smart, J. J. C.
Philosophy and Scientific Realism
168 pp. 1963. (3rd Impression 1967.) 25s.

Smythies, J. R. (Ed.)
Brain and Mind
Contributors: Lord Brain, John Beloff, C. J. Ducasse, Antony Flew,
Hartwig Kuhlenbeck, D. M. MacKay, H. H. Price, Anthony Quinton and
J. R. Smythies
288 pp. 1965. 40s.

Science and E.S.P.
Contributors: Gilbert Murray, H. H. Price, Rosalind Heywood, Cyril Burt,
C. D. Broad, Francis Huxley and John Beloff
320 pp. about 40s.

Taylor, Charles
The Explanation of Behaviour
288 pp. 1964. (2nd Impression 1965.) 40s.

Williams, Bernard, and Montefiore, Alan
British Analytical Philosophy
352 pp. 1965. (2nd Impression 1967.) 45s.

4

International Library of Philosophy and Scientific Method
(Demy 8vo)

Wittgenstein, Ludwig
Tractatus Logico-Philosophicus
The German text of the *Logisch-Philosophische Abhandlung* with a new
translation by D. F. Pears and B. F. McGuinness. Introduction by Bertrand
Russell
188 pp. 1961. (3rd Impression 1966.) 21s.

Wright, Georg Henrik Von
Norm and Action
A Logical Enquiry. The Gifford Lectures
232 pp. 1963. (2nd Impression 1964.) 32s.

The Varieties of Goodness
The Gifford Lectures
236 pp. 1963. (3rd Impression 1966.) 28s.

Zinkernagel, Peter
Conditions for Description
Translated from the Danish by Olaf Lindum
272 pp. 1962. 37s. 6d.

International Library of Psychology, Philosophy, and Scientific Method
(Demy 8vo)

PHILOSOPHY

Anton, John Peter
Aristotle's Theory of Contrariety
276 pp. 1957. 25s.

Bentham, J.
The Theory of Fictions
Introduction by C. K. Ogden
214 pp. 1932. 30s.

Black, Max
The Nature of Mathematics
A Critical Survey
242 pp. 1933. (5th Impression 1965.) 28s.

Bluck, R. S.
Plato's Phaedo
A Translation with Introduction, Notes and Appendices
226 pp. 1955. 21s.

Broad, C. D.
Scientific Thought
556 pp. 1923. (4th Impression 1952.) 40s.

Five Types of Ethical Theory
322 pp. 1930. (9th Impression 1967.) 30s.

The Mind and Its Place in Nature
694 pp. 1925. (7th Impression 1962.) 55s. See also Lean, Martin

Buchler, Justus (Ed.)
The Philosophy of Peirce
Selected Writings
412 pp. 1940. (3rd Impression 1956.) 35s.

Burtt, E. A.
The Metaphysical Foundations of Modern Physical Science
A Historical and Critical Essay
364 pp. 2nd (revised) edition 1932. (5th Impression 1964.) 35s.

6

International Library of Psychology, Philosophy, and Scientific Method
(Demy 8vo)

Carnap, Rudolf
The Logical Syntax of Language
Translated from the German by Amethe Smeaton
376 pp. 1937. (7th Impression 1967.) 40s.

Chwistek, Leon
The Limits of Science
Outline of Logic and of the Methodology of the Exact Sciences
With Introduction and Appendix by Helen Charlotte Brodie
414 pp. 2nd edition 1949. 32s.

Cornford, F. M.
Plato's Theory of Knowledge
The Theaetetus and Sophist of Plato
Translated with a running commentary
358 pp. 1935. (7th Impression 1967.) 28s.

Plato's Cosmology
The Timaeus of Plato
Translated with a running commentary
402 pp. Frontispiece. 1937. (5th Impression 1966.) 45s.

Plato and Parmenides
Parmenides' *Way of Truth* and Plato's *Parmenides*
Translated with a running commentary
280 pp 1939 (5th Impression 1964.) 32s.

Crawshay-Williams, Rupert
Methods and Criteria of Reasoning
An Inquiry into the Structure of Controversy
312 pp. 1957. 32s.

Fritz, Charles A.
Bertrand Russell's Construction of the External World
252 pp. 1952. 30s.

Hulme, T. E.
Speculations
Essays on Humanism and the Philosophy of Art
Edited by Herbert Read. Foreword and Frontispiece by Jacob Epstein
296 pp. 2nd edition 1936. (6th Impression 1965.) 32s.

Lange, Frederick Albert
The History of Materialism
And Criticism of its Present Importance
With an Introduction by Bertrand Russell, F.R.S. Translated from the German
by Ernest Chester Thomas
1,146 pp. 1925. (3rd Impression 1957.) 70s.

International Library of Psychology, Philosophy, and Scientific Method
(Demy 8vo)

Lazerowitz, Morris
The Structure of Metaphysics
With a Foreword by John Wisdom
262 pp. 1955. (2nd Impression 1963.) 30s.

Lean, Martin
Sense-Perception and Matter
A Critical Analysis of C. D. Broad's Theory of Perception
234 pp. 1953. 25s.

Lodge, Rupert C.
Plato's Theory of Art
332 pp. 1953. 25s.

The Philosophy of Plato
366 pp. 1956. 32s.

Mannheim, Karl
Ideology and Utopia
An Introduction to the Sociology of Knowledge
With a Preface by Louis Wirth. Translated from the German by Louis Wirth and Edward Shils
360 pp. 1954. (2nd Impression 1966.) 30s.

Moore, G. E.
Philosophical Studies
360 pp. 1922. (6th Impression 1965.) 35s. See also Ramsey, F. P.

Ogden, C. K., and Richards, I. A.
The Meaning of Meaning
A Study of the Influence of Language upon Thought and of the Science of Symbolism
With supplementary essays by B. Malinowski and F. G. Crookshank
394 pp. 10th Edition 1949. (6th Impression 1967.) 32s.
See also Bentham, J.

Peirce, Charles, *see* Buchler, J.

Ramsey, Frank Plumpton
The Foundations of Mathematics and other Logical Essays
Edited by R. B. Braithwaite. Preface by G. E. Moore
318 pp. 1931. (4th Impression 1965.) 35s.

Richards, I. A.
Principles of Literary Criticism
312 pp. 2nd edition. 1926. (17th Impression 1966.) 30s.

Mencius on the Mind. Experiments in Multiple Definition
190 pp. 1932. (2nd Impression 1964.) 28s.

Russell, Bertrand, *see* Fritz C. A.; Lange, F. A.; Wittgenstein, L.

8

International Library of Psychology, Philosophy, and Scientific Method
(Demy 8vo)

Smart, Ninian
Reasons and Faiths
An Investigation of Religious Discourse, Christian and Non-Christian
230 pp. 1958. (2nd Impression 1965.) 28s.

Vaihinger, H.
The Philosophy of As If
A System of the Theoretical, Practical and Religious Fictions of Mankind
Translated by C. K. Ogden
428 pp. 2nd edition 1935. (4th Impression 1965.) 45s.

Wittgenstein, Ludwig
Tractatus Logico-Philosophicus
With an Introduction by Bertrand Russell, F.R.S., German text with an English translation en regard
216 pp. 1922. (9th Impression 1962.) 21s.
For the Pears-McGuinness translation—*see page 5*

Wright, Georg Henrik von
Logical Studies
214 pp. 1957. (2nd Impression 1967.) 28s.

Zeller, Eduard
Outlines of the History of Greek Philosophy
Revised by Dr. Wilhelm Nestle. Translated from the German by L. R. Palmer
248 pp. 13th (revised) edition 1931. (5th Impression 1963.) 28s.

PSYCHOLOGY

Adler, Alfred
The Practice and Theory of Individual Psychology
Translated by P. Radin
368 pp. 2nd (revised) edition 1929. (8th Impression 1964.) 30s.

Eng, Helga
The Psychology of Children's Drawings
From the First Stroke to the Coloured Drawing
240 pp. 8 colour plates. 139 figures. 2nd edition 1954. (3rd Impression 1966.) 40s.

Jung, C. G.
Psychological Types
or The Psychology of Individuation
Translated from the German and with a Preface by H. Godwin Baynes
696 pp. 1923. (12th Impression 1964.) 45s.

International Library of Psychology, Philosophy, and Scientific Method

(Demy 8vo)

Koffka, Kurt
The Growth of the Mind
An Introduction to Child-Psychology
Translated from the German by Robert Morris Ogden
456 pp. 16 figures. 2nd edition (revised) 1928. (6th Impression 1965.) 45s.
Principles of Gestalt Psychology
740 pp. 112 figures. 39 tables. 1935. (5th Impression 1962.) 60s.

Malinowski, Bronislaw
Crime and Custom in Savage Society
152 pp. 6 plates. 1926. (8th Impression 1966.) 21s.
Sex and Repression in Savage Society
290 pp. 1927. (4th Impression 1953.) 28s.
See also Ogden, C. K.

Murphy, Gardner
An Historical Introduction to Modern Psychology
488 pp. 5th edition (revised) 1949. (6th Impression 1967.) 40s.

Paget, R.
Human Speech
Some Observations, Experiments, and Conclusions as to the Nature, Origin, Purpose and Possible Improvement of Human Speech
374 pp. 5 plates. 1930. (2nd Impression 1963.) 42s.

Petermann, Bruno
The Gestalt Theory and the Problem of Configuration
Translated from the German by Meyer Fortes
364 pp. 20 figures. 1932. (2nd Impression 1950.) 25s.

Piaget, Jean
The Language and Thought of the Child
Preface by E. Claparède. Translated from the French by Marjorie Gabain
220 pp. 3rd edition (revised and enlarged) 1959. (3rd Impression 1966.) 30s.

Judgment and Reasoning in the Child
Translated from the French by Marjorie Warden
276 pp. 1928 (4th Impression 1966.) 28s.

The Child's Conception of the World
Translated from the French by Joan and Andrew Tomlinson
408 pp. 1929. (4th Impression 1964.) 40s.

International Library of Psychology, Philosophy, and Scientific Method *(Demy 8vo)*

Piaget, Jean *(continued)*

The Child's Conception of Physical Causality
Translated from the French by Marjorie Gabain
(3rd Impression 1965.) 30s.

The Moral Judgment of the Child
Translated from the French by Marjorie Gabain
438 pp. 1932. (4th Impression 1965.) 35s.

The Psychology of Intelligence
Translated from the French by Malcolm Piercy and D. E. Berlyne
198 pp. 1950. (4th Impression 1964.) 18s.

The Child's Conception of Number
Translated from the French by C. Gattegno and F. M. Hodgson
266 pp. 1952. (3rd Impression 1964.) 25s.

The Origin of Intelligence in the Child
Translated from the French by Margaret Cook
448 pp. 1953. (2nd Impression 1966.) 42s.

The Child's Conception of Geometry
In collaboration with Bärbel Inhelder and Alina Szeminska. Translated from the French by E. A. Lunzer
428 pp. 1960. (2nd Impression 1966.) 45s.

Piaget, Jean and Inhelder, Bärbel
The Child's Conception of Space
Translated from the French by F. J. Langdon and J. L. Lunzer
512 pp. 29 figures. 1956 (3rd Impression 1967.) 42s.

Roback, A. A.
The Psychology of Character
With a Survey of Personality in General
786 pp. 3rd edition (revised and enlarged 1952.) 50s.

Smythies, J. R.
Analysis of Perception
With a Preface by Sir Russell Brain, Bt.
162 pp. 1956. 21s.

van der Hoop, J. H.
Character and the Unconscious
A Critical Exposition of the Psychology of Freud and Jung
Translated from the German by Elizabeth Trevelyan
240 pp. 1923. (2nd Impression 1950.) 20s.

Woodger, J. H.
Biological Principles
508 pp. 1929. (Reissued with a new Introduction 1966.) 60s.